Uniting the Dual Torah

Uniting the Dual Torah

SIFRA AND THE PROBLEM OF THE MISHNAH

JACOB NEUSNER

The Institute for Advanced Study

Brown University

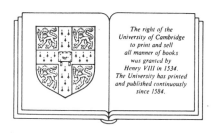

The right of the
University of Cambridge
to print and sell
all manner of books
wus granted by
Henry VIII in 1534.
The University has printed
and published continuously
since 1584.

CAMBRIDGE UNIVERSITY PRESS

Cambridge

New York   Port Chester

Melbourne   Sydney

Published by the Press Syndicate of the University of Cambridge
The Pitt Building, Trumpington Street, Cambridge CB2 1RP
40 West 20th Street, New York, NY 10011, USA
10 Stamford Road, Oakleigh, Melbourne 3166, Australia

© Cambridge University Press 1990

First published 1990

Printed in the United States of America

Library of Congress Cataloging-in-Publication Data

Neusner, Jacob, 1932–
   Uniting the dual Torah : Sifra and problem of the Mishnah / Jacob
Neuser.
      p.   cm.
   Includes bibliographical references.
   ISBN 0-521-38125-8
   1. Sifra – Relations to Mishnah.   2. Mishnah – Relations to Sifra.
3. Tradition (Judaism)   I. Title.
BM517.S63N49   1990
296.1'4–dc20   89-17320
                                                                          CIP

British Library Cataloguing in Publication Data

Uniting the Dual Torah : Sifra and the problem of the
   Mishnah.
   1. Judaism. Talmud-Critical studies
   I. Neusner, Jacob, 1932–
   296.1'206

ISBN 0-521-38125-8 hard covers

For my best friend and best companion,
who is my wife,
SUZANNE RICHTER NEUSNER

a rollicking book, and one I have most enjoyed writing,
goes to the person I have most enjoyed knowing

with the gift of whatever love I know how to give
to the only person to whom I have ever given it

on the occasion, and in celebration, of
our twenty-fifth wedding anniversary

March 15, 1989

zeh mah sheyesh

Contents

Preface

The theme of this book is how a remarkable authorship set forth a distinctive solution to a long-standing problem in the theology, literature, and law of the Judaism of the Dual Torah. The problem was posed by the character and standing of the Mishnah. From the moment of its promulgation as the basis for the law of Judaism, the Mishnah was represented as authoritative. Therefore, in the context of the life of Israel, the Mishnah enjoyed its standing as *torah,* divine revelation, which yet was clearly not like The Torah revealed by God to Moses at Sinai. To that problem there were two solutions: the successor documents that undertook the exegesis, amplification, and application of the Mishnah and that presented by the authorship of Sifra. The solution proposed by the successor authorities to the Mishnah, in Tosefta, ca. A.D. 300, the Talmud of the Land of Israel or Yerushalmi, ca. A.D. 400, and the Talmud of Babylonia or Bavli, ca. A.D. 600, was to treat the word or conception, *torah,* as a common noun, signifying, among other things, process, status, or classification. Then the Mishnah found ample place for itself within the capacious classification, *torah.*

The solution proposed by the authorship of Sifra was to treat the word, *torah,* as solely a proper noun, The Torah, but *also* to insist that the Mishnah found a fully legitimate position within The Torah. That solution required the authorship of the Mishnah to undertake a profound critique of the logic of the Mishnah, both as that logic dictated the correct joining of two or more sentences into a cogent thought and as that logic governed the formation of propositions for analysis. In fact, the authorship of Sifra set forth a systematic critique of the Mishnah in its principal definitive traits: its topical program and arrangement, its principles of cogent discourse, and its logic of critical analysis and probative demonstration of propositions. Furthermore, it set forth a sizable portion of the Mishnah's contents, as these pertained to the book of Leviticus, within its own definition of the correct topical program and arrangement, its own principles of cogent discourse, and its own logic of critical analysis and proof.

This book, therefore, proposes the thesis that these two solutions came to full expression in the works of exegesis and amplification that adopted the Mishnah, the oral Torah, as the base text, and in the single work of exegesis and amplification that adopted Scripture, in the particular form of the book of Leviticus, as the base text. In the prologue I explain the thesis of this book and what I conceive to be at stake. In the shank of the book I develop the thesis. Simply, at stake in the Tosefta and two Talmuds, on the one side, and in Sifra on the other,[1] was how to unite the dual Torah. That is what I mean by "Sifra and the problem of the Mishnah."

The program of the book is simple. In Chapters One and Two I describe the problem of the Mishnah as I conceive it to have confronted the heirs and successors of the framers of that document. Chapter Three then presents a sample of Sifra, including 6 of the 277 chapters of the writing. Chapter Four forms my theoretical statement and is the center-piece of the book. Chapters Five and Six attend to formal questions of the order and organization of propositions and topics, on the one side, and the logic of cogent discourse on the other. Chapters Seven and Eight turn to the deep structure of logic: how we set forth and prove propositions. There I define the probative logic of hierarchical classification, compari-son and contrast of like and unlike, that forms the foundation for all learning in antiquity; we call it *Listenwissenschaft.* I identify the particu-lar traits of mind that characterize the Mishnah's framer's utilization of the logic of hierarchical classification and then show in detail the Sifra's authorship's sustained and stunning critique of the application of that logic. In Chapter Eight, I explain how that same authorship turned and rehabilitated *Listenwissenschaft* by showing the correct mode of defin-ing classifications and comparing and contrasting categories in hierar-chical order.

In this way I lay forth the proposition of this book, that in order to re-present the dual Torah in a single, whole statement, the authorship of Sifra set forth a sustained critique of practical reason. It was in their deep search into the written Torah that they found the principles of probative logic for the demonstration of the unity of two components of the Torah, oral and written. The underlying theological premise, of course, was that The Torah portrayed for humanity the workings of the mind of God, just as creation portrayed the workings of the hand of God. Therefore, when our authorship penetrated into the workings of the intellect revealed in The Torah, they entered into the mind of God.

For the purpose of interpreting the results of this book, I have invoked the metaphor of "critique," suggesting that the authorship of Sifra has presented an attack upon, and a critique of, the logic of the Mishnah. But an equally valid metaphor may be provided by academic discourse. The Mishnah and Sifra coexisted in the curriculum of the master–disciple circles of the Judaism of the Dual Torah. Therefore, the authorship of Sifra represents one view of logic, that of the Mishnah, a different, and complementary view, of how to solve the same problems of taxonomic logic. Readers who prefer to see the data I set forth within a less colorful metaphor than the one I have used – a metaphor that represents one authorship severely criticizing the thought processes of a prior authorship – will find no argument from me.

Let me place the present work into its proximate and broad context. As to the former, the book takes its place as second within a trilogy of studies of Sifra. The first is the first complete translation of Sifra into any language, published as follows:

Sifra. An Analytical Translation. Atlanta, 1988: Scholars Press for Brown Judaic Studies. I. *Introduction and Vayyiqra Dibura Denedabah and Vayiqqra Dibura Dehobah.*

Sifra. An Analytical Translation. Atlanta, 1988: Scholars Press for Brown Judaic Studies. II. *Sav, Shemini, Tazria, Negaim, Mesora, and Zabim.*

Sifra. An Analytical Translation. Atlanta, 1988: Scholars Press for Brown Judaic Studies. III. *Aharé Mot, Qedoshim, Emor, Behar, and Behuqotai.*

The third, summmarized in the Appendix so far as the results pertain to this book, is *Sifra in Perspective: The Documentary Comparison of the Midrashim of Ancient Judaism,* Atlanta, 1988: Scholars Press for Brown Judaic Studies.

Since I present in this book numerous abstracts of my translation, I had best explain my intent and philosophy for translating Sifra in the present context. My translation provides the document with its first consecutive numbering system as well as its first detailed formal analysis. The translation on which this study rests is one that I call *form analytical.* In this translation, now in print, I prepare a way to answer the questions, such as those treated here, that can be addressed on the basis of a form analytical reading of a document when it is considered whole and complete, from beginning to end.

The correct methodological approach to the study of any document on its own terms is dictated by established procedures in all humanistic learning in the West. First, we have to allow a document such as Sifra to speak for itself. Its authorship's own choices as to aesthetic and substantive questions alike must give its testimony. The choices of that authorship on how to express its ideas constitute the single authoritative

commentary to the document.[2] In translating, that means that the traits
of the document demand attention on their own, without an *a priori*
premise as to the origin, purpose, or character of the writing before us.
The beginning of criticism is a translation that makes possible independent analysis, sustained inquiry into objective traits of evidence,
analysis of the indicative characteristics of that evidence, and interpretation through comparison and contrast of the outcome of that analysis and
inquiry. The methodological requirements of contemporary humanistic
inquiry dictate the emprirical approach taken in my translation of Sifra as
of the two Sifrés and the other Midrash compilations produced in the
formative age of the Judaism of the Dual Torah. In the bibliography I
specify the larger context of this work of translation and phenomenological analysis.

JACOB NEUSNER

Program in Judaic Studies
Brown University
Providence, Rhode Island

Notes

[1] I shall deal with the standing of Sifré to Numbers and Sifré to Deuteronomy in
respect to the Mishnah in the companion volume to this one, *Sifra in Context*. At
this point I have no need to claim for Sifra utterly unique traits or standing,
though I do maintain for our authorship a genuinely singular cast of mind.

[2] The conception that the medieval commentaries tell us of the original meaning of an ancient document need not detain us. When my translations are
criticized as ignorant for ignoring what Rashi has to say about a passage in the
Talmud of Babylonia, I marvel that my intent has registered. For that is not out of
"ignorance" but entirely intentional. I began this mode of reading the rabbinic
texts with the Mishnah, insisting that the Mishnah constitutes its own best
exegesis, and that when people say things in one way and not in some other, that
constitutes a signal as to their intent and meaning. I extended that same critical
hermeneutics to principal documents of the rabbinic canon, and hope to complete the task. No one doubts that the received exegetical tradition contains
points of interest, particularly as to the possible meanings of words and phrases.

Prologue

I. The Thesis of This Book

This book proposes to demonstrate that the authorship of Sifra composed
the one (and the only truly successful) document to accomplish the
union of the two Torahs not merely formally but through the interior
structure of thought. It was by means of the critique of practical logic and
the rehabilitation of the probative logic of hierarchical classification
(Listenwissenschaft), in particular, that the authorship of Sifra accomplished this remarkable feat of intellect. That authorship achieved the
(re-)union of the two Torahs into a single cogent statement within the
framework of the written Torah by penetrating into the deep composition of logic that underlay the creation of the world in its correct
components, rightly classified, and in its right order, as portrayed by the
Torah. Specifically, by systematically demolishing the logic that sustains
an autonomous Mishnah and by equally thoroughly demonstrating the
dependency, for the identification of the correct classification of things,
not upon the traits of things viewed in the abstract, but upon the
classification of things by Scripture, the framers of Sifra recast the two
parts of the Torah into a single coherent statement through unitary and
cogent discourse.

   At stake, therefore, for our authorship is the dependency of the Mishnah upon Scripture, at least for the encompassing case of the book of
Leviticus.[1] So in choosing, as to form, the base text of Scripture, the
authorship of Sifra made its entire statement *in nuce.* Then by composing
a document that for very long stretches cannot have been put together
without the Mishnah and, at the same time, subjecting the generative
logical principles of the Mishnah to devastating critique, that same authorship took up its mediating position. The destruction of the Mishnah
as an autonomous and free-standing statement, based upon its own logic,

1

is followed by the reconstruction of (large tracts of the Mishnah) as a statement wholly within, and in accord with, the logic and program of the written Torah in Leviticus.[2] Quite how they did so requires the studies presented in this book, each in its logical position, beginning to end. I, therefore, represent as a triumph of intellect the work of the authorship of Sifra, as we now know it in its recurrent and fixed forms of rhetoric and logic and equally permanent protocol of relationships with other documents, particularly Scripture and Mishnah (with Tosefta). What we have in Sifra is simply one of the great, original, and successful works of the critical mind (and, in an odd sense, I should claim also, aesthetics.[3]) in the Judaism of the dual Torah as it emerged from late antiquity. Let me explain the question that is answered in this book by inquiry into the deep structure of the logic of coherent discourse and cogent thought expressed in uniting the Torah through rewriting Scripture.

The former, and dominant, approach to uniting the two Torahs, oral and written, into a single cogent statement, involved reading the written Torah into the oral. In form, this was done through inserting into the oral Torah a long sequence of proof texts. That is the solution taken by the authorities who received the Mishnah, the initial and authoritative writing down of the oral Torah, and who subjected it to four hundred years of amplification, paraphrase, and internal augmentation. They carried out that solution through the Tosefta, ca, A.D. 300, then the Talmud of the Land of Israel, ca. A.D. 400, and then, in the most successful and thorough manner, through the Talmud of Babylonia, ca. A.D. 600. The other solution required reading the oral Torah into the written one, by inserting into the written Torah citations and allusions to the oral one, and also by demonstrating, on both philosophical and theological grounds, the utter subordination and dependency of the oral Torah, the Mishnah, to the written Torah – while at the same time defending and vindicating that same oral Torah.

II.   Dating Sifra, Documentary Discourse and an Authorship

We do not know when Sifra reached closure, or precisely what "closure" might mean. Indeed, to say precisely what we mean by "Sifra" requires attention. For we cannot be certain that everything now printed in what we call "Sifra" was there at the outset, when the document was finally closed by its original authorship. An incremental process of copying, adding, and changing affects all writings that reach us from antiquity; before printing, everything was in flux. Although, as in the case of many documents out of Greco–Roman antiquity, we have rich manuscript traditions on the basis of which to produce critical texts, in the case of

the Judaic holy books, we have paltry evidence, none of it within centuries of the time at which, people generally assume, Sifra was finally
redacted. In fact, manuscript testimony begins long after the Muslim
conquest of the Middle East brought to an end the period we identify as
"late antiquity," that is, the age in which the Judaism of the dual Torah
took form and produced its principal documents. Although Sifra, among
other writings, is nearly universally held to have been redacted before
the Talmud of Babylonia, the final document of the formative age of the
Judaism under study, in ca. A.D. 600, that premise has no bearing upon
our work. As stated previously, I do not propose to explain a trait of the
document, let alone an opinion expressed in the writing, by appeal to a
particular historical event, identifying the particular historical setting or
context in which our authorship concluded its work, and to which (as a
matter of definition) that authorship proposed to make its statement.
There is no *terminus ante quem* that plays a role in the argument of this
book. I also do not know that statements attributed by our authorship to
particular authorities of a period prior to the (unknown) time of redaction really were said by those to whom they are assigned. Accordingly,
we have no *terminus a quo.*

Finally, as I have already suggested, I cannot demonstrate that everything now in our hands was in that original (theoretical) Sifra that
supposedly was closed at a particular time in a particular place; I should
never exclude the probability that, prior to printing, copyists added
materials they thought belonged in this document. The state of manuscript evidence, so satisfyingly assembled for us in the part now published by Peofessor and Rabbi Louis Finkelstein, does strongly suggest
that what we have is what those original redactors gave us, more or less,
and that variations in contents contributed by later copyists proved
trivial.[4] But even though I believe Finkelstein has demonstrated that fact
for the generality of our document, in no way does my thesis concerning
it appeal to the "original" Sifra or exclude from discourse and analysis a
single line I deem to be "added later." That entire mode of scholarship
seems to me to yield uninteresting results, precisely because it aims at a
positive judgment, a precision, not possible in the state of the evidence
with which we deal.

What I do maintain is that our document reveals a fixed rhetorical,
logical, and even topical program, which we may distinguish from the
fixed rhetorical, logical, and topical programs of other documents of its
classification. It is a singular species within its genus. I demonstrate that
fact in the companion work, *Sifra in Context,* and need not review the
demonstration here. The result may be stated very simply, and with
heavy emphasis.

Fundamental to our document are certain recurrent structures of rhetoric, logic, and topic. These must be identified as the generative and definitive structures of the writing. People can, and surely did, borrow from a corpus of ready-made statements, for example, paragraphs, but what they did with them when they were making Sifra was always dictated by a protocol of a highly conventional and formal character, conventional in logic, formal in rhetoric, and fixed as to program and proposition.

Now whether a single authorship made the whole, or whether the document grew incrementally over the period of a week, a month, a year, a century, or a millennium, I do not know; no one does. However, it is beyond doubt that throughout the period of formation the process was not agglutinative but patterned and paradigmatic, and that the paradigm established its paramount presence at the very onset of the process of agglutination. The very formal, conventional character of the writing before us, its structurally repetitive chararacter, its limited repertoire not only of forms but also of intellectual initiatives – these demonstrated traits define Sifra and only Sifra and, therefore, were present at the point at which, whatever antecedent conceptions of writings were utilized, the authorship of Sifra undertook to form and frame this document in particular. To express that fact, I have appealed to the conception of not a single author, which is beyond demonstration though possible, but of an authorship, a body of composers, working at an indeterminate time and place, all bound by a single protocol of generative conceptions and a distinctive protocol as to rhetoric and logic.

III.   What Do We Mean by an Authorship?

By definition a composite document such as ours has no single author. But since it exhibits a cogent character, a work such as Sifra, therefore, derives from a considered set of decisions of a rhetorical, logical, and topical order. To be sure, as I have stressed, we do not know for how long the authorship that formed Sifra flourished. Until medieval times, we have no authoritative evidence in the form of dated manuscripts for any document of the Judaism of the dual Torah. In addition, we do not know that what we now call Sifra existed in late antiquity. However, we do stand on solid ground in maintaining that the cogent discourse that defines the document's rhetoric, topic, and logic marked the document from its original stages. Logic prescribes that, if we are unable to assign the document to a particular point of origin, we gain out of the definitive paradigm of rhetoric, topic, and logic a clear picture of the sustaining position of the authorship at hand *ab origine.* Others, joining the creative work of handing on the document, added what they chose, but, as we recognize, solely in line with the established principles of public discourse.

Accordingly, a composite document such as ours has no single author. But as I show in the companion study of *Sifra in Context,* as a coherent statement in both form and proposition, Sifra exhibits a cogent character. Therefore, it derives from a considered set of decisions of a rhetorical, logical, and topical order, that is, Sifra derives from an authorship, a collectivity of consensus about this particular writing.[5]

Again, it is the uniformity of rhetoric, topic, and logic that justifies the claim to treat the document as cogent, even though later tradents joined the process of formulation and formation. When in due course I propose to relate the indicative traits of the document to the circumstance within the unfolding canon I believe definitive for the document, I refer not to any single paragraph or chapter, let alone a statement within one, but to the definitive and indicative traits of the whole, logic, rhetoric, topic alike, and these in the larger context of the canonical program of the framers of the dual Torah in the late fourth, fifth, and sixth centuries.

IV. Defining "The" Sifra

What requires this careful definition of what we can, and cannot, mean when we refer to "*the*" Sifra? I have now emphasized that the work of the authorship of Sifra reaches us only through a long process of copying and recopying. Accordingly, we cannot be certain that the Hebrew version in our hands is the one originally sent into the world by the authorship of the document. If, therefore, we propose to represent the traits of mind and intellect of the authorship responsible for Sifra, we cannot appeal to any one detail, for example, a given paragraph or pericope. That singleton may or may not have found a place in the original version(s), produced by the authorship that bears responsibility for the writing and that has defined and guaranteed the consensus constituted, to begin with, by Sifra. We do not have the original manuscript that stated what the initial authorship wished to say. We do not even come within a millenium of that original authorship.

The state of manuscript evidence, whether rich or impoverished, settles few important questions as to the original intent and statement of the responsible authorship. If we wish to know anything at all about the document as its authorship created it, we have to appeal not to particular statements but to the character of the document as a whole, as evidenced in each and every one of its parts. General and ubiquitous traits of rhetoric and logic can be imitated by later copyist-authors, adding their own message to the document as it passes through their hands. But they cannot be invented – and, by definition, they do represent the intent and plan of the original authorship. In addition, we may even appeal to overall traits of the topical plan and program of the document for evidence of the initial program, even though one or another subject or specific proposition cannot be reliably imputed to that original author-ship. The way we solve the problem of the parlous character of the manuscript tradition and evidence of any rabbinic document of late antiquity – and every document reaches us only by means of the most dubious manuscript tradition – is to conduct an analysis of the traits of the whole: what defines in all of the parts the indicative character of rhetoric, logic, and topic? When we can answer those questions, we may "introduce" our document, that is to say, answer such basic questions about the classification and definition of the writing as permit us to understand and make sense of that writing. This method, of course, disavows those critics who argue that, until all manuscript evidence has been collated (which critics call "the making of a critical text"), no work of description, analysis, and interpretation is possible.[6]

Moreover, critics who mount an argument based on the inadequacy of available textual evidence ignore the stress, in the work done today on the history of religion for Judaism, upon the ubiquitous traits of form, including the formalization of rhetoric, the prevalence of a given (docu-mentary) logic, and the recurrence and conventionality of a given (docu-mentary) topical program. No one known to me composes a history of religion, for a Judaism, based on the premise that the texts we now have accurately and in every detail represent the original statement of the initial authorship. Quite to the contrary, it is because of the uncertainty of our textual tradition and its available representation that the entire emphasis lies on uniformities and continuities, within a document, of a given convention in rhetoric, logic, and topic. Therefore, whereas the internal evidence supplied by that authorship deals with no speculation on the circumstance of composition or the purpose of publication, the phenomenological study presented here rests upon sound foundations. The questions under discussion involve not the history of manuscripts but the definitive structure and generative character of the document itself.

To conclude: Whereas in antiquity books or other important writings (e.g., letters and treatises) bore the name of the author or at least an attribution (e.g., Aristotle's or Paul's name), no document in the canon of Judaism produced in late antiquity bore a named author. No document in that canon contains within itself a definitive statement of date of com-position, a defined place or circumstance in which the book is written, a sustained argument to which we readily gain access, or any of the other usual indicators by which we define the authorship, the context, and the circumstance of a book. There is a reason for that fact. The purpose of the sages who in the aggregate created the canonical writings of the Judaism of the dual Torah is served by not specifying differentiating traits such as time, place, and identity of the author or the authorship. The canon –

"the one whole Torah of Moses, our rabbi" – presents single books as undifferentiated episodes in a timeless, ahistorical setting: Torah revealed to Moses by God at Mount Sinai, but written down long afterward. That theological conviction about the canon overall denies us information to introduce the book at hand, that is, to say, what it is. Without the usual indicators, then, how are we to read our document on its own terms, so as to answer the question: what is this book? When, where, why was it written? What does it mean?

Lacking clear answers to these questions, we turn to the evidence the document does provide: its salient traits of plan and program as displayed by intrinsic evidence. By plan I mean simply the literary traits before us. The intellectual program, so far as we can define it, derives from those same literary traits: From *how* the book's authorship persistently and ubiquitously presents its messages, we hope to learn *what* important points that authorship proposed to impart. In effect these two go together: form and meaning, structure and sustained polemic. Proposing to define the document at hand, we begin from the outside, with formal traits, and work our way inwards, toward the deciphering of the messages contained within those recurrent points of interest and stress, as signified in form. Only by seeing the document whole and simultaneous will we gain the rudiments of a definition. Describing and defining bits and pieces would yield no encompassing description of the whole. If we ask, therefore, what is this book, we begin with the entirety of the document. That is the approach I have taken in succession to each document of the Judaism of the Dual Torah.

Among the three definitive or indicative traits of a piece of sustained writing – rhetoric, logic, and topic – the first is the easiest to characterize, since it is, by definition, recurrent and repetitive. The logic or principle of cogent discourse, which imparts (in the mind of the authorship) intelligibility, comes to formal expression in rhetoric, so we commonly move from description of rhetoric to analysis of the logical foundations of rhetoric. And, under normal circumstances, the third and most difficult point of entry into a definition of the document is its topical program. Here, because the authorship treats more than a single topic, that is diffuse. Furthermore, it is the indicative trait of the document least likely to form connections to other documents, authorships' preferring, after all, to say something fresh or at least something old in a new way. By "the" Sifra, therefore, I mean the protocol of fixed traits of rhetoric, logic, and, within the methodical program outlined in the companion study, even topic that mark this document and no other, identifying "the" Sifra as a species within the genus of which it forms a component.

This statement explains why I have to ask the reader to stipulate the result of the companion study on *Sifra in Context,* a polythetic definition of the document as a singular species within not a single genus but multiple genera. The only way I can treat the problem of uniting the Dual Torah as solved by our authorship is to ask for the reader's indulgence in conceding, for the sake of argument, the distinctive character of this piece of writing, that is to say, to permit me to speak of "the" Sifra (obviously, by merely saying, "Sifra" without further qualification). Given the challenges and problems to that mode of speech, I believe it is no small concession. But, for the moment, we will do our work as though I had demonstrated what in fact will be set forth presently. The order of argument is dictated, for me, by the simple fact that the problem at hand is the fresher and more interesting of the two: What does our authorship accomplish and why? And later on, a more familiar issue, which I have addressed, method and substance alike, for nearly all of the Midrash compilations of consequence: On what basis do I claim that our authorship has written a book of its own, not merely a formless and aimless scrapbook of this and that? Now to the issue at hand: how to unify the two constituents of the Dual Torah, the written and the oral.

Notes

[1] That our authorship can have demonstrated the same propositions of topical program and order, logic of cogent discourse, and logic of probative demonstration of propositions, for other parts of the Mishnah that relate to other legal codes in the Mosaic composite is beyond all doubt shown in the two Sifrés. We have no counterpart for Exodus, and, of course, there are sizable tracts of the Mishnah that stand out of all relationship to Scripture. But the program of our document certainly is not particular to the book of Leviticus, and the polemic and propositions encompass the entirety of the dual Torah, wherever finally written down.

[2] While this is a wholly phenomenological study, I might observe that an ideal historical setting in which the issues I think worked out here proved urgent will be a Karaite one, where the opposed parties either deny that there was an oral Torah at all, or affirm that the oral Torah stands wholly autonomous of the written one. The authorship before us then adopted a mediating position, within the principles of Karaism concerning the written Torah, restating the basic propositions, so far as relevant, of the oral Torah, Scripture and Mishnah, respectively. But they did this with a philosophical profundity that required closest attention to the critique of applied reason, so that the destruction of the Mishnah as a free-standing statement was accomplished not merely formally (as I originally thought in my *History of the Mishnaic Law of Purities. VII. Negaim. Sifra* [Leiden, 1976: E. J. Brill]), but, as I demonstrate, in terms of inner logical structure. Unfortunately, I do not know when Sifra reached closure. Was it only in Karaite times and did Sifra address as its distinctive and urgent question, the twin-challenges of Karaism and extreme rabbinism? Nonetheless, the same issue

— sola scriptura, only a written Torah from Sinai, as against the Mishnah as oral tradition of autonomous standing — assuredly occupied much attention from the very origin of the Mishnah itself, as tractate Avot shows us. I do know that one paramount issue within the documentary statement of Sifra's authorship is the sustained attack on the taxonomic, hierarchical logic of the Mishnah and the equally protracted demonstration of the other logic that our authorship proposes. All of this becomes clear in the pages of this book and its companions, fore and aft.

3   There is an odd and compelling beauty in Sifra. One's first impression may well be that of tedium. But once we understand what is happening at any given passage and grasp the problem facing our authorship, we realize the resources of critical intellect and imagination that sustain the discourse they set forth. As I was developing my translation with the help of Professor Bernard Mandelbaum, I was very often taken with his admiration for the document as such, not merely for the many fine statements it contains, just as I was swept away by the flow of discourse, argument, and even rhetoric. That is why I think we have an aesthetic triumph in hand, even though, admittedly, it is one that works its magic through repetition, the wearing down of the independence of the reader and the reshaping of reading into a single fixed pattern. Recognition of the familiar is only part of the result, however. The other part is the discovery of surprise within the repeated and the familiar. This is not an exegetical–eisegetical counterpart to Ravel's interminable and offensive *Bolero* — not at all!

4   The exaggeration of the variety and extent of variations in readings of the ancient documents is meant to intimidate all other sorts of studies but collections and arrangements of variant readings. But no one who understands form-analysis can take fright before the fulminations of the collectors and arrangers of variants, who grasp only what they collect and do not understand the ways in which, when framing questions in one way rather than another, we amply take account of the variations in readings of this, that, and the other thing. We return to this matter in a moment.

5   Nothing in this book rests upon the allegation that Sifra is unique or sui generis, and no statement made alleges that our authorship was the only one to propose uniting the dual Torah in the manner set forth here. I do think that only a polythetic taxonomy permits us to compare and contrast Sifra to the two Sifrés, and, moreover, that the shared traits among the three documents ordinarily grouped as "the halakhic midrashim" (often with the Mekhilta attributed to R. Ishmael!) are imputed more than inherent. But that is a problem to be addressed elsewhere.

6   The single explicit statement on the matter comes from Peter Schaefer, "Research into Rabbinic Literature: An Attempt to Define the *Status Quaestionis,*" *Journal of Jewish Studies* 37 (1986): 146–152. This article in no way succeeds in its announced purpose, and its discussion of the matter at hand is uncomprehending and (alas) rather pretentious. But others in less explicit ways have raised the issue, not perceiving that that issue had formed one generative consideraion for my defining my work as I have. The other was the impossibility of demonstrating which attributions to named authorities are valid, which not. Schaefer does not seem to grasp the principles of form-analysis and how that

approach to the text takes full account of the complexity of manuscript variations – when and where there is a rich manuscript tradition at all. His conception, because there are so many representations of a document, we can say nothing at all about the document in its "original" form, is not wrong; it is simply beside the point, when, as in the rabbinic writings, documents follow exceedingly well-defined and limited formal, rhetorical, and logical programs. Schaefer's work on the Hekhalot fragments brought him into contact with a corpus of materials of a chaotic character, dealing with a document (if it ever was a single document at all) in no way comparable to the well-formed and rigidly formalized rabbinic writings, such as the Mishnah, Sifra, and the two Sifrés. So he has generalized from a set of writings that may or may not even fall into the tradition of formulation and transmission subject to the discipline of the rabbinic movement and institutions. Schaefer does not seem to have understood the results of Y. N. Epstein's monumental study of Mishnah variants, *Mabo lenusah hammishnah,* or perhaps he has misunderstood the forest for the trees, the trees for the leaves, in pronouncing the forest and the trees to comprise only leaves. For what Epstein demonstrated was that the variations are trivial, the basic structures uniform (e.g., as to the shape and structure of the Mishnah as a whole). Furthermore, Schaefer has not understood how others, working with different types of writings altogether, indeed have taken full account of problems to which he has accused colleagues of being utterly oblivious. The ultimately nihilistic position he has propounded depends upon his own unwillingness to consider the solutions of others to problems that he has declared beyond solution, rather than to criticize those solutions if he understands them and can propose interesting criticisms of them. On the whole, I think we may value Schaefer's own collections of variants without following him into the cul de sac defined by his anti-intellectual nihilism.

CHAPTER ONE

The Problem of the Mishnah

I. The Problem of the Mishnah

When, in ca. A.D. 200, the Mishnah reached closure and was received and adopted as law by the state-sanctioned Jewish governments in both the Roman empire, in the land of Israel, and Iran, in Babylonia, respectively, the function and character of the document precipitated a considerable crisis. Politically and theologically presented as the foundation for the everyday administration of the affairs of Jewry, the Mishnah ignored the politics of the sponsoring regimes. Essentially ahistorical, the code hardly identified as authoritative any known political institution, let alone the patriarchate in the land of Israel, the exilarchate in Babylonia. True, that political–institutional flaw (from the viewpoint of the sponsoring authorities) scarcely can have proved critical.

But silence of the authorship of the Mishnah on the theological call for their document presented not a chronic but an acute issue. Since Jews generally accepted the authority of Moses at Sinai, failure to claim for the document a clear and explicit relationship to the Torah of Moses defined that issue. Why should people accept as authoritative the rulings of this piece of writing? Omitting reference to a theological, as much as to a political myth, the authorship of the Mishnah also failed to signal the relationship between their document and Scripture. Since, for all Judaisms, Hebrew Scriptures in general, and the Pentateuch, in particular, represented God's will for Israel, silence on that matter provoked considerable response. I will now describe in detail the political, theological, and literary difficulties presented by the Mishnah to any theory that the Mishnah formed part of God's revelation to Moses at Sinai.

Laws issued to define what people were supposed to do could not stand by themselves; they had to receive the imprimatur of heaven, that is, they had to be given the status of revelation. Accordingly, to make its

11

way in Israelite life, the Mishnah as a constitution and code demanded for itself a theory of beginnings at (or in relation to) Sinai, with Moses, from God. The character of the Mishnah itself hardly won confidence that, on the face of it, the document formed part of, or derived from Sinai. It was originally published through oral formulation and oral transmission, that is, in the medium of memorization. However, it had been in the medium of writing that, in the view of all of Israel until about A.D. 200, God had been understood to reveal the divine word and will. The Torah was a written book. People who claimed to receive further messages from God usually wrote them down. They had three choices in securing acceptance of their account. All three involved linking the new to the old.

In claiming to hand on revelation, they could, first, sign their books with the names of biblical heroes. Second, they could imitate the style of biblical Hebrew. Third, they could present an exegesis of existing written verses, validating their ideas by supplying proof texts for them. From the closure of the Torah literature in the time of Ezra, circa 450 B.C., to the time of the Mishnah, nearly seven hundred years later, we do not have a single book alleged to be holy and, at the same time, standing entirely out of relationship to the Holy Scriptures of ancient Israel. The pseudepigraphic writings fall into the first category, the Essene writings at Qumran into the second and third. We may point also to the Gospels, which take as a principal problem demonstrating how Jesus had fulfilled the prophetic promises of the Old Testament and in other ways carried forward and even embodied Israel's Scripture.

Insofar as a piece of Jewish writing did not find a place in relationship to Scripture, its author laid no claim to present a holy book. The contrast between Jubilees and the Testaments of the Patriarchs, with their constant and close harping on biblical matters, and the several books of Maccabees, shows the differences. The former claim to present God's revealed truth, the latter, history. So a book was holy because in style, in authorship, or in (alleged) origin it continued Scripture, finding a place, therefore, (at least in the author's mind) within the canon, or because it provided an exposition on Scripture's meaning. But the Mishnah made no such claim. It entirely ignored the style of biblical Hebrew, speaking in a quite different kind of Hebrew altogether. It is silent on its authorship through sixty-two of the sixty-three tractates (the claims of Abot are post facto). In any event, nowhere does the Mishnah contain the claim that God had inspired the authors of the document. These are not given biblical names and certainly are not alleged to have been biblical saints. Most of the book's named authorities flourished within the same century as its anonymous arrangers and redactors, not in remote antiquity. Above all, the Mishnah contains scarcely a handful of exegeses of Scripture. These, where they occur, play a trivial and tangential role. Here then is the problem of the Mishnah: different from Scripture in language and style, indifferent to the claim of authorship by a biblical hero or divine inspiration, stunningly aloof from allusion to verses of Scripture for nearly the whole of its discourse – yet authoritative for Israel.

The Mishnah was not a statement of theory alone, telling only how things will be in the eschaton. Nor was it a wholly sectarian document, reporting the view of a group without standing or influence in the larger life of Israel. True, in some measure it bears both of these traits of eschatology and sectarian provenance. But the Mishnah was (and is) law for Israel. It entered the government and courts of the Jewish people, both in the motherland and also overseas, as the authoritative constitution of the courts of Judaism. The advent of the Mishnah, therefore, marked a turning in the life of the nation–religion. The document demanded explanation and apology. And the one thing one could not do, as a Jew in third-century Tiberias, Sepphoris, Caesarea, or Beth Shearim, in Galilee, was ignore the thing. True, one might refer solely to ancient Scripture and tradition and live life out within the inherited patterns of the familiar Israelite religion–culture. But as soon as one dealt with the Jewish government in charge of everyday life – went to court over the damages done to a crop by a neighbor's ox, for instance – one came up against a law in addition to the law of Scripture, a document the principles of which governed and settled all matters. As a result, the Mishnah rapidly came to confront the life of Israel. The people who knew the Mishnah, the rabbis or sages, came to dominate that life. And their claim, in accord with the Mishnah, to exercise authority and the right to impose heavenly sanction came to perplex.

II. The Two Solutions to the Problem of the Mishnah

Allow me to begin with a brief survey of the repertoire of responses that were attempted over the next 400 years.

One response was represented by the claim that the authorities of the Mishnah stood in a chain of tradition that extended back to Sinai. This claim, however, stated explicitly in the Mishnah's first apologetic, tractate Avot, that circulated from approximately a generation beyond the promulgation of the Mishnah itself, required amplification and concrete demonstration. The word *torah* as a common noun, as spoke of a status or classification of sayings. A saying was *torah*, that is, enjoyed the status of or fell into the classification of *torah*, if it stood in the line of tradition from Sinai.

A second and distinct response took the same view of *torah* as a common noun. This response was to treat the Mishnah as subordinate to, and dependant upon, Scripture. Then *torah* was what fell into the classification of the revelation of *Torah* by God to Moses at Sinai. The way of providing what was needed within that theory was to link statements of the Mishnah to statements ("proof texts") of Scripture. The Tosefta, ca. 300, a compilation of citations of, and comments upon, the Mishnah, together with some autonomous materials that may have reached closure in the period in which the work of redaction of the Mishnah continued, as well as the Talmud of the Land of Israel, ca. 400, fairly systematically did just that.

The former solution treated Torah with a small *t*, that is to say, as a generic classification, and identified the Mishnah with the Torah revealed to Moses at Sinai by claiming a place for the Mishnah's authorities in the process of tradition and transmission that brought torah – no longer, the Torah, the specific writing comprising the Five Books of Moses – to contemporary Israel, the Jewish people. It was a theological solution, expressed through ideas, attitudes, implicit claims, but not through sustained rewriting of either Scripture or the Mishnah.

The latter solution, by contrast, concerned the specific and concrete statements of the Mishnah and required a literary, not merely a theological, statement, one precise and specific to passages of the Mishnah, one after the other. What was demanded by the claim that the Mishnah depended upon, but, therefore, enjoyed the standing of, Scripture, was a line-by-line commentary upon the Mishnah in light of Scripture. But this too, I stress, treated *torah* as a common noun.

The third way, which I will describe in the shank of this book, would set aside the two solutions, the theological and the literary, and explore the more profound issues of the fundamental and generative structure of right thought, yielding, as a matter of fact, both Scripture and the Mishnah. This approach insisted that *torah* always was a proper noun. There was and is, only The Torah. But this – The Torah – demanded expansion and vast amplification. When we know the principles of logical structure and especially those of hierarchical classification that animate The Torah, we can undertake part of the task of expansion and amplification, that is, join in the processes of thought that, in the mind of God, yielded The Torah. For when we know how God thought in giving The Torah to Moses at Sinai, and so account for the classifications and their ordering in the very creation of the world, we can ourselves enter into The Torah and participate in its processes. But in this simple typology I have moved far ahead of my story. I will return to the problem of the Mishnah and describe its parameters. I will begin with an explanation of why The Torah became dual, so that an intellectual labor of uniting the two components of the dual Torah provoked the deep thought represented by the canon of Judaism in its formative time, from the second through the sixth centuries of the Common Era.

III. The Conception of the Dual Torah

To understand the most important symbolic trait of Judaism in its formative age, the development of the notion of a dual Torah, written and
oral, we must first return to the tractate Avot and its rendition of the
chain of tradition that led from Sinai to the authorities of the Mishnah:

> 1. Moses received Torah at Sinai and handed it on to Joshua, Joshua
> to elders, and elders to prophets. And prophets handed it on to the
> men of the great assembly. They said three things: Be prudent in
> judgment. Raise up many disciples. Make a fence for the Torah.

What we see is the claim that at Sinai Moses received not only the
Scriptures – the Torah everyone knew, that is, the written Torah – but
something beyond. This something falls into the classification of *torah,*
revelation, but is not contained within the written Torah. We know that
because the sayings assigned to the authorities in the chain of tradition
do not cite Scripture but cite wisdom of another source. In time to come,
this other source of *torah* would be understood as a memorized Torah,
that is, the other half of the "one whole Torah of Moses, our rabbi."
Finally, the doctrine of the dual Torah would emerge whole and complete, encompassing all of the sayings of the recognized sages, not only in
ancient times but in the present day. Then the Judaic system of the dual
Torah would encompass revelation not out of the past – "tradition" – but
the revelation consisting in the Torah-teaching of today's sage. That
teaching did not derive from the past, from "tradition," and Judaism
never constituted a traditional religion. That teaching derived from today's sage, teaching Torah. Judaism as a living religion of everyday
revelation from God to Israel in the present condition attains its full and
complete definition: the religion of God's revelation, Torah in the here
and now.

The question of the standing and status of the Mishnah invoked the
conception of revelation of an other-than-written character from Sinai.
Upon its closure, the Mishnah gained an exalted political status as the
constitution of Jewish government of the Land of Israel. Accordingly, the
clerks who knew and applied its law had to explain the standing of that
law, meaning its relationship to the law of the Torah. But the Mishnah
provided no account of itself. Unlike biblical law codes, the Mishnah
begins with no myth of its own origin and ends with no doxology.
Discourse commences in the middle of things and ends abruptly. What
follows from such laconic rambling is that the exact status of the document required definition entirely outside the framework of the document itself. The framers of the Mishnah gave no hint of the nature of their

book, so the Mishnah reached the political world of Israel without a trace of self-conscious explanation or any theory of validation.

The one thing that is clear, alas, is negative. The framers of the Mishnah nowhere claim, implicitly or explicitly, that what they have written forms part of the Torah, enjoys the status of God's revelation to Moses at Sinai, or even systematically carries forward secondary exposition and application of what Moses wrote down in the wilderness. Later on, perhaps 200 years beyond the closure of the Mishnah, the need to explain the standing and origin of the Mishnah led later sages to posit two things. First, God's revelation of The Torah at Sinai encompassed the Mishnah as much as Scripture. Second, the Mishnah was handed on through oral formulation and oral transmission from Sinai to the framers of the document as we have it. These two convictions, fully exposed in the ninth-century letter of Sherira, an important rabbinical authority in Babylonia, in fact emerge from the references of both Talmuds to the dual Torah. One part is in writing. The other was oral and now is in the Mishnah.

As for the Mishnah itself, however, it contains not a hint that anyone has heard such a tale. The earliest apologists for the Mishnah, represented in Avot and the Tosefta alike, know nothing of the fully realized myth of the dual Torah of Sinai. It may be that the authors of those documents stood too close to the Mishnah to see the Mishnah's standing as a problem or to recognize the task of accounting for its origins. Certainly they never refer to the Mishnah as something out there, nor speak of the document as autonomous and complete. Only the two Talmuds reveal that conception – alongside their mythic explanation of where the document came from and why it should be obeyed. So the Yerushalmi marks the change. In any event, the absence of explicit expression of such a claim in behalf of the Mishnah requires little specification. It is just not there.

But the absence of an implicit claim demands explanation. When ancient Jews wanted to gain for their writings the status of revelation, of *torah,* or at least to link what they thought to what the Torah had said, they could do one of four things. They could sign the name of a holy man of old, for instance, Adam, Enoch, Ezra. They could imitate the Hebrew style of Scripture. They could claim that God had spoken to them. They could, at the very least, cite a verse of Scripture and impute to the cited passage their own opinion. These four methods – pseudepigraphy, stylistic imitation (hence, forgery), claim of direct revelation from God, and eisegesis – found no favor with the Mishnah's framers. To the contrary, they signed no name to their book. Their Hebrew was new in its syntax and morphology, completely unlike that of the Mosaic writings of the Pentateuch. They never claimed that God had anything to do with their opinions. They rarely cited a verse of Scripture as authority. It follows that, whatever the authors of the Mishnah said about their document, the implicit character of the book tells us that they did not claim God had dictated or even approved what they had to say. Why not? The framers simply ignored all the validating conventions of the world in which they lived. And, as I have said, they failed to make explicit use of any others. It follows that we do not know whether the Mishnah was supposed to be part of the Torah or to enjoy a clearly defined relationship to the existing Torah. We also do not know what else, if not the Torah, was meant to endow the Mishnah's laws with heavenly sanction. To state matters simply, we do not know what the framers of the Mishnah said they had made, nor do we know what the people who received and were supposed to obey the Mishnah thought they possessed.

IV.   Torah in the Mishnah

A survey of the uses of the word *Torah* in the Mishnah provides us with an account of what the framers of the Mishnah, founders of what would emerge as rabbinic Judaism, understood by that term. But it will not tell us how they related their own ideas to the Torah, nor shall we find a trace of evidence of that fully articulated way of life – in use of the word *Torah* to categorize and classify persons, places, things, relationships, all manner of abstractions – that we find exposed in some later redacted writings. True, the Mishnah places a high value upon studying the Torah and upon the status of the sage. The following characteristic sayings speaks of a *mamzer,* that is, one born of parents who had no legal right to wed, a serious disability in a caste society such as the one at hand, as against an *am haares,* understood here simply as an ignorant person. A "*mamzer*-disciple of a sage takes priority over a high-priest *am-haares,*" as at Mishnah-tractate Horayot 3:8. But that judgment, distinctive though it is, cannot settle the question. All it shows is that the Mishnah pays due honor to the sage. But if the Mishnah does not claim to constitute part of the Torah, then what makes a sage a sage is not mastery of the Mishnah in particular. What we have in hand merely continues the established and familiar position of the wisdom writers of old. Wisdom is important. Knowledge of the Torah is definitive. But to maintain that position, one need hardly profess the fully articulated Torah myth of rabbinic Judaism. Proof of that fact, after all, is the character of the entire wisdom literature prior to the Mishnah itself.

So the issue is clearly drawn. It is not whether we find in the Mishnah exaggerated claims about the priority of the disciple of a sage. We do find such claims. The issue is whether we find in the Mishnah the assertion that whatever the sage has on the authority of his master goes back to

Sinai. We seek a definitive view that what the sage says falls into the classification of Torah, just as what Scripture says constitutes Torah from God to Moses. That is what distinguishes wisdom from the Torah as it emerges in the context of rabbinic Judaism. The simple fact is that we do not find the Torah in the Mishnah, and, in the Mishnah's authorship's representation of their writing, the Mishnah is not part of the Torah.

When the authors of the Mishnah surveyed the landscape of Israelite writings down to their own time, they saw only Sinai, that is, what we now know as Scripture. Based on the documents they cite or mention, we can say with certainty that they knew the pentateuchal law. We may take for granted that they accepted as divine revelation also the Prophets and the Writings, to which they occasionally make reference. That they regarded as a single composition, that is, as revelation, the Torah, Prophets, and Writings appears from their references to the Torah, as a specific "book", and to a Torah-scroll. Accordingly, one important meaning associated with the word *Torah* was concrete in the extreme. The Torah was a particular book or sets of books, regarded as holy, revealed to Moses at Sinai. That fact presents no surprise, since the Torah-scroll(s) had existed, it is generally assumed, for many centuries before the closure of the Mishnah in 200 A.D.

What is surprising is that everything from the formation of the canon of the Torah to their own day seems to have proved null in their eyes. Between the Mishnah and Mount Sinai lay a vast, empty plain. From the perspective of the Torah myth as they must have known it, from Moses and the prophets, to before Judah the Patriarch, lay a great wasteland. So the concrete and physical meaning attaching to the word *Torah,* that is, the Torah, the Torah revealed by God to Moses at Mount Sinai (including the books of the Prophets and the Writings), bore a contrary implication. Beyond The Torah there was no torah. Besides the Pentateuch, Prophets, and Writings, not only did no physical scroll deserve veneration, but no corpus of writings demanded obedience. So the very limited sense in which the words *the Torah* were used passed a stern judgment upon everything else, including all the other writings that we know circulated widely, in which other Jews alleged that God had spoken and said "these things."

The range of the excluded possibilities that other Jews explored demands no survey. But, in a moment, we will take a passing glance at another Judaism of this same time and place. What other possibilities have been neglected? They encompass everything, not only the Gospels (by 200 A.D. long since in the hands of outsiders), but secret books, history books, psalms, wisdom writings, rejected works of prophecy – everything excluded from any biblical canon by whoever determined there should be a canon. If the library of the Essenes at Qumran tells us what might have been, then we must regard as remarkably impoverished the (imaginary) library that would have served the authors of the Mishnah: The Book of Books, but nothing else. We seldom see so stern, so austere a vision of what commands the status of holy revelation among Judaisms over time. The tastes of the Mishnah's authors express a kind of literary iconoclasm, but with a difference. The literary icons did survive in the churches of Christendom. But, in their own society and sacred setting, the judgment of Mishnah's authors would prevail from its time to ours. Nothing in the Judaisms of the heritage from the Hebrew Scripture's time to the Mishnah's day would survive the implacable rejection of the framers of the Mishnah, unless under Christian auspices or buried in caves. Therefore, when we take up that first and simplest meaning associated with the word *Torah* or The Torah, we confront a stunning judgment: this and nothing else, this alone, the thing alone of its kind and no other thing of similar kind.

V.   How Mishnah-Tractates Actually Relate to the Written Torah

Treating the issue of the standing and character of the Mishnah, within the community that received the document as authoritative, as settled by the provision of proof texts for individual statements by itself presented no final solution. For with the claim that the Mishnah stood in relationship to The Torah revealed by God to Moses at Sinai a range of questions were precipitated. That same claim, presumably required for political reasons as much as for considerations of theological logic, defined the problem of the Mishnah in a very particular way, as we already recognize. As we now realize, the Mishnah had to be brought into alignment with The Torah of Moses. The final solution to the problem of the Mishnah was to identify that document as half of a two-part revelation, or Torah, one in writing, the other oral. But that mythico–theological solution itself raised more questions than it settled, and it was, in any case, a long time in coming. Before proceeding, let me characterize the actual facts of the matter, that is to say, the relationship between the Mishnah and Scripture. Among the sixty-two tractates of the Mishnah (omitting reference to tractate Avot, which is not part of the Mishnah as originally promulgated, differing as to form, rhetoric, logic, and topical program), we find three relationships to Scripture.

First, there are tractates that simply repeat in their own words precisely what Scripture has to say, and, at best, serve to amplify and complete the basic ideas of Scripture. For example, all of the cultic tractates of the second division, the one on Appointed Times, which tell what one is supposed to do in the Temple on the various special days of the year, and the bulk of the cultic tractates of the fifth division, which deals with Holy Things, simply restate facts of Scripture. For another example, all of those tractates of the sixth division, on Purities, which specify sources of uncleanness, depend completely on information supplied by Scripture. I have demonstrated in detail that every important statement in Niddah, on menstrual uncleanness, and the most fundamental notions of Zabim, on the uncleanness of the person with flux referred to in Leviticus Chapter Fifteen, as well as every detail in Negaim, on the uncleanness of the person or house suffering the uncleanness described at Leviticus Chapters Thirteen and Fourteen – all of these tractates serve only to restate the basic facts of Scripture and to complement those facts with other important ones.

Second, there are tractates that take up facts of Scripture but work them out in an unpredictable way. A supposition concerning what is important about the facts, utterly remote from the supposition of Scripture, will explain why the Mishnah tractates under discussion say such original things when confronting Scripturally-provided facts. For example, Scripture takes for granted that the red cow will be burned in a state of uncleanness, because it is burned outside the camp or Temple. The priestly writers cannot have imagined that a state of cultic cleanness was to be attained outside of the cult. The absolute datum of tractate Parah, by contrast, is that cultic cleanness can be attained outside of the "tent of meeting." The red cow was to be burned in a state of cleanness even exceeding that cultic cleanness required in the Temple itself. The problematic that generates the intellectual agendum of Parah, therefore, is how to work out the conduct of the rite of burning the cow in relationship to the Temple: Is it to be done in exactly the same way, or in exactly the opposite way? This mode of contrastive and analogical thinking helps us to understand the generative problematic of such tractates as Erubin and Besah, to mention only two.

Third, there are many tractates that either take up problems in no way suggested by Scripture, or begin from facts, at best, merely relevant to facts of Scripture. In the former category are Tohorot, on the cleanness of foods, with its companion, Uqsin; Demai, on doubtfully tithed produce; Tamid, on the conduct of the daily whole-offering; Baba Batra, on rules of real estate transactions and certain other commercial and property relationships, and so on. In the latter category are Ohalot, which spins out its strange problems within the theory that a tent and a utensil are to be compared to one another (!); Kelim, on the susceptibility to uncleanness of various sorts of utensils; Miqvaot, on the sorts of water that effect purification from uncleanness; Ketubot and Gittin, on the documents of marriage and divorce; and many others. These tractates draw on facts of Scripture. But the problem confronted in these tractates in no way responds to problems important to Scripture. What we have here is a prior program of inquiry, which will make ample provision for facts of Scripture in an inquiry generated essentially outside of the framework of Scripture. First comes the problem or topic, then – if possible – comes attention to Scripture.

The simple facts of the matter just now adduced in evidence cannot have made much difference to the third and fourth century theologians who confronted the issue. But any position – from complete autonomy to complete dependence of the Mishnah upon Scripture – can have found support in the evidence. Some tractates merely repeat what we find in Scripture. The Mishnah in no way is so remote from Scripture as its (merely formal) omission of citations of verses of Scripture suggests. But in topical, logical, and rhetorical program, the Mishnah in no way can be described as contingent upon, and secondary to, Scripture, as many of its third through seventh century apologists claimed. The authorship of the Mishnah ignored the entire linguistic heritage of Scripture, writing in a Hebrew of a different character altogether from that of Scripture; they appealed for inner cogency not to narrative, such as predominates in Scripture, but to the logic of hierarchical classification; and large tracts of the Mishnah treat not merely problems distinctive to the document but even topics that have no counterpart whatsoever in Scripture. At the same time, Scripture confronted the framers of the Mishnah as revelation, not merely as a source of facts.

The framers of the Mishnah had their own world with which to deal. They made statements in the framework and fellowship of their own age and generation. They were bound, therefore, to come to Scripture with a set of questions generated other than in Scripture. They brought their own ideas about what was going to be important in Scripture. This is perfectly natural. The philosophers of the Mishnah conceded to Scripture the highest authority. Nonetheless, what they chose to hear, within the authoritative statements of Scripture, will in the end form a statement of its own. Although all of Scripture is authoritative, only some of Scripture is relevant. As a result, the framers and philosophers of the tradition of the Mishnah came to Scripture when they had reason to. That is to say, they brought to Scripture a program of questions and inquiries, all highly selective and framed essentially among themselves. That is why their program itself constituted a statement upon the meaning of Scripture. They and their apologists of one sort hastened to add that their program consisted of a statement of the meaning of Scripture.

In part, we must affirm the truth of that claim. When the framers of the Mishnah speak about the priestly passages of the Mosaic law codes, to take one stunning example, with deep insight they perceive profound layers of meaning embedded in those codes. What they have done with the Priestly Code (called P), moreover, they also have done, though I think less coherently, with the bulk of the Deuteronomic laws and with some of those of the Covenant Code. But their exegetical triumph – exegetical, not merely eisegetical – lies in their handling of the complex corpus of materials of the Priestly Code. The intellectual acumen exhibited by the framers of the Mishnah in dealing with issues of Leviticus, for instance, finds no counterpart in the address to those same topics in the Essene writings of Qumran. The choice of points of stress and special concern, in any event, represents an act of selection, not of mere repetition. For others will have selected and then claimed merely to paraphrase totally different passages of Scripture, not in the Mosaic codes to begin with. Prophecy makes its impact on the holy books of other Israelites of the same ancient times, as, for instance, Q (Quelle: prior source), Matthew, and Mark. Surely we must concede that, in reading those passages, other writers, interested in history and salvation, displayed that same perspicacity as did the framers of the Mishnaic tradition who interpreted the priestly code as they did and so formed a theory of Israel's sanctification. It is in the nature of Scripture itself that such should be the case. The same Scripture that gives us the prophets gives us the Pentateuch as well – and gives priority to the Pentateuchal codes as the revelation of God to Moses. As a result, the appeal to the facts of the Mishnah's relationship to Scripture has no bearing upon the issue at hand.

VI.   The Two Solutions to the Problem of the Mishnah

Two solutions to the problem of the Mishnah in relationship to Scripture presented themselves. One of them, the more influential of the two, proposed to show that, while standing by itself, the Mishnah rested on Scripture. Scripture, therefore, would be read into the Mishnah. To use the language of the Torah myth, the written Torah would be adduced in evidence of propositions of the oral Torah. The premise then was that the two Torahs stood distinct from one another. Therefore, each of the two Torahs would come to full expression on its own, as a literary entity essentially in isolation from the other. A statement of the Torah would be dual, just as the Torah was dual, one emergent on the base of the oral Torah, the Mishnah, the other in the Scriptures, such as were read, for example, in the synagogues.

That is the premise of all documents of the Judaism of the dual Torah. Every writing but one would represent the oral Torah by invoking the text of the Mishnah as the base, and all other materials, whether proof texts of Scripture or discourses of sages, as dependent, for order and structure – therefore, for proportion, balance, composition, and cogency – upon the Mishnah. Then the Torah, the one whole Torah of Moses, our rabbi, as later on matters came to mythic characterization, came to full expression in two distinct statements. Scripture remained always autonomous, and, bearing a vast and welcome burden of amplification and articulation, the Mishnah too remained always an entity unto itself. That theory of the dual Torah always bifurcated yielded most of the literature of the Judaism of the dual Torah that emerged from late antiquity.

But, as I have suggested, there was the authorship of one document that dissented, and that was Sifra's authorship. They attempted to set forth the dual Torah as a single, cogent statement, reading the Mishnah into Scripture not merely for proposition but for expression of proposition. On the surface that decision represented a literary, not merely a theological, judgment. But within the deep structure of thought, it was far more than a mere matter of how to select and organize propositions. Presenting the two Torahs in a single statement constituted an experiment in logic, that logic, in particular, that made cogent thought possible, and that transformed facts into propositions, and propositions into judgments more or less consequential. To demonstrate the profound layers of thought upon which the authorship of Sifra erected its remarkable writing will require much exposition. At this point, it suffices to warn that our authorship did something no one else in Judaic antiquity even imagined attempting to do: to state the dual Torah in a single, coherent, cogent piece of writing, a piece of writing in which new thought came to expression in a very particular medium indeed.

Nor is that medium difficult to describe in formal terms. Whereas the Mishnah's other apologists wrote the written Torah into the Mishnah, Sifra's authorship wrote the oral Torah into Scripture. That is to say, the other of the two approaches to the problem of the Mishnah, the one of Sifra, initially claimed to demonstrate that the Mishnah found its correct place within the written Torah itself. Instead of citing verses of Scripture in the context of the Mishnah, the authorship of Sifra cited passages of the Mishnah in the context of Scripture, Leviticus in particular. However, allow me to concentrate on the other solution, the one that characterized authorities from Avot and the Tosefta through the Bavli, which we may call "the appeal to the Torah for a solution to the problem of the Mishnah."

VII. The Mishnah as an Autonomous Component of the Torah

The prevailing theory, reaching expression in all the successor writings of the Mishnah except for Sifra, generated two, contradictory positions. Both rested on the premise of the autonomy of the Mishnah and in literary form preserved the Mishnah as a free-standing piece of writing. Only the Sifra, as I said, would dismiss the claim of the Mishnah to any independent standing whatever and would in literary form deny to the Mishnah all indication of autonomy. Within the contrary theory, the autonomous Mishnah would be portrayed as either a Torah independent of, and correlative with, Scripture, hence the oral Torah and the written Torah as two distinct writings, or as a secondary and dependent amplification of the written Torah. Let us dwell on these two mutually antagonistic, and yet fundamentally coherent, descriptions of the Mishnah as a free-standing writing.

First, and more radically, the Mishnah constitutes revelation, that is, *torah* as generic, with a small *t.* Here the more simple sense claims that the Mishnah falls into the (open) classification of torah, deriving from the same authority, and consequently enjoying the same standing as any other writing of the same genus (meaning: Scripture). The Mishnah, proposition by proposition, too is a statement of revelation: "torah [not the Torah meaning the Five Books of Moses alone] revealed to Moses at Sinai." But this part of revelation has come down in a form different from the well-known, written part, the Scripture, and, in fact, constitutes its own tradition. For a long time it was handed down orally, not in writing, until given the written formulation now before us in the Mishnah. This sort of apologetic for the Mishnah appears, to begin with, in Abot, with its stunning opening chapter, linking Moses on Sinai through the ages to the earliest-named authorities of the Mishnah itself, the five pairs, on down to Shammai and Hillel. Because some of the named authorities in the chain of tradition appear throughout the materials of the Mishnah, the claim is that what these people say comes to them from Sinai through the processes of qabbalah and massoret — handing down, "traditioning."

Therefore, the reason (from the perspective of the Torah myth of the Mishnah) that the Mishnah does not cite Scripture is that it does not have to. It stands on the same plane and enjoys the same authority as Scripture. The apologists for the Mishnah explored a position not entirely alien to prior Judaic authorships, if not those of the particular Judaism at hand. For this same radical position characterized the writings of people who signed to their books the names of biblical authorities, for example, Baruch or Ezra. But the claim in behalf of the Mishnah is still more extreme than that taken by those pseudepigraphic writers, who imitated the style of Scripture, or who claimed to speak within that same gift of revelation as Moses. How so? It is one thing to say one's holy book is Scripture because it is like Scripture, or to claim that the author of the holy book has a revelation independent of that of Moses. These two positions concede to The Torah of Moses priority over their own holy books. Yet the Mishnah's apologists made no such concession, when they allege that the Mishnah is part of The Torah of Moses. Instead they appealed to the highest possible authority in the Israelite framework, claiming the most one can claim in behalf of the book that, in fact, bears the names of men who lived fifty years before the apologists themselves. So the Mishnah, for the apologists in tractate Avot, is free standing, autonomous torah, that is, revelation from God through precisely those same authorities, revelation or the part of the Torah that happens to come down in oral form and that happens to have been preserved in the names of authorities other than those mentioned in the Scriptures, for example, Simeon the Righteous or Hillel or Gamaliel or even Judah the Partiarch, sponsor of the Mishnah.

What of the other position? It is that the Mishnah is authoritative not because it is *torah* in the generic sense, but because it simply amplifies or depends upon The Torah, in the particular sense of the Five Books of Moses. The earliest exegetical strata of the two Talmuds and the legal–exegetical writings produced in the 200 years after the closure of the Mishnah took the position that the Mishnah is wholly dependent upon Scripture and authoritative, in the status (*but not the classification!*) of the Torah, because of that dependency. Whatever is of worth in the Mishnah can be shown to derive directly from Scripture. As a result, the Mishnah was represented as distinct from, and subordinate to, Scripture. This position is expressed in an obvious way. Once the Talmuds cite a Mishnah pericope, they commonly ask, "What is the source of these words?" And the answer invariably is, "As it is said in Scripture." This constitutes not only a powerful defense for the revealed truth of the Mishnah. It present, also, a stunning judgment upon the standing (and, as a matter of fact, the classification) of the Mishnah. For when the exegetes find themselves constrained to add proof texts, they admit the need to acknowledge that the Mishnah is not (part of) The Torah but only a secondary expression or amplification of The Torah.

That judgment upon the Mishnah forms part of the polemic of Sifra's authorship – but only part of it. Sifra's authorship conducts a sustained polemic against the failure of the Mishnah to cite Scripture very much or systematically to link its ideas to Scripture through the medium of formal demonstration by exegesis. Sifra's rhetorical exegesis, as we will see, follows a standard redactional form. Scripture will be cited. Then a statement will be made about its meaning, or a statement of law correlative to that Scripture will be given. That statement sometimes cites the Mishnah, often verbatim. Finally, the author of Sifra invariably states, "Now is that not (merely) logical?" And the point of that statement will be: Can this position not be gained through the working of mere logic based upon facts supplied (to be sure) by Scripture? The polemical power of Sifra lies in its repetitive demonstration that the stated position, citation of a Mishnah pericope, is not only not the product of logic, but is, and only can be, the product of exegesis of Scripture. That is only part of the matter, as I will explain, but that component of the larger judgment of Sifra's authorship does make the point that the Mishnah is subordinated to Scripture and validated only through Scripture. In that regard, the authorship of Sifra stands at one with the position of the authorships of the other successor writings, even though Sifra's writers carried to a much more profound level of thought the critique of the Mishnah. They did so by rethinking the logical foundations of the entire Torah. But, again, I have moved ahead of my story.

The polemic of Sifra, the Tosefta, and the Talmuds is against the positions that, first, what the Mishnah says (in the Mishnah's own words) is merely logical; and that, second, the position taken by the Mishnah can have been reached in any way other than through a grammatical and syntactical exegesis of Scripture. That other way, the way of reading the Scripture through philosophical logic or practical reason, is explicitly rejected time and again. Philosophical logic and applied reason are inadequate. Formal exegesis is shown to be not only adequate, but necessary, indeed inexorable. It follows that Sifra undertakes to demonstrate precisely what the framers of the opening pericopes of the Talmud's treatment of the Mishnah's successive units of thought also wish to show. The Mishnah is not autonomous, independent, or correlative, (i.e., separate but equal). It is contingent, secondary, and derivative, resting wholly on the foundations of the (written) revelation of God to Moses at Mount Sinai. Therein, too, lies the authority of the Mishnah as tradition.

To review, there are two positions that would rapidly take shape when the Mishnah was published. First, tradition in the form of the Mishnah is deemed autonomous of Scripture and enjoys the same authority as that of Scripture. The reason is that Scripture and ("oral") tradition are merely two media for conveying a single corpus of revealed law and doctrine. Second, tradition in the form of the Mishnah is true because it is not autonomous of Scripture. Tradition is secondary and dependent upon Scripture. The authority of the Mishnah is the authority of Moses. That authority comes to the Mishnah directly and in an unmediated way, because the Mishnah's words were said by God to Moses at Mount Sinai and faithfully transmitted through a process of oral formulation and oral transmission from that time until those words were written down by Judah the Patriarch at the end of the second century. Or, that authority comes to the Mishnah indirectly, in a way mediated through the written Scriptures.

What the Mishnah says is what the Scripture says, rightly interpreted. The authority of tradition lies in its correct interpretation of the Scripture. Tradition bears no autonomous authority, is not an independent entity, correlative with Scripture. A very elaborate (and insufferably dull) technology of exegesis of grammar and syntax is needed to build the bridge between tradition as contained in the Mishnah and Scripture, the original utensil shaped by God and revealed to Moses to convey the truth of revelation to the community of Israel.

VIII.   From Proper Noun to Common Noun: The Torah Myth and the Problem of the Mishnah

Clearly, all views of the Mishnah as a free standing, even subordinated, writing in the setting of the Torah appealed to the conception of the Torah as an open canon. That is to say, Torah served as the definition of a classification (for the theory of the Mishnah as a species of the genus, Torah), or of a status (for the theory of the Mishnah as a dependent statement of the Torah). The conception of the Torah as a particular piece of writing, but as a piece of writing subject to continuous revision from within, such as the authorship of the Mishnah exposed, differed and stood as an idiosyncratic notion. If we ask ourselves what was at stake in the two positions, a simple answer appears. The authorship of Sifra saw the Torah as a particular thing, but one capable of expansion and revision. The writers of the other successor documents, Tosefta and the two Talmuds in particular, were prepared to define the Torah as Torah, either as generic within a classification system or as having status within a system of hierarchization. The authorship of Sifra, therefore, imputed to the word *Torah* only a single meaning, The Torah, the Five Books of Moses, then revising the limited conception of what those books (or, at least, the book of Leviticus) comprised. The writers of the other documents imputed to the word *Torah* the sense of a classification or a status, treating the word in an abstract, not only a concrete way, that is to say: as a common noun, not a proper noun. And within that small difference unfolds the tale told here. We can understand how radical a position emerges in Sifra only when we see that position as rejection of a protracted process of the articulation of the contrary one.

Let us consider how, for most of the Judaisms of antiquity, and for most of the writers of the books of the Judaism of the dual Torah, the word *Torah* moved from a proper to a common noun.[1] The Torah of Moses clearly occupied a critical place in all systems of Judaism from the closure of the Torah book, the Pentateuch, in the time of Ezra onward. But, as we have already noticed, among the successor writers to the Mishnah, the Torah, as the book, developed into an abstract and encompassing symbol, so that in most of the canonical writings of the Judaism of the dual Torah, everything was contained in that one thing. When we speak of *torah,* in the bulk of the rabbinical literature of late antiquity, we no longer denote a particular book, on the one side, or the contents of such a book, on the other. Instead, we connote a broad range of clearly distinct categories of common noun and verb, concrete fact and abstract relationship alike.

What are the common nouns that *torah* as generic, torah with a small *t* connotes? "Torah" stands for a kind of human being. It connotes a social status and a sort of social group. It refers to a type of social relationship. It further denotes a legal status and differentiates among legal norms. As symbolic abstraction, the word encompasses things and persons, actions and status, points of social differentiation and legal and normative standing, as well as "revealed truth." In all, the main points of insistence of the whole of Israel's life and history come to full symbolic expression in that single word. If people wanted to explain how they would be saved, they would use the word *Torah*. If they wished to sort out their parlous relationships with gentiles, they would use the world *Torah*. Torah stood for salvation and accounted for Israel's worldly condition and the hope, for both individual and nation alike, of life in the world to come. For the kind of Judaism under discussion, therefore, the word *Torah* stood for everything. The Torah symbolized the whole, at once and entire. When, therefore, we wish to describe the unfolding of the definitive doctrine of Judaism in its formative period, the first exercise consists in paying close attention to the meanings imputed to a single word for everyone in the Judaism of the dual Torah except for, and until, Sifra's authorship.

Every detail of the religious system at hand exhibits essentially the same point of insistence, captured in the simple notion of the Torah as the generative symbol, the total, exhaustive expression of the system as a whole. That is why the definitive ritual of the Judaism under study consisted in studying the Torah as the generative symbol, the total, exhaustive expression of the system as a whole. That is why the definitive myth explained that one who studied Torah would become holy, like Moses "our rabbi," and like God, in whose image humanity was made and whose Torah provided the plan and the model for what God wanted of a humanity created in his image. As for Christians it was in Christ God made flesh, so the framers of the system of Judaism at hand found in the Torah that image of God to which Israel should aspire, and to which the sage in fact conformed.

The meaning of the several meanings of the Torah then requires only brief explanation.

1.   When the Torah refers to a particular thing, it is to a scroll containing divinely revealed words. The authorship of Sifra will concur, but differ: It is a particular thing, in their case, the book of Leviticus. But then that book or scroll ("sifra") gains a new definition of its own.

2.   The Torah may further refer to revelation, not as an object but as a corpus of doctrine.

3.   When one "does Torah," the disciple "studies" or "learns," and the

master "teaches," Torah. Hence while the word *Torah* never appears as a verb, it does refer to an act.

4. The word also bears a quite separate sense, torah as category or classification or corpus of rules, for example, "the torah of driving a car" is a usage entirely acceptable to some documents. This generic usage of the word does occur.

5. The word *Torah* very commonly refers to a status, distinct from and above another status, as "teachings of Torah" as against "teachings of scribes." For the two Talmuds that distinction is absolutely critical to the entire hermeneutic enterprise. But it is important even in the Mishnah.

6. Obviously, no account of the meaning of the word *Torah* can ignore the distinction between the two Torahs, written and oral. It is important only in the secondary stages of the formation of the literature.

7. Finally, the word *Torah* refers to a source of salvation, often fully worked out in stories about how the individual and the nation will be saved through Torah. In general, the sense of the word *salvation* is not complicated. It is simply salvation in the way in which Deuteronomy and the Deuteronomic historians understand it: Kings who do what God wants win battles, those who do not, lose. So here too, people who study and do Torah are saved from sickness and death, and the way Israel can save itself from its condition of degradation also is through Torah.

The transformation of the word *Torah* from a proper noun, referring to the Pentateuch, to a common noun bearing diverse connotations and serving various purposes, provided a final solution to the problem of the Mishnah. Meaning no longer "the Torah," but "torah" as classification, the Mishnah fell into the classification of torah because its authorities stood in the chain of tradition of Sinai. When "torah" referred to standing or status, the Mishnah enjoyed the status of torah, because it depended upon the authority of the Torah revealed by God to Moses at Sinai. In both of these ways, therefore, people could readily answer the question of the Mishnah's authority in both politics and theology.

In order to grasp precisely how torah as a common noun served, we turn to the solutions the Mishnah worked out in the two Talmuds in succession: the one a broadening of the common noun to encompass within the status of torah the sages of the Mishnah, the other a revising of the literature that belonged to the classification of torah to state, all together and all at once, in a single statement, the one whole Torah of Moses, our rabbi. It is the Talmud of the Land of Israel that in the unfolding of the canonical writings first fully exposed the conception of the sage as torah, and the Talmud of Babylonia that re-presented the Torah, uniting the dual Torah in the ultimate statement that defined the Judaism of the dual Torah from then to now.

Notes

[1]   In my *Torah: From Scroll to Symbol in Talmudic Judaism.* (Second printing: Atlanta, 1988: Scholars Press for Brown Judaic Studies), I trace the progess of the word *Torah* from proper to common noun. But in that work I did not realize that the word in some writings retained only, or mainly, its sense as a proper noun, referring to the Torah-scroll, the Pentateuch, the Five Books of Moses in particular. So the formulation of matters here moves beyond the results set forth there.

CHAPTER TWO

Torah as a Common Noun:
The Solution of the Talmuds

I. Building on the Structure of the Mishnah:
The Solution of the Talmuds

The character and uses of the Mishnah made necessary the formation of the Talmuds, its constant exegetical companions. For with the processes of exegesis and application of the Mishnah came the labor of collecting and arranging these exegeses, in correlation with the Mishnah, read line by line and paragraph by paragraph. The result was the formation of ad hoc and episodic amplifications and clarifications, which ultimately comprised the first stratum of the two Talmuds. The process, once applied to the Mishnah, overspread the limits of that document. Within the work of exegesis of Scripture was the correlative labor of organizing what had been said verse by verse, following the structure of a book of the Hebrew Bible. The sorts of things the sages who framed the Talmuds did to the Mishnah, they then went and did to Scripture. Just as the Mishnah was subjected to an exegesis consisting of citation and gloss, so Scripture was addressed in the same way by sages of the same circles. But the Mishnah framed the focus of initial interest and its requirements then dictated what would be done with Scripture. The documents all focus attention on the Mishnah in particular. Three of them, the Tosefta and the two Talmuds, the Talmud of the Land of Israel, a.k.a. the Yerushalmi, ca. A.D. 400, and the Talmud of Babylonia, a.k.a. the Bavli, ca. A.D. 600, organize everything at hand around the redactional structure supplied by the Mishnah itself.[1]

The framers of both Talmuds present their materials around the Mishnah, working out whatever they wish to say in the form of a commentary upon, or amplification of, the oral Torah. Formally, therefore, both sets of authors rely upon the Mishnah as the lattice for the vines they wish to display. That their work constitutes far more than a mere commentary or

31

amplification hardly requires demonstration. For one thing, both authorships made radical choices, within the Mishnah, concerning the topics to be subjected to amplification as well as those to be ignored. Second, both groups of writers likewise break up the Mishnah into small and isolated units of discourse, rather than allowing the Mishnah's majestic and well-composed statements of thought to work out a proposition on a given theme with the precision and forethought that, in point of fact, characterized Mishnaic discourse. Third, both authorships begin their analysis of most sentences or paragraphs of the Mishnah with a single question: What is the source of this statement? And both answer in one way: "as it is said," followed by a citation of a verse of the written Torah. These are only three of the many, fundamental ways in which the authorships of both Talmuds have chosen to build upon the foundations of the Mishnah a structure of thought quite their own. Each group of writers made its statement, in its way, of matters of concern to it, while maintaining the pretense that at issue was merely the sense, or harmony, or exposition, of what the Mishnah had already laid down, so long before, as Torah.

Both documents addressed the problem of making of the dual Torah a single statement by a labor of re-presenting the written Torah, in topic, program, and structure within the framework of the oral one. That choice forms part of their larger character as discourses built on the Mishnah. But, for the issue at hand, that fact in no way diminishes the implications for our inquiry. Once the Mishnah, and not Scripture, defines the program of discourse, then Scripture proves, in point of fact, secondary and of diminished interest. Its contribution to the larger project of making the statement of the Torah in a single, sustained way, such as both Talmuds accomplished, is then ancillary: a source of proof texts. Then the written Torah in the nature of things was not asked to carry out the tasks, as to topic, order, structure, program, that were assigned to the oral one: this, then not that. Consequently, the emergent statement of the Torah, in the Yerushalmi's thirty-nine tractates and the Bavli's thirty-seven, appealed for order and sense to the oral Torah.

The reason that both writings relied for structure on the oral, rather than the written, Torah, is that, in each case, reading the word *torah* as generic made it unimportant to turn for plan and structure to Scripture in particular, that is to say, to the (written) Torah. As a common noun, *torah* encompassed not only a document but persons; it supplied not only authoritative teachings contained within its words but also status to persons and teachings not contained within its words (but, it would be assumed, implicit in them). When Scripture, not the Mishnah, defined traits of order, supplied the program of discourse, and dictated structure, then, correspondingly, none had to appeal to classification of *torah* or status as torah. So the two form matching opposites: The structure of the written Torah will impart to *torah* the definition of a proper noun, the structure of the oral Torah will require that *torah* serve as a common noun. And, it would follow, the representation of *torah* as a common noun will take on a heavy burden of meaning, as, we will now see, is the case for the Yerushalmi.

Along parallel lines, the task of formulating and expressing in a single statement the united Torah, written and oral, will entail a merely formal, and in no way substantive or profound and penetrating, re-presentation of torah – not The Torah at all. The Bavli will show us with great clarity what uniting the dual Torah yielded, when all that was at stake was setting within the same capacious (Mishnaic) utensil the two Torahs, revised and reframed by the Torah authorities of the age, the sages themselves. For at stake in both Yerushalmi and Bavli is the sage as liv-ing *torah,* and the person of the sage forms the union of the two Torahs. The Yerushalmi's authors would set forth the sage as living *torah,* and, in that context, the Bavli's authors would proceed to set side by side the written and the oral Torahs, unifying them in no profound way at all, but taking as premise the unity of the two in the person and learning of the sage.[2]

II. The Yerushalmi and the Union of the Torah in the Person of the Sage

The Mishnah is held in the Talmud of the Land of Israel to be equivalent to Scripture (Yerushalmi, Horayyot 3:5). But the Mishnah is not called (the oral) Torah. Still, once the Mishnah entered the status of torah, such as was taken for granted was possible since "torah" referred to a status, not merely a particular book or Scripture, it would take but a short step to a theory of the Mishnah as part of the revelation at Sinai – hence, oral Torah. In the first Talmud we find the first glimmerings of an effort to theorize in general, not merely in detail, about how specific teachings of Mishnah relate to specific teachings of Scripture. The citing of scriptural proof texts for Mishnah propositions, after all, would not have caused much surprise to the framers of the Mishnah; they themselves included such passages, though not often. But what conception of the Torah underlies such initiatives, and how do Yerushalmi sages propose to explain the phenomenon of the Mishnah as a whole? The following passage provides one statement. It refers to the assertion (M. Hag. 1:8D) that the laws on cultic cleanness presented in the Mishnah rest on deep and solid foundations in the Scripture.

Y. Hagigah 1:7

[V A]   The laws of the Sabbath [M. 1:8B]: R. Jonah said R. Hama bar Uqba raised the question [in reference to M. Hag. 1:8D's view that there are many verses of Scripture on cleanness], "And lo, it is written only, 'Nevertheless a spring or a cistern holding water shall be clean; but whatever touches their carcass shall be unclean' (Lev. 11:36). And from this verse you derive many laws. [So how can M. Hag. 1:8D say what it does about many verses for laws of cultic cleanness?]"

[B]   R. Zeira in the name of R. Yohanan: "If a law comes to hand and you do not know its nature, do not discard it for another one, for lo, many laws were stated to Moses at Sinai, and all of them have been embedded in the Mishnah."

The truly striking assertion appears at B. The Mishnah now is claimed to contain statements made by God to Moses. Just how these statements found their way into the Mishnah, and which passages of the Mishnah contain them, we do not know. Given the fundamental assertion at hand, however, that is hardly important. The passage proceeds to a further, and far more consequential proposition. It asserts that part of the Torah was written down, and part was preserved in memory and transmitted orally. In context, moreover, that distinction must encompass the Mishnah, thus explaining its origin as part of the Torah. Here is a clear and unmistakable expression of the distinction between two forms in which a single Torah was revealed and handed on at Mount Sinai, part in writing, part orally.

Whereas the passage below does not make use of the language, Torah-in-writing and Torah-by-memory, it does refer to "the written" and "the oral." Therefore, I believe it fully justifiable to supply the word *Torah* in square brackets. The reader will note, however, that the word *Torah* likewise does not occur in parts K or L. Only when the passage reaches its climax, at M, does it break down into a number of categories – Scripture, Mishnah, Talmud, laws, and lore. It there makes the additional point that everything comes from Moses at Sinai. The fully articulated theory of two Torahs (not merely one Torah in two forms) does not reach final expression in this passage. But short of explicit allusion to Torah-in-writing and Torah-by-memory, which (so far as I am able to discern) we find mainly in the Talmud of Babylonia, the ultimate theory of Torah of formative Judaism is at hand in what follows.

Y. Hagigah 1:7

[V D]   R. Zeirah in the name of R. Eleazar: " 'Were I to write for him my laws by ten thousands, they would be regarded as a strange thing' (Hos. 8:12). Now is the greater part of the Torah written down? [Surely not. The oral part is much greater.] But more abundant are the matters which are derived by exegesis from the written [Torah] than those derived by exegesis from the oral [Torah]."

[E]   And is that so?

[F]   But more cherished are those matters which rest upon the written [Torah] than those which rest upon the oral [Torah].

[J]   R. Haggai in the name of R. Samuel bar Nahman, "Some teachings were handed on orally, and some things were handed on in writing, and we do not know which of them is the more precious. But on the basis of that which is written, 'And the Lord said to Moses, Write these words; in accordance with these words I have made a covenant with you and with Israel' (Ex. 34:27), [we conclude] that the ones which are handed on orally are the more precious."

[K]   R. Yohanan and R. Yudan b. R. Simeon – One said, "If you have kept what is preserved orally and also kept what is in writing, I shall make a convenant with you, and if not, I shall not make a convenant with you."

[L]   The other said, "If you have kept what is preserved orally and you have kept what is preserved is writing, you shall receive a reward, and if not, you shall not receive a reward."

[M]   [With reference to Deut. 9:10: "And on them was written according to all the words which the Lord spoke with you in the mount,"] said R. Joshua b. Levi, "He could have written, 'On them,' but wrote, 'And on them.' He could have written, 'All,' but wrote, 'According to all.' He could have written, 'Words,' but wrote 'The words.' [These then serve as three encompassing clauses, serving to include] Scripture, Mishnah, Talmud, laws, and lore. Even what an experienced student in the future is going to teach before his master already has been stated to Moses at Sinai."

[N]   What is the Scriptural basis for this view?

[O]   "There is no remembrance of former things, nor will there be any remembrance of later things yet to happen among those who come after" (Qoh. 1:11).

[P]   If someone says, "See, this is a new thing," his fellow will answer him, saying to him, "This has been around before us for a long time."

Here we have explicit evidence that people believed part of the Torah had been preserved not in writing but orally. Linking that part to the Mishnah remains a matter of implication. But it surely is probable when we are told that the Mishnah contains Torah traditions revealed at Sinai. From that view it requires only a small step to the allegation that the Mishnah is part of the Torah, the oral part.

In the story that follows, we will see that because people observed the rules of the Torah, they expected to be saved. And if they did not observe, they accepted their punishment. So Torah now stands for something more than revelation and life of study, and (it goes without saying) the sage now appears as a holy, not merely a learned, man. This is because his knowledge of the Torah has transformed him. Accordingly, we deal with a category of stories that portray Torah as a matter of status of persons, not only writings, and that will reach its culmination in the numerous explicit descriptions of sages as Torah in classification and status alike, hence, as it happens in the present system, also as source of salvation.

Y. Taanit 3:8

[II A]   Levi ben Sisi: troops came to his town. He took a scroll of the Torah and went up to the roof and said, "Lord of the ages! If a single word of this scroll of the Torah has been nullified [in our town], let them come up against us, and if not, let them go their way."

[B]   Forthwith people went looking for the troops but did not find them [because they had gone their way].

[C]   A disciple of his did the same thing, and his hand withered, but the troops went their way.

[D]   A disciple of his disciple did the same thing. His hand did not wither, but they also did not go their way.

[E]   This illustrates the following apothegm: You can't insult an idiot, and dead skin does not feel the scalpel.

What is interesting here is how categories or taxa (singular: taxon) into which the word *Torah* previously fell have been absorbed and superseded in a new taxon. The Torah is an object: "He took a scroll . . ." It — the object – also contains, that is, constitutes, God's revelation to Israel: "If a single word . . ." The outcome of the revelation is to form an ongoing way of life, embodied in the sage himself: "A disciple of his did the same thing . . ." The sage plays an intimate part in the supernatural event: "His hand withered . . ." Now can we categorize this story as a statement that the Torah constitutes a particular object, or a source of divine revelation, or a way of life? Yes and no.

The Torah here stands not only for the things we already have catalogued. It represents one more thing that takes in all the others. Torah is a source of salvation. How so? The Torah stands for, or constitutes, the way in which the people of Israel save themselves from marauders. This straightforward sense of salvation will not have surprised the author of Deuteronomy. In the canonical documents prior to the Yerushalmi, we look in vain for sayings or stories that fall into such a category. True, we may take for granted that everyone always believed that, in general, Israel would be saved by obedience to the Torah. That claim would not have surprised any Israelite writers from the first prophets down through the final redactors of the Pentateuch in the time of Ezra and onward through the next 700 years. But, in the rabbinical corpus from the Mishnah forward, the specific assertion that by taking up the scroll of the Torah and standing on the roof of one's house, confronting God in heaven, a sage in particular could take action against the expected invasion – that kind of claim is not located, so far as I know, in any composition surveyed thus far.

This new usage of Torah found in the Talmud of the Land of Israel emerges from a group of stories not readily classified in our established categories. All of these stories treat the word *Torah* (whether scroll, contents, or act of study) as source and guarantor of salvation. Accordingly, evoking the word *Torah* forms the centerpiece of a theory of Israel's history, on the one side, and an account of the teleology of the entire system, on the other. Torah indeed has ceased to constitute a specific thing or even a category or classification when stories about studying the Torah yield not a judgment as to status (i.e., praise for the learned man) but promise for supernatural blessing now and salvation in time to come.

III. The Bavli and the Union of the Torah in a Single Cogent Statement

Approximately 90 percent of the Yerushalmi's units of discourse in my sample probe of five tractates dealt with the Mishnah[3] in the Mishnah's terms and framework. Hence, we may conclude that the principal, though not sole, focus of discourse in the Yerushalmi was the amplification of the Mishnah. By contrast, in the Bavli, we find that, varying from tractate to tractate, as high a proportion as 40 percent of the units of discourse of a given tractate may focus upon Scripture rather than the Mishnah. Thus, for the framers of the Bavli, Scripture, the written Torah, served, alongside the Mishnah, as the fundamental structure of the organization of discourse and the definition of the order of thought. In addition, for the authorship of the Bavli, the two Torahs, oral and written, were to be set forth in a single statement, side by side, in a formal relationship. Unfortunately, the Bavli's authorship united the dual Torah by entirely formal means. So far as there was a profound and substantive union of the two Torahs, it would take place in an other-than-literary context.

These statements on how the two Talmuds approach the problem of uniting the dual Torah begin in the context of comparison of the (later) Bavli with the (earlier) Yerushalmi. The Yerushalmi then forms the base against which the Bavli is to be defined. The comparison of the Bavli to the Yerushalmi, we know, presents the one important and demonstrable difference between them. Whereas the Yerushalmi rarely makes intensive use of Scripture as the framework for the composition of units of discourse and the organization of several such units of discourse into a large-scale and sustained statement, the Bavli often does. In general, the Bavli does so from four to six times more frequently than does the Yerushalmi.[4] In the Bavli's tractates (varying to be sure by reason of subject matter), we may discern that as much as a third of the units of discourse focus not upon the Mishnah but upon Scripture. The Yerushalmi's equivalent proportions in no way correspond. The Bavli's writers and redactors made up Scripture by units of discourse on a large scale. They built out of such units of discourse enormous and sustained constructions. The Yerushalmi's writers and redactors less commonly did the former and never did the latter, so what is distinctive to the Bavli has now to return to center stage. The Bavli's authorship joined for redactional purposes and, therefore, formed into a single, if deeply seamed, statement the two media of the Torah, one of which the Yerushalmi's authors had neglected. Therefore, the difference between the Bavli and the Yerushalmi is the Bavli's far more ample use of Scripture not only for proof, nor even only for truth, but solely the Bavli's resort to Scripture for the redaction and organization of large-scale discourse. In the Bavli, the Scripture serves alongside the Mishnah and in volume is not enormously less than it. In the Bavli, Scripture and the Mishnah together define structure and impart proportion and organization. By contrast, in the Yerushalmi, Scripture forms an important component of the canon. But it does not dictate lines of order and main beams of structure.

IV.   An Example of Uniting the Dual Torah in the Bavli

Since the preceding discussion has proceeded in general terms, I will provide an example of how the framers of the Bavli set side by side a Mishnah passage and its amplification, then a set of verses of Scripture and exegesis thereof. The Mishnah passage refers to various persons who do not have a portion in the world to come. The passage is worked out in its own terms. Then verses of Scripture relevant to those who are named, but not relevant to the proposition of the Mishnah that those who are named are deprived of their portion in the world to come, are set forth in their own terms. This brief snippet suffices to show the reader how the Bavli's editors provide an account of the two Torahs in a single sustained passage. In the Epilogue, we will see why this approach to uniting the two Torahs succeeded, whereas the approach taken by the authorship of Sifra did not.

Mishnah-Tractate Sanhedrin 11:2

A. *Three kings and four ordinary folk have no portion in the world to come.*

B. *Three kings: Jeroboam, Ahab, and Manasseh.*

C. *R. Judah says, "Manasseh has a portion in the world to come,*

D. *"since it is said, 'And he prayed to him and he was entreated of him and heard his supplication and brought him again to Jerusalem into his kingdom' "* (2 Chr. 33:13).

E. *They said to him, "To his kingdom he brought him back, but to the life of the world to come he did not bring him back."*

F. *Four ordinary folk: Balaam, Doeg, Ahitophel, and Gehazi.*

We now briefly consider an amplification of the Mishnah passage above, and then see how, side by side, the Bavli's framers set a systematic amplification of a passage of Scripture.

CCX.

A. *Four ordinary folk: Balaam, Doeg, Ahitophel, and Gehazi [M. 11:2F]:*

B. [The name] Balaam [means] not with [the rest of] the people [using the same consonants], [who will inherit the world to come].

C. Another interpretation: Balaam, because he devoured the people.

D. "Son of Beor" means that he had sexual relations with a cow [a play on the consonants of the word for Beor].

CCXI.

A. It was taught on Tannaite authority:

B. Beor, Cushan-rishathaim, and Laban, the Syrian, are one and the same person.

C. Beor: because he had sexual relations with a cow.

D. Cushan-rishathaim [two acts of wickednesss], for he commited two acts of wickedness against Israel, one in the time of Jacob and one in the time of the Judges.

E. But what is his real name? It was Laban the Aramaean.

Now to a citation of Scripture and a systematic amplification of what is cited. What we will see is a treatment (Num. 22:7ff.) without any interest at all in the Mishnah passage with which we commenced. Here is an example of how the Bavli's framers set Mishnah and Scripture passages side by side and work out the meanings of both.

CCXIV.

A. "And the elders of Moab and the elders of Midian departed" (Num. 22:7):

B. It was taught on Tannaite authority:

C. There was never peace between Midian and Moab. The matter may be compared to two dogs who were in a kennel, barking at one another.

D. A wolf came and attacked one. The other said, "If I do not help him today, he will kill him, and tomorrow he will come against me."

E. So the two dogs went and killed the wolf.

F. Said R. Pappa, "This is in line with what people say: 'The weasel and the cat can make a banquet on the fat of the unlucky.' "

The verses in sequence are now taken up. Amplification and fairly systematic treatment of Numbers (Num) 22 in no way serve the requirements of the Mishnah pericope cited at the outset. The thrust of exegesis derives from Scripture's, not the Mishnah's, statements, even though the topic important to the Mishnah directs our attention to the passage of Scripture that will be subjected to exegesis. That is what we understand when we realize that the Mishnah supplies the lattice; but, we will now see, Scripture nourishes the luxuriant foliage, all on its own.

CCXV.

A. "And the princess of Moab abode with Balaam" (Num. 22:8):

B. And as to the princess of Midian, where had they gone?

C. When he said to them, "Lodge here this night and I will bring you word again [as the Lord shall speak to me]," (Num. 22:8), they said, "Does any father hate his son? [No chance!]"

CCXVI.

A. Said R. Nahman, "Hutzbah, even against heaven, serves some good. To begin with, it is written, 'You shall not go with them' (Num. 22:12), and then it is said, 'Rise up and go with them' " (Num. 22:20).

B. Said R. Sheshet, "Hutzbah is dominion without a crown.

C. "For it is written, 'And I am this day weak, though anointed king, and these men, the sons of Zeruiah, be too hard for me' " (2 Sam. 3:39). [Freedman, *Sanhedrin* p. 717, n. 1: Thus their boldness and impudence outweighed sovereignty.]

CCXVII.

A. Said R. Yohanan, "Balaam had one crippled foot, for it is written, 'And he walked haltingly' (Num. 23:3).

B. "Samson had two crippled feet, as it is said, 'An adder in the path that bites the horses' heels' (Gen. 49:17). [Freedman, *Sanhedrin,* p. 717, n. 3: This was a prophecy of Samson. " 'An adder in the path' is taken to mean that he would have to slither along like an adder, being lame in both feet."]

C. "Balaam was blind in one eye, as it is said, 'Whose eye is open' (Num. 24:3).

D. "He practiced enchantment with his penis.

E. "Here it is written, 'Falling but having his eyes open' (Num. 24:3), and elsewhere: 'And Haman was fallen on the bed whereon Esther was' " (Est. 7:8).

F. It has been stated on Amoraic authority:

G. Mar Zutra said, "He practiced enchantment with his penis."

H. Mar, son of Rabina, said, "He had sexual relations with his ass."

I. As to the view that he practiced enchantment with his penis it is as we have just now stated.

J. As to the view that he had sexual relations with his ass:

K. Here it is written, "He bowed, he lay down as a lion and as a great lion" (Num. 24:9), and elsewhere it is written, "At her feet [105B] he bowed, he fell" (Jud. 5:27).

CCXVIII.

A. "He knows the mind of the most high" (Num. 24:16):

B. Now if he did not know the mind of his own beast, how could he have known the mind of the most high?

C. What is the case of the mind of his beast?

D. People said to him, "What is the reason that you did not ride on your horse?"

E. He said to them, "I put it out to graze in fresh pasture."

F. [The ass] said to him, "Am I not your ass" (Num. 22:30) [That shows he rode an ass, not a horse.]

G. "[You are] merely for carrying loads."

H. "Upon whom you rode" (Num. 22:30).

I. "It was a happenstance."

J. "Ever since I was yours, until this day" (Num. 22:30).

K. [The ass continued,] "And not only so, but I serve you for sexual relations by night."

L. Here it is written, "Did I ever do so to you" (Num. 22:30) and elsewhere it is written, "Let her serve as his companion." [The same word is used, proving that sexual relations took place as with David and the maiden in his old age.]

M. Then what is the meaning of the statement, "He knows the mind of the Most High" (Num. 24:16)?

N. He knew how to tell the exact time at which the Holy One, blessed be he, was angry.

O. That is in line with what the prophet said to Israel, "O my people, remember now what Balak, king of Moab, consulted, and what Balaam the son of Beor answered him from Shittim to Gilgal, that you may know the righteousness of the Lord" (Mic. 6:5).

P. What is the meaning of the statement, "That you may know the righteousness of the Lord" (Mic. 6:5)?

Q. Said the Holy One, blessed be he, to Israel, "Know that I have done many acts of charity with you, that I did not get angry with you in the time of the wicked Balaam.

R. "For if I had become angry during all those days, there would not remain out of (the enemies of) Israel a shred or a remnant."

S. That is in line with what Balaam said to Balak, "How shall I curse one whom God has not cursed? Or shall I rage, when the Lord has not raged?" (Num. 23:8).

T. This teaches that for all those days the Lord had not been angry.

U. But: "God is angry every day" (Ps. 7:12).

V. And how long does his anger last? It is a moment, for it is said, "For his anger endures but a moment, but his favor is life" (Ps. 30:5).

W. If you wish, I shall propose, "Come, my people, enter into your chambers and shut your doors about you, hide yourself as it were for a brief moment, until the indignation be past" (Is. 26:20).

X. When is he angry? It is in the first three hours [of the day], when the comb of the cock is white.

Y. But it is white all the time?

Z. All the other time it has red streaks, but when God is angry, there are no red streaks in it.

Whereas, we may explain the interest of our authorship in the cited passages of the book of Numbers, we cannot maintain that their intent bore any relationship to Mishnah exegesis. Mishnah's topic draws attention to the verses of Scripture in which that topic is paramount. Then the verses of Scripture, viewed on their own, define the generative questions or problems requiring attention. Accordingly, the passages at hand are joined together by the Bavli's editorship with those that precede in such wise that the oral and the written Torahs stand side by side, correlated, separate if not wholly equal, given the Mishnah's definitive structural position.

This brief example then provides a good instance of addressing both Torahs, oral, then written, treated separately but in a single passage. When we see how Sifra's authorship joins the two Torahs, the Bavli's mode of doing so will stand forth as not "how people do things in general" but as the consequence of a choice and a judgment. For in Sifra, with its foundation in the order and structure of the written Torah, the two Torahs do not stand side by side; to the contrary, where a given topic is under discussion, the distinct units of the Mishnah are subordinated not only in order and program, but in discourse. Sifra makes a single statement out of the two components of the Torah, uniting the dual Torahs by re-presenting the oral one within the unfolding discourse of the written one. In the nature of things, that cogent statement of two parts of the Torah as one then portrays everything all together and all at once. It is not a mere formal effect but a substantive and logical initiative, for to re-present the two as one, our authorship finds it has to enter into the deepest layers of thought and to find the unity of the two Torahs in the union of thought that precipitates and generates them both.

V.   Formally Unifying the Dual Torah

Even though, as I insist, what the Bavli's framers do to unite the dual Torah stands for a choice and a judgment, still, to that authorship, matters cannot have appeared as other than natural and "traditional." For the authorship of the Bavli carried forward a long-established enterprise in the forging of links between the Mishnah and Scripture. But the organizers and redactors of the materials compiled in the Bavli did something unprecedented in the Tosefta and quite uncommon in the Yerushalmi. As we saw in the brief passage just presented, they allowed sustained passages of Scripture to serve, as much as sustained and not merely episodic passages of the Mishnah served, as main beams in the composition of structure and order. In a single document, the Mishnah and Scripture functioned together and for the first time in much the same way. The original thesis, that the Mishnah depended upon the written Torah, thus all of its statements were linked to proof texts of Scripture, now gave way to its natural and complete fulfillment. Once sets of verses of Scripture could be isolated and in their continuity made to provide a focus of discourse just as the Mishnah did, Scripture would join the

Mishnah in a single statement, cut down and reshaped to conform to the model of the Mishnah. Thus, through the Bavli, Scripture joined the Mishnah in a new union of mythic language creating one whole Torah.

In so revising Scripture as to recast it into that same discursive and rhetorical framework that defined how and where the Mishnah would serve, the authors – that is, the framers of larger-scale units of discourse, ultimate redactors alike – made their unique contribution. Imposing a literary and redactional unity upon documents so remarkably disparate in every respect as the Mishnah and Scripture, the Bavli's authorship created something both entirely their own and in no way original to them: the Torah, that is, Judaism, in its final and complete statement.

However, the Bavli's creation of a single statement of the dual Torah was solely formal. In presenting a summa of Judaism, the Bavli joined the two streams that, like the Missouri and the Mississippi at St. Louis, had until its time flowed separate and distinct within the same banks. The one stream, coursing from the source of the Mishnah, and the other stream, emanating from the source of Scripture, had mingled only in eddies, at the edges. But the banks of the mighty river had been set from Sinai, and (in the mythic dimension) the two streams had been meant to flow together as one river. In the Yerushalmi, Scripture found a place along the sides. The Mishnah formed the main stream. In the collections of scriptural exegesis (Midrashim, except for Sifra and in much diminished measure the two Sifrés), Scripture had flowed down the center, wholly apart from the Mishnah. In the Bavli, for the first time, the waters mingled in the middle – there, but not in the depths. Discourse was common only for formal reasons, not sustained, not such as to permit the interpenetration of the two Torahs. True, the Bavli for the first time from Sinai (to speak within the Torah myth) joined together in a whole and complete way, in both literary form and doctrinal substance, the one whole Torah of Moses, our rabbi. But, within the framework of the Bavli, the two components of the Torah remained autonomous, correlative, and distinct entities: voices in harmony, but singing a fugue, not one chorus, one melody, one musical line, all together and all at once. Sifra's authorship would compose of the dual Torah that kind of music.

Because Bavli's writers accomplished the nearly perfect union of Scripture and Mishnah in a single document, the Bavli became Israel's fullest Torah. But, again, this union was only nearly perfect and merely at the surface. To demonstrate the greater union that occured, at a more profound level of thought, not merely at the superficial level of formal discourse about topics, I will devote the rest of this book to the Sifra's authorship of the two Torahs. Indeed Sifra's authorship made not only a single statement of the dual Torah, but a single statement *that spoke a single language of logic and cogent thought* – an accomplishment the

Bavli's authorship never even attempted. If the Bavli became the definitive mode of uniting the dual Torah, it is because the Bavli proved accessible, in a way in which the profound reflection of Sifra's authorship cannot ever have proved accessible. That is why when the people of the Torah, Israel, the Jewish people, for the next fifteen hundred years, wished to approach the Mishnah, it was through the reading of the Bavli. That is why when that same people wished to address Scripture, it was through the reading of the Bavli.

As a result, Sifra remained inaccessible, a locked treasury, a cave barred by rocks: a source of diverse texts and explanations, a repository, along with other repositories, of miscellanies. It was not understood for what it was, a sustained and cogent statement of the dual Torah in a single discourse. It formed a re-presentation, in which the written Torah defined the program, the rhetoric, the structure, above all, the logic of cogent thought, encompassing also, as a matter of fact, the oral Torah, the Mishnah, as well.

We now turn to a sizable sample of Sifra, so that readers may encounter for themselves the definitive traits I propose, in the chapters that follow, to describe, analyze, and interpret within the framework of this book. I will show how, by doing things in one way rather than in some other, the authorship of Sifra succeeded in setting for their own statement, their re-presentation, of the dual Torah, as a single, cogent account, entirely on its own, as much as the Bavli stood on its own: the alternative version of the dual Torah as one. The Bavli set the two Torahs side by side, and that, a mere formality, was easy to grasp.[5] Sifra's authorship insisted that a single mode of thought, that of the written Torah, dictated the how, as much as the what, of revelation and the inquiry into revelation. And that, so penetrating into the center of intellect, was difficult to grasp, and, I think, never was grasped. It is the way not taken.

Notes

[1] The two Torahs, oral, in the two Talmuds, and written, in the Midrash compilations, therefore, unfolded side by side, in a process that correlated but was essentially distinct within each document. The type of discourse and the mode of organizing the literary result of discourse suitable for the one document served the other as well. The same people did both for the same reasons. So to the Tosefta, Sifra, and the Yerushalmi alike, the paramount issue was Scripture, not merely its authority but especially its sheer mass of information. The decisive importance of the advent of the Mishnah in precipitating the vast exegetical enterprise represented by the books at hand emerges from a simple fact. This is the argument of my *Midrash in Context: Exegesis in Formative Judaism* (Second printing: Atlanta, 1988: Scholars Press for Brown Judaic Studies).
[2] We return to this matter in the Epilogue.

3   See my *The Talmud of the Land of Israel. A Preliminary Translation. 35. Introduction. Taxonomy* (Chicago, 1985: University of Chicago Press).

4   *Judaism. The Classic Statement. The Evidence of the Bavli* (Chicago, 1986: University of Chicago Press).

5   But there were other, better reasons for the success of the Bavli, specified in the Epilogue.

CHAPTER THREE

A Sample of Sifra

I. Introduction to the Translation

Before proceeding, let us turn to the other mode of uniting the dual Torah. We consider a translation of a sample of Sifra, 6 chapters of the 277 into which both available printed versions (identified presently) divide the document. In this way the reader will have a clear picture of the working of the document as a whole. Sifra, like all other writings of the dual Torah produced in late antiquity, is rhetorically, logically, and topically a uniform statement, repetitious in its basic structure, a fixed form in rhetoric and pattern of modes of thought. Together with the translation, I remark on matters pertinent to the description of the document as a whole.

In my translation I mark each of the smallest whole units of thought with a letter, each of the completed propositions of thought (that we might call "paragraphs") with an Arabic numeral, and entire cogent statements or arguments with a Roman numeral. I anticipate that, however the exegesis of the text may improve upon my basic translation and revise and correct details of sense imputed to words and phrases, the fundamental analytical structure I have identified and presented will endure, as it has for every other document in the rabbinic canon I have translated.[1] In the present case I have ignored the paragraphing of the printed document and made up my own. The reason is that the printed versions in the Hebrew break up sustained and protracted discussions, on the one side, or present as a single discourse two or more whole and completed units of thought, on the other. My division of the chapters of the document, however, follows the received one in the printed text.

What follows is an analytical translation, one in which I make immediately visible the principal and indicative literary traits of the Hebrew, so highlighting the distinctive character of rhetoric and logic of the

47

original. I paragraph the whole units of thought, from the smallest building blocks of discourse upward, and indicate the larger compositions, their beginnings and endings. On the basis of that presentation, readers may perform their own form analyses, inquiries into modes of logical discourse, and other studies that tell us, in aesthetics as much as in theology, the authorship's message and meaning. For any distinction between method and message, form and meaning, obliterates the power of discourse attained in this compilation – as in any other component of the canon of Judaism.

I translate the text of Shachne Koleditzky, *Sifra debé Rab. Hu Sefer Torat Kohanim* (Jerusalem, 1961), and the commentary, printed there, of Rabbenu Hillel b. R. Eliaqim. I also consulted I. H. Weiss, *Sifra* (Vienna 1862, reprinted New York, 1946). My preference for Koleditzky's edition is because of the superior apparatus and larger type faces, and also because Rabbenu Hillel's commentary is exceedingly illuminating. I ordinarily inserted into my translation the emendations of Elijah of Vilna, where these seemed to me materially to affect the meaning. I have made use of two type faces to present the translation of Sifra. Words in bold type face appear both in Sifra and in the Mishnah or in the Tosefta. Bold type face thus signifies materials common to both documents. Words in regular type occur only in Sifra.

II   Sifra to Leviticus 25:1–17 = Sifra Parashat Behar Chapters 245 through 250

Let us begin by reviewing the verses of Scripture that form the structure and dictate the order of discourse in the passage of Sifra we take as our sample. Nothing in what follows is comprehensible without knowledge of the order, program, and propositions of the scriptural passage at hand. That means that, when and where the Mishnah is cited, it will be solely in the context of Scripture's presentation of the topic. A detailed picture of what Sifra's authorship wishes to say concerning scriptural topics would demonstrate that the propositions and problematic concerning a given topic derive in the main from what is settled as law in the Mishnah. That makes all the more striking the form of discourse. We deal with Leviticus 25:1–17, as follows:

> "The Lord said to Moses on Mount Sinai," Say to the people of Israel, When you come into the land which I give you, the land shall keep a sabbath to the Lord. Six years you shall sow your field, and six years you shall prune your vineyard and gather in its fruits; but in the seventh year there shall be a sabbath of solemn rest for the land, a sabbath to the Lord; you shall not sow your field or prune your

vineyard. What grows of itself in your harvest you shall not reap, and the grapes of your undressed vine you shall not gather; it shall be a year of solemn rest for the land. The sabbath of the land shall provide food for you, for yourself and for your male and female slaves and for your hired servant and the sojourner who lives with you; for your cattle also and for the beasts that are in your land all its yield shall be for food (Lev. 25:1–7).

"And you shall count for yourself seven weeks of years, seven times seven years, so that the time of the seven weeks of years shall be to you forty-nine years. Then you shall send abroad the ram's horn on the tenth day of the seventh month; on the day of atonement you shall send abroad the trumpet throughout all your land. And you shall hallow the fiftieth year and proclaim liberty throughout the land to all its inhabitants; it shall be a jubilee for you, when each of you shall return to his property and each of you shall return to his family. A jubilee shall that fiftieth year be to you; in it you shall neither sow nor reap what grows of itself, nor gather the grapes from the undressed vines. For it is a jubilee, it shall be holy to you, you shall eat what it yields out of the field (Lev. 25:8–12).

"In this year of jubilee each of you shall return to his property. And if you sell a property to your neighbor or buy from your neighbor, you shall not wrong [here: defraud by reason of overcharge] one another. According to the number of years after the jubilee, you shall buy from your neighbor, and according to the number of years for crops he shall sell to you. If the years are many you shall increase the price, and if the years are few you shall diminish the price, for it is the number of the crops that he is selling to you. You shall not wrong one another, but you shall fear your God: for I am the Lord your God" (Lev. 25:13–17).

245. Parashat Behar Parashah 1

CCXLV:I.1   A.   The Lord said to Moses on Mount Sinai:

B.   "What has the topic of the sabbatical year of the land to do in particular with Mount Sinai [that of all subjects, this is the one that is explicitly tied to revelation at Sinai]?"

C.   Is it not the fact that all religious duties were announced at Sinai?

D.   The point is that just as in the case of the sabbatical year both the governing principles and the details were announced from Sinai,

E.   so all of the other religious duties' governing principles and details were announced from Sinai.

2.   A.   "When you come [into the land which I give you, the land shall keep a sabbath to the Lord]:"

B.   Might one suppose that the sabbatical year was to take effect once they had reached Transjordan?

C.   Scripture says, "into the land."

D.   It is that particular land.

E.   Might one suppose that the sabbatical year was to take effect once they had reached Ammon and Moab?

F.   Scripture says, "Which I give you,"

G.   and not to Ammon and Moab.

H.   And on what basis do you maintain that when they had conquered the land but not divided it, divided it among familiars but not among fathers' houses so that each individual does not yet recognize his share –

I.   might one suppose that they should be responsible to observe the sabbatical year?

J.   Scripture says, "[Six years you shall sow] your field,"

K.   meaning, each one should recognize his own field.

L.   ". . . your vineyard:"

M.   meaning, each one should recognize his own vineyard.

N.   You turn out to rule:

O.   **Once the Israelites had crossed the Jordan, they incurred liability to separate dough offering and to observe the prohibition against eating the fruit of fruit trees for the first three years after planting and the prohibition against eating produce of the new growing season prior to the waving of the sheaf of new grain [that is, on the fifteenth of Nisan].**

P.   **When the sixteenth of Nisan came, they incurred liability to wave the sheaf of new grain.**

Q.   **With the passage of fifty days from then they incurred the liability to the offering of the Two Loaves.**

R.   **At the fourteenth year they became liable for the separate of tithes.**

S.   **They they began to count the years of the sabbatical cycle, and in the twenty-first year after entry into the land, they observed the sabbatical year.**

T.   **In the sixty-fourth year they observed the first Jubilee [T. Men. 6:20].**

2.   A.   "the land shall keep a sabbath to the Lord:"

B.   might one suppose that the sabbath should involve not digging pits, ditches, and wells, not repairing immersion-pools?

C.   Scripture says, "you shall not sow your field or prune your vineyard" –

D.   I know that the prohibition extends only to sowing.

E.   How do I know that it covers also sowing, pruning, ploughing, hoeing, weeding, clearing, and cutting down?

F.   Scripture says, "your field you shall not . . . your vineyard . . . you shall not:"

G.   none of the work that is ordinarily done in your field and in your vineyard.

3.   A.   And how do we know that farmers may not fertilize, prune trees, smoke the leaves or cover over with powder for fertilizer?

B.   Scripture says, "your field you shall not . . ."

4.   A.   And how do we know that farmers may not trim trees, nip off dry shoots, trim trees?

B.   Scripture says, "your field you shall not . . ."

5.   A.   Since scripture says, "you shall not sow your field or prune your vineyard,"

B.   might one suppose that the farmer also may not hoe under the olive trees, fill in the holes under the olive trees, or dig between one tree and the next?

C.   Scripture says, "you shall not sow your field or prune your vineyard" –

D.   sowing and pruning were subject to the general prohibition of field labor. Why then were they singled out?

E.   It was to build an anology through them, as follows:

F.   what is distinctive in sowing and pruning is that they are forms of labor carried on on the ground or on a tree.

G.   So I know that subject to the prohibition are also other forms of labor that are carried on on the ground or on a tree, [excluding from the prohibition, therefore, the types of labor listed at B].

6.   A.   Might one suppose that the Jubilee year should count in the years of the sabbatical cycle?

B.   Scripture says, "six years you shall sow your field or prune your vineyard" –

C.   years of sowing count in the years of the sabbatical cycle, but the Jubilee year [in which the prohibitions of the seventh year are in force],

D.   but the Jubilee year does not count in the years of the sabbatical cycle.

7.   A.   And how do we know that in **the case of rice, durra, millet, and sesame, which took root before the new year [of the seventh year], that the farmer may collect them in the seventh year [since they are not part of the crop of that year but of the prior year] [M. Shebiit 2:7 A–D] (translation Louis Newman, *The Sanctity of the Seventh Year. A Study of Mishnah-Tractate Shebiit* [Chico, 1983: Scholars Press for Brown Judaic Studies] pp. 34–5)?**

B.   Scripture says, "and gather in its fruits . . . in the seventh year."

C.   Then might one suppose that even though in the sixth year they had not yet taken root [one may still harvest them in the seventh year]?

D.   Scripture says, "Six years you shall sow your field, and six years you shall prune your vineyard and gather in its fruits" –

E.   in the six years they sow and in the six years they gather,

F.   but they do not sow in the sixth year and gather in the seventh.

8.   A.   R. Jonathan b. Joseph says, "How do we know that in the case of a crop that reached a third of its growth prior to the New Year, you may gather in the crop in the seventh year?

B.   "Scripture says, 'and gather in its fruits,"

C.   "once it has reached a third of its full growth [prior] to the advent of the seventh year."

The process of inclusion and exclusion accounts for nearly the entire exposition. The opening, redactional observation and the next, methodical opening give way to a sustained and cogent inquiry: what forms of labor in the sabbatical year are permitted, what prohibited, in the fields and vineyards? No. 2 undertakes the exclusion of labor not dealing with the production of agricultural produce and the inclusion under the prohibition of labor that serves the interests of the crop, 2.B, E. Nos. 3, 4, and 5 carry forward that same fundamental exercise. In the Mishnah, some sort of generalization or list (it is the same thing) is likely to have emerged; here we are left with the governing analogy. No. 7 rests on the same proof text that is under discussion. Therefore, the framers have not allowed the principle they wish to lay out to dictate omissions of material relevant on account of the principles of aggregation and conglomeration that govern a different kind of composition altogether. No. 7 introduces yet another distinct principle, given its place in order for the same reason as the foregoing: its proof text positions the principle here. The point is that wheras crops that have grown in the seventh year are prohibited, those of the sixth, spilling over into the seventh, are not. No. 8 makes that same point. The upshot is that the principle of composition is fundamentally exegetical, in that (whether made up or ready made) set-piece compositions are laid out in accord with the sequence of the verses, and, for the piece at hand, there is no pretense at the presentation of a sustained and sequential program of principles, propositions, or even modes of argument.

246. Parashat Behar Pereq 1

CCXLVI:I.1   A.   And how do we know that the thirty days prior to the New Year on which the seventh year commences are deemed equivalent to the sabbatical year [so that the prohibitions of the sabbatical year apply a month prior to the commencement of that year]?

B.   Scripture says, "but in the seventh year there shall be a sabbath of solemn rest for the land."

2.   A.   In this connection sages have said:

B.   "White figs which appear in the seventh year – the restrictions of the sabbatical year apply to them in the second year of the new sabbatical cycle, rather than in the seventh year itself, because they take three years to ripen fully."

C.   R. Judah says, "Persian figs which appear in the seventh year – the restrictions of the sabbatical year apply to them in the year following the sabbatical year, that is, in the first year of the new sabbatical cycle rather than in the seventh year itself, because they take two years to ripen fully."

D.   Sages said to him, "They ruled concerning white figs alone" (translation Louis Newman, *The Sanctity of the Seventh Year. A Study of Mishnah-Tractate Shebiit* [Chico, 1983: Scholars Press for Brown Judaic Studies] pp. 37–8).

3.   A.   "a sabbath of solemn rest for the land, [a sabbath to the Lord]:"

B.   Just as is said with reference to the Sabbath that celebrates creation, "a sabbath of solemn rest for the Lord," so in reference to the seventh year, "a sabbath to the Lord."

4.   A.   "you shall not sow your field or prune your vineyard:"

B.   all kinds of labor that pertain to your field,

C.   all kinds of labor that pertain to your vineyard.

5.   A.   "What grows of itself in your harvest you shall not reap:"

B.   On the foundation of this statement sages founded the rule that what grows of itself is forbidden in the seventh year.

6.   A.   "and the grapes of your undressed vine you shall not gather:"

B.   From what is cultivated in the land you shall not cut grapes, but you may cut grapes from what is left as ownerless property. [Once a crop is declared ownerless, anyone may come and make use of it.]

7.   A.   ". . . you shall not gather:"

B.   You may not gather in the way in which people usually gather.

C.   In this connection sages have said:

D.   "Figs of the Sabbatical year – they do not dry them in the ordinary drying place, but one does dry them in a deserted place [where one does not ordinarily process figs]. They do not trample grapes of the sabbatical year in a vat, but one does trample them in a trough. And they do not prepare olives of the sabbatical year in an olive-press or with an olive-crusher, but one does crush them and place them in a small press."

E.   R. Simeon says, "One even grinds them in an olive press and places them in a small press in order to complete the processing of the olives" [M. Shebiit 8:6A–H] (translation Louis Newman, *The Sanctity of the Seventh Year. A Study of Mishnah-Tractate Shebiit* [Chico, 1983: Scholars Press for Brown Judaic Studies] pp. 64–5).

8.   A.   "a sabbath of solemn rest:"

B.   Once the seventh year has come to an end, even though the produce of that year continue under the rule of release of that year, one may nonetheless undertake work on the fruit tree itself,

C.   even though the produce remains prohibited until the fifth day of the month of Shebat.

9.   A.   "The sabbath of the land shall provide food for you:"

B.   what derives from the rest period of the land you may eat.

C.   But you may not consume what has been kept in preserve.

D.   In this connection sages have said,

E.   "As regards a field that was improved during the sabbatical year –

F.   the House of Shammai say, "Other Israelites do not eat of its produce that grows during the sabbatical year."

G.   The House of Hillel say, "They do eat produce of this field that grows during the sabbatical year. [Israelites who did not commit transgression of cultivating the field are not deprived of their right to eat produce of the sabbatical year.]

H.   The House of Shammai say, "They do not eat produce of the sabbatical year when it was given by the owner of a field as a favor."

I.   The House of Hillel say, "They eat produce of the sabbatical year whether or not it was given by the owner of the field as a favor."

J.   R. Judah says, "The rulings attributed to the Houses are reversed, for this is among the lenient rulings of the House of Shammai and the stringent rulings of the House of Hillel" [M. Shebiit 4:2F–K (translation Louis Newman, *The Sanctity of the Seventh Year. A Study of Mishnah-Tractate Shebiit* [Chico, 1983: Scholars Press for Brown Judaic Studies] pp. 51–2.

10.   A.   "[The sabbath of the land shall provide food] for you:"

B.   not for others.

11.   A.   "food:"

B.   not for presenting meal offerings from that produce, nor for presenting drink offerings from it.

12. A. "for yourself and for your male and female slaves:"

    B. What is the point of Scripture here?

    C. Since is is said, "[For six years you shall sow your land and gather in its yield, but the seventh year you shall let it rest and lie fallow,] that the poor of your people may eat; and what they leave the wild beasts may eat. You shall do likewise with your vineyard and with your olive orchard]" (Ex. 23:10–11),

    D. I might have supposed that produce of the seventh year may be eaten only by the poor alone.

    E. How do I know that even the rich may eat it?

    F. Scripture says, "for yourself and for your male and female slaves."

    G. Lo, wealthy landowners are covered, bondmen and bond-women are covered.

    H. Then why is it written, "that the poor of your people may eat"?

    I. "The poor, but not the rich, may consume the available crop after the removal of stored crops from the household," the words of R. Judah.

    J. R. Yosé says, "All the same are the poor and the rich: all of them may consume the crop after the time for the removal of stored crops from the household has come."

13. A. Another matter concerning the statement, "that the poor of your people may eat; [and what they leave the wild beasts may eat]:"

    B. What is suitable for human consumption is given to human beings.

    C. What is suitable for animals is given to animals.

14. A. "and for your hired servant and the sojourner:"

    B. from among gentiles,

15. A. "who lives with you:"

    B. this serves to encompass guests.

16. A. "for your cattle also and for the domesticated beasts:"

    B. What is the point of Scripture here [for the point can be made without specifying both categories of beasts]?

    C. If a wild beast, which is not within your domain, lo, it may eat [produce of the seventh year],

    D. a domesticated cattle, which is within your domain, surely should eat produce of the seventh year!

    E. If that were the case, then I should say, let the farmer collect produce for his domesticated beast and let the beast consume the fodder without limit of time,

    F. in which case how am I to carry out the requirement of

removing stored produce of the seventh year along with the produce that serves for human consumption?

G.   Then is the domesticated beast truly going to eat produce without limit [ignoring the limit imposed by the requirement of removal]?

H.   When Scripture says, therefore, "for your cattle also and for the domesticated beasts,"

I.   it draws an analogy between the domesticated beast and the wild beast, indicating,

J.   so long as a wild beast finds produce of a given sort growing wild in the field, a domesticated beast may eat produce of that same sort in the barn. But when the produce of that sort has disappeared from the field, then the produce of the same species is no longer to be made available to the domesticated beast in the barn. [The law requires people to remove produce of the sabbatical year from their homes when edibles of the same species are no longer available for people to gather from the field; once all vegetables of a certain type have been gathered or have dried up, people may not longer retain in storage similar vegetables in their homes (Newman, *Sanctity of the Seventh Year*, p. 179). This same rule extends to fodder.]

17.   A.   "that are in your land [all its yield shall be for food]:"

B.   what is in your land is for people to people eat.

C.   Food is not to be exported as Aqilas exported food for his workers in Pandos.

D.   Said R. Simeon, "I heard explicitly that they export produce to Syria but not abroad."

18.   A.   "shall be for food:"

B.   even for kindling a lamp, even for use as a dye.

19.   A.   "all its yield:"

B.   This teaches that only produce is eaten.

C.   In this connection sages have said:

D.   "After what time during the sabbatical year do they gather and eat the fruit of trees? [Gathering fruit too early in the ripening process is prohibited. By doing so the farmer would prevent fruit that grows during the sabbatical year from being used as food.]

E.   "As regards unripe figs, from the time that they begin to glisten the farmer may eat them as a random snack together with his bread in the field.

F.   "After they have ripened, he may gather them into his house and eat them.

G.   "And similarly, when figs have ripened during the

other years of the sabbatical cycle, they become liable to the separation of tithes.

H. "As regards unripe grapes, from the time that they produce liquid, the farmer may eat them with his bread in the field.

I. "After they have ripened, he may gather them into his house and eat them.

J. "And similarly when the grapes have ripened during the other years of the sabbatical cycle, they become liable to the separation of tithes.

K. "As regards olives, from the time a seah of olives yields a quarter log of oil, the farmer may crush them and eat them in the field. When a seah of olives yields a half log of oil, he may press them and anoint himself in the field.

L. "When a seah of olives yields a third of its total eventual output, that is, a full log of oil, he may press the olives in the field and gather them into his house.

M. "And similarly, when the olives have reached a third of their eventual yield during the other years of the sabbatical cycle, they become liable to the separation of tithes.

N. "And as regards the fruit of all other trees, the season during other years when they become liable to the separation of tithes is the season during the sabbatical year when they may be eaten, [M. Shebiit 4:7–9A–W, translation and commentary by Newman, *Sanctity of the Seventh Year*, p. 106].

20. A. "for food:"

 B. and not to use it for aromatic sprinkling,

 C. not to make ointment with it,

 D. not to make poultices with it,

 E. and not to make an emetic with it.

There is an on-going interchange with the Mishnah and the Tosefta, but I cannot predict what in those documents will capture the attention of our authorship and what will not. Nos. 1, 7, 9, and 19 (which encompasses No. 18) all direct us to the prior documents. No. 4 presents a generalization without particulars. No. 5 alludes to a rule but does not cite it. No. 6 works out an exclusion. No. 8 makes an important point, which is that the prohibition of field labor ends at the conclusion of the year, even though produce that derives from the sabbatical year remains prohibited until mid-winter. The sequences of Nos. 10–11, 13–15, 17, and 20 go through the more conventional exclusionary process. Nos. 12 and 16 then ask whether a logical argument will have yielded a conclusion without the detailed specifics of Scripture and proves that it will not (in saying so I follow Hillel's reading of the passage). Clearly, our authorship draws heavily upon the available documents, and when it does so, it has only limited interest in points of intersection or even contact.

247. Parashat Behar Parashah 2

CCXLVII:I.1   A.   ["And you shall count for yourself seven weeks of years, seven times seven years, so that the time of the seven weeks of years shall be to you forty-nine years. Then you shall send abroad the ram's horn on the tenth day of the seventh month; on the day of atonement you shall send abroad the trumpet throughout all your land. And you shall hallow the fiftieth year and proclaim liberty throughout the land to all its inhabitants; it shall be a jubilee for you, when each of you shall return to his property and each of you shall return to his family. A jubilee shall that fiftieth year be to you; in it you shall neither sow nor reap what grows of itself, nor gather the grapes from the undressed vines. For it is a jubilee; it shall be holy to you; you shall eat what it yields out of the field" (Lev. 25:8–12.)]
   B.   "And you shall count for yourself:"
   C.   in a court.
2.   A.   "seven weeks:"
   B.   Might one suppose that at issue are seven weeks of days [that is, forty-nine days]?
   C.   Scripture says, "seven weeks of years."
   D.   If it is "seven weeks of years," then is the sense that one should count out seven sabbatical years in sequence and then observe the jubilee?
   E.   Scripture says, "seven years seven times."
   F.   Thus, since Scripture makes the point through these two verses, [we can prove it,] but had Scripture not done so, we should not have been able to prove it.
3.   A.   And how do we know that one counts the years of the septennate?
   B.   Scripture says, "[seven weeks of years, seven times seven years,] so that the time of the seven weeks of years shall be to you [forty-nine years]."
   C.   How do we know that one counts the years of the jubilee?
   D.   Scripture says, "forty-nine years."
   E.   "And how do we know that one observes the seventh year without reference to the jubilee?
   F.   "Scripture says, 'seven weeks of years.'
   G.   "And how do we know that one observes the jubilee year without reference to the sabbatical cycle?
   H.   "Scripture says, 'forty-nine years,'" the words of R. Judah.

I. And sages say, "The seventh year applies without regard to the jubilee, but the jubilee applies only if the seventh year goes along with it."

4. A. And how do we know that the jubilee is announced with the ram's horn?

B. Scripture says, "Then you shall send abroad the ram's horn."

C. I know only that the ram's horn is used for the jubilee. How do I know that it also applies in the new year?

D. Scripture says, "And how do we know that the sounding of the trumpets on the New Year is with the ram's horn?"

E. Scripture says, "Then you shall send abroad the ram's horn for sounding [a quavering note] on the tenth day of the seventh month; on the day of atonement you shall send abroad the ram's horn throughout all your land" (Lev. 25:9).

F. Why does Scripture refer to the seventh month?

G. Lo, it is the sounding of the horn appropriate to the seventh month, and what is that? It is the ram's horn.

H. So too the sounding of the horn for the New Year is to be on the ram's horn.

I. And how do we know that before the quavering notes of the horn are to be notes of the same plane?

J. Scripture says, "Then you shall send abroad the ram's horn for sounding [a quavering note]."

K. And how do we know that after the quavering notes of the horn are to be notes on the same plane?

L. Scripture says, "Then you shall send abroad the ram's horn."

M. I know only that this applies to the proclamation of the Jubilee [to which Lev. 25 makes reference].

N. How do I know that the same rule applies to the New Year?

O. Scripture says, "Then you shall send abroad the ram's horn for sounding [a quavering note] on the tenth day of the seventh month; on the day of atonement" –

P. Why again does Scripture refer to the seventh month?

Q. Lo, the sounding of the horn throughout the entire seventh month is to be like this.

R. Just as the notes prior and after the wavering notes are to be on the same plane, so in connection with the quavering notes of the New Year, the notes prior and the notes after the quavering notes are to be on the same plane.

5. A. "on the [tenth] day:"

B. by day and not by night.

6. A. "on the day of atonement:"

B. even on the Sabbath.

7. A. "you shall send abroad the trumpet throughout all your land:"

B. this teaches that every individual is obligated in this regard.

8. A. Might one suppose that even the sounding of the ram's horn on the new year overrides the restrictions of the Sabbath "throughout your land"?

B. Scripture says, "Then you shall send abroad the ram's horn on the tenth day of the seventh month."

C. Since it is said, "on the day of atonement," do I not know that that is the tenth day of the month?

D. If so, why is reference made to the tenth day of the month?

E. Doing so on the tenth of the month overrides the restrictions of the Sabbath throughout your land, but the sounding of the ram's horn for the New Year does not override the restrictions of the Sabbath throughout your land but only in the court alone.

The expected restrictions ("this, not that") and inclusions and exclusions occupy Nos. 1–3. Of special note is the interest in how the proof is derived, not only on the upshot of the inquiry, at Nos. 2 and 3. The rest covers familiar ground.

248. Parashat Behar Pereq 2

CCXLVIII:I.1   A.   "And you shall sanctify the fiftieth year [and proclaim liberty throughout the land to all its inhabitants; it shall be a jubilee for you, when each of you shall return to his property and each of you shall return to his family. A jubilee shall that fiftieth year be to you; in it you shall neither sow nor reap what grows of itself, nor gather the grapes from the undressed vines. For it is a jubilee; it shall be holy to you; you shall eat what it yields out of the field]:"

B. What is the point of Scripture?

C. Since it is said, "[Then you shall send abroad the ram's horn] on the tenth day of the seventh month,"

D. I might then have reached the conclusion that the year can be sanctified only on the tenth day, [so that if it was not proclaimed holy on that day, it would not be observed as holy].

E. So when Scripture says, "And you shall sanctify the fiftieth year," it teaches that the year had become consecrated from the New Year [and the rite only announced and confirmed that fact].

2. A. Said R. Yohanan b. Beroqah, "Subjugated bondmen were not freed to return to their homes, nor were fields returned to their masters, but people ate, drank, and celebrated, with crowns on their heads,

B. "[from the New Year] until the Day of Atonement of that year arrived.

C. "Once the Day of Atonement had arrived, they would sound the ram's horn,

D. "then fields would revert to their original owners and bondmen would be freed to go home.

3. A. "and proclaim liberty throughout the land to all its inhabitants:"

B. "liberty" refers only to freedom.

C. Said R. Judah, "What is the sense of the word for freedom? [Since it shares consonants with the word for "go around,"] it is like a traveller who is licensed to go around and carry his goods through the whole district [Jastrow, p. 289]."

4. A. "its inhabitants:"

B. when they are actually living on the land, not when they have gone into exile from it.

C. If they were living on it, but if the tribes of Judah were assimilated with the tribes of Benjamin, and of Benjamin in Judah, might one suppose that the Jubilee would still apply?

D. Scripture says, "its inhabitants" – "to all its inhabitants,"

E. meaning that, since the tribe of Reuben and Gad and the half-tribe of Manasseh, the Jubilee years have been annulled.

5. A. "it shall be a jubilee:

B. "even though there has been no release, even though the ram's horn has not been sounded.

C. "Or might one suppose that there is a Jubilee even though the slaves have not been sent forth?

D. "Scripture says, 'it . . .,' " the words of R. Judah.

E. R. Yosé says, " 'it shall be a jubilee:'

F. "even though there has been no release, even though the slaves have not been sent forth.

G. "Then might one suppose that there is a Jubilee even though the ram's horn has not been sounded?

H. "Scripture says, 'it . . .' "

I. Said R. Yosé, "[Following GRA:] Since one verse of Scripture serves to include, and another one serves to exclude, how come I maintain that there can be a Jubilee without the sending forth of the slaves, but there cannot be a Jubilee without the sounding of the ram's horn?

J. "Since a verse of Scripture makes the matter depend on the sounding of the ram's horn, while another verse of Scripture makes the matter depend on the sending forth of the slaves,

K. "the sounding of the ram,'s horn depends upon the action of the court, while the sending forth of the slaves depends on the actions of each individual.

6. A. "when each of you shall return to his property and each of you shall return to his family:"

B. Said R. Eliezer b. Jacob, "Concerning what classification of slave does Scripture speak here?

C. "If it concerns a [Hebrew slave] sold for six years, that of course has already been dealt with. And if it concerns a person sold for a year or two, that of course has already been dealt with.

D. "The passage therefore addresses only the case of the slave who before the Jubilee has had his ear pierced to the door jamb so as to serve in perpetuity.

E. "The Jubilee serves to release him."

7. A. Another teaching concerning the verse, "when each of you shall return to his property and each of you shall return to his family:"

B. "To the family that is assumed to be his family he returns [regaining their status, even if it is very exalted]," the words of R. Meir.

C. R. Jadah says, "To his property and his family he returns, and he does not return to the status that is possessed by the family."

D. And the same rule applies to the person guilty of manslaughter when he returns from his exile on the death of the high priest.

8. A. "shall return:"

B. encompassing a woman.

No. 1 makes the point that the Jubilee begins with the New Year, not the Day of Atonement. No. 2 explains what happens in the interval. No. 3 then provides an etymology for the word *freedom*. None of this has any keen interest in the amplification of the rules at hand or can be called exegetical. It is at No. 4 that the process of exclusion and inclusion begins. Then No. 5 raises the issue of what is essential to the rite, another component of the work of definition through inclusion and exclusion. The text is somewhat in disarray. No. 6 and 8 conclude the work of inclusion. No. 7 raises an extraneous point.

249. Parashat Behar Pereq 3

CCXLIX:I:1 A. ["A jubilee shall that fiftieth year be to you; in it you shall neither sow nor reap what grows of itself, nor gather the grapes from the undressed vines. For it is a jubilee; it shall be holy to you; you shall eat what it yields out of the field. In this year of jubilee each of you shall return to his property" (Lev. 25:11–13).]

B. "it shall be a jubilee for you:"

C. Might one suppose that when the year begins, the sanctification should take effect from the New Year, and when the year comes to an end, it should be drawn out to the Day of Atonement,

D. for, after all, time is added from the profane to the consecrated spell?

E. Scripture says, "it shall be a jubilee for you. . . . A jubilee shall that fiftieth year be to you:"

F. the sanctification lasts, therefore, only to the New Year.

2. A. "in it you shall neither sow nor reap what grows of itself, nor gather the grapes from the undressed vines:"

B. Precisely the rules that apply to the seventh year apply to the Jubilee year.

3. A. "For it is a jubilee; it shall be holy to you:"

B. Just as the holiness of a crop that is holy affects money that is paid for the crop, so the seventh year's holiness affects money that is paid for the crop of the seventh year.

C. Then might one say, just as what has been consecrated is so redeemed by the payment of money as to go forth into unconsecrated status while the money paid for it is held to be holy, so in the case of the produce of the seventh year the rule is the same?

D. Scripture states, "it [shall be holy to you]," meaning, it remains in its status of sanctification [even though exchanged for money].

E. One turns out to rule:

F. **[In the case of one who sold produce of the sabbatical year, used the money received to purchase some other produce, and then exchanged this produce, in turn, for still other produce,] the very last produce obtained in this manner is subjected to the laws of the Sabbatical year, and the produce itself [that is, the original produce of the sabbatical year, remains] forbidden [and subject to the restrictions of the sabbatical year] [M. Shebiit 8:7D–E [Newman, *The Sanctity of the Seventh Year,* p. 171].**

G. How so?

H. If with produce of the seventh year one purchased meat, this and that [the produce, the meat] must be removed at the time of the removal of preserved crops in the seventh year.

I. If one purchased fish with the meat, the meat has dropped out and the fish has entered into consideration; if then for the fish, oil, the fish drops out and and the oil is affected.

J. [Accordingly,] **[in the case of one who sold produce of the sabbatical year, used the money received to purchase some other produce, and then exchanged this produce, in turn, for still other produce,] the very last produce obtained in this** manner is subjected to the laws of the Sabbatical year, and the produce itself [that is, the original produce of the sabbatical year, remains] forbidden [and subject to the restrictions of the sabbatical year].

4. A. "you shall eat what it yields out of the field:"

B. So long as ownerless produce of a given species is growing in the fields, people may continue to retain in their homes and eat produce of the same species that they have stored in their homes [M. Shebiit 9:4A, Newman, *The Sanctity of the Seventh Year*, p. 187].

C. When ownerless produce of a given species has disappeared from the fields, people cease to retain in their homes and eat produce of the same species that they have stored in their homes.

D. In this connection stages have ruled:

E. One who pickles three types of vegetables of the sabbatical year together in a single jar, –

F. R. Eliezer says, "They may continue to eat these vegetables by virtue of the fact that the vegetable which ordinarily is the first of the three to disappear from the field is still growing. [That is, once the first of these vegetables disappears from the field, all the vegetables in the jar are subject to removal.]"

G. R. Joshua says, "They may eat any of these vegetables even by virtue of the fact that the vegetable which ordinarily is the last to disappear from the field is still growing. ["That is, only when the last of these vegetables has disappeared from the field are the contents of the jar as a whole subject to removal.]"

H. Rabban Gamaliel says, "As each type of vegetable disappears from the field, one must remove that type of vegetable from the jar."

I. And the decided law accords with Rabban Gamaliel's ruling.

J. R. Simeon says, "All vegetables are regarded as a single species of produce with respect to the laws of removal."

K. They may eat purslane of the sabbatical year anywhere in the land of Israel until all types of vegetables disappear from the valley of Beit Netofah [M. Shebiit 9:5A–G, Newman, *The Sanctity of the Seventh Year*, pp. 189–190].

5. A. "In this year of jubilee [each of you shall return to his property]:"

B. this year sets slaves free, but the seventh year does not set slaves free.

C. But is the opposite of that proposition not a matter of logical inference?

D. If the advent of the Jubilee year, which does not release monetary debts, releases slaves, the seventh year, which does release monetary debts, surely should release slaves!

E. Scripture states, "In this year of jubilee [each of you shall return to his property]:"

F. this year sets slaves free, but the seventh year does not set slaves free.

G. Then there is an argument a fortiori that the Jubilee year also should release monetary debts:

H. if the seventh year, which does not set slaves free, does have the effect of releasing monetary debts, the Jubilee year, which does set slaves free, surely should have the effect of releasing monetary debts!

I. Scripture says, "[At the end of every seven years you shall grant a release.] And this is the manner of release: there shall release [every creditor what he has lent to his neighbor]" (Dt. 15:1-2).

J. it is the advent of the seventh year that remits monetary debts, but the Jubilee year does not remit monetary debts.

K. And the Jubilee year effects the release of slaves, while the advent of the seventh year does not effect the freeing of the slaves.

6. A. "In this year of jubilee each of you shall return to his property:"

B. this serves to encompass the case of one who sells a field, whose son then went and redeemed it [purchasing it from the buyer]. In the Jubilee year the field reverts to the father.

The clarification now draws heavily on materials previously defined, which means that our authorship conceives its readership to be following their statements consecutively. That contradicts the conventional repetition of the same points in response to the same set of words in diverse passages. But No. 2 leaves no doubt as to the expectation of our authorhsip in the matter, which means that where we have repetition, it is for formal and aesthetic reasons, not for the purpose of exposition of an important proposition. No. 3 then leads us to the program of the Mishnah, which allows us to give an example of No. 2.B's generalization. No. 4 then follows suit. The only important point comes with No. 5, which compares the Jubilee year and the seventh year, a matter that allows us also to touch base with Deuteronomy 15:1ff., the counterpart passage, and (implicitly) to make the point that each passage contributes something fresh.

250. Parashat Behar Parashah 3

CCL:I.1 A. ["And if you sell a property to your neighbor or buy from your neighbor:"]

B. How do we know that, when one sells a property, one should sell only to "your neighbor"?

C. Scripture says, "And if you sell a property to your neighbor."

D. And how do we know that, when one buys a property, one should buy only from "your neighbor"?

E. Scripture says, "or buy from your neighbor."

F. I know only that these rules pertain to real estate transactions, concerning which Scripture speaks.

G. How do we know that the law encompasses movables?

H. Scripture says, "sell a property,"

I. which serves to encompass movables.

J. How do we know that **the claim of fraud for overcharge [above true value] does not apply to real estate transactions [M. Baba Mesia 4:9B]?**

K. Scripture says, "or buy from your neighbor . . . you shall not wrong" [meaning, there will be no claim of overcharge].

L. As to movables, there can be a claim of fraud through overcharge, but as to real estate there can be no such claim.

M. And how do we know that, **as to the sale of slaves, there can be no claim of fraud by reason of overcharge [Mishnah-tractate Baba Mesia 4:9B]?**

N. Scripture says, "[You may also buy from among the strangers who sojourn with you and their families that are with you, who have been born in your land; and they may be your property.] You may bequeath them to your sons after you, to inherit as a possession for ever" (Lev. 25:45–46).

O. Just as inherited property is not subject to a claim of fraud by reason of overcharge, so slaves are not subject to a claim of fraud by reason of overcharge.

P. And how do we know that, **as to the redemption of things that have been consecrated to the temple, there can be no claim of fraud by reason of overcharge [M. Baba Mesia 4:9B]?**

Q. Scripture says, "you shall not wrong one another," omitting reference to what has been consecrated to the temple. [If one overpays to redeem the dedicated object, there is no recourse.]

S. How do we know that **a claim of fraud by reason of overcharge does not apply to deeds [M. Baba Mesia 4:9B]?**

T. Scripture says, "sell a property" –

U. what is singular in such a thing is that one has sold the palpable object or bought the palpable object,

T. so excluded are deeds, in which case one has not bought or sold a palpable object, but only the evidence that these represent real things.

U. Therefore, if one has sold deeds for the purposes of using them for clothing, there can be a claim of fraud by reason of overcharge.

2. A. "you shall not wrong [here: defraud by reason of overcharge] one another:"

B. this refers to fraud in monetary transactions.

C. Might one suppose that at issue is fraud in words?

D. When Scripture says, "You shall not wrong one another" (Lev. 25:17), lo, at issue is fraud accomplished through words.

E. Lo, how then am I to interpret " 'you shall not wrong [here: defraud by reason of overcharge] one another:' "

F. this refers to fraud in monetary transactions.

3. A. And how much of an overcharge is involved in fraud?

B. **Defrauding involves an overcharge of four pieces of silver for what one has brought for twenty-four pieces of silver to the sela** –

C. **a sixth of the purchase price of an object.**

D. **How long is it permitted to return a defective sela? For the length of time it takes to show to a storekeeper or an expert.**

E. **R. Tarfon gave instructions in Lydda: "Fraud is an overcharge of eight pieces of silver to a sela, one third of the purchase price," so the merchants of Lydda rejoiced.**

F. **He said to them, "All day long it is permitted to retract."**

G. **They said to him, "Let R. Tarfon leave us where we were."**

H. **And they reverted to conduct matters in accord with the ruling of the sages [M. Baba Mesia 4:3A–K].**

4. A. **All the same are the buyer and the seller: both are subject to the law of fraud.**

B. **And just as fraud applies to an ordinary person, so it applies to a merchant.**

C. **R. Judah says, "Fraud does not apply to a mechant."**

D. **He who has been subjected to fraud – his hand is on top.**

E. **If he wanted, he says to him, "Return my money."**

F. **Or if we wanted he says to him, "Give me back the amount of the fraud" [M. Baba Mesia 4:4A–F].**

5. A. **How much may a sela be defective and still not fall under the rule of fraud?**

B. **R. Meir says, "Four issars, at an issar to a denar." R. Judah says, "Four pondions, at a pondion to a denar." R. Simeon says, "Eight pondions, at two pondions to a denar" [M. Baba Mesia 4:5A–D].**

6. A. **How long is it permitted to return a defective sela?**

B. **In large towns, for the length of time it takes to show the coin to a money changer.**

C. **And in villages, up to the eve of the Sabbath [M. Baba Mesia 4:6A–C]**

D. **For so it is customary for the market to be held in large towns from one Friday to the next [Tosefta-tractate Baba Mesia 3:20D].**

E. **But if the one who gave the coin refuses to take it back, he has no valid claim against the other except for resentment.**

F. **One may give such a coin in exchange for produce in the status of second tithe, for easy transportation to Jerusalem, and need not scruple, for it is only churlishness [to refuse a slightly depreciated coin] [M. Baba Mesia 4:6D–H].**

7. A. "you shall not wrong [here: defraud by reason of overcharge] one another:"

B. I know then that the law covers men [since in the Hebrew "one another" is "a man, his brother"].

C. How do I know that a woman is not to be defrauded by a man?

D. or a man by a woman?

E. Scripture says, ". . . another" –

F. covering all cases.

8. A. **[All the same are the buyer and the seller: both are subject to the law of fraud.]. Just as fraud applies to an ordinary person, so it applies to a merchant.**

B. **R. Judah says, "If an act of fraud is committed by a merchant against a common person, the latter may enter a claim of fraud. If it is committed by an ordinary person against a merchant, the latter may not enter a claim of fraud. [A claim of fraud by reason of overcharge over true value cannot be entered by a merchant]" [M. Baba Mesia 4:4A–C].**

9. A. I know only that the law covers dealings between one merchant and another.

B. How do I know that as to dealings between a merchant and an ordinary person, an ordinary person and a merchant, an ordinary person and another ordinary person, [one may enter claims of fraud by reason of overcharge from true value]?

C. Scripture says, ". . . another" –

D. covering all cases.

The basic proposition of No. 1 is to prove on the basis of Scripture the inclusions and exclusions, as to a claim of fraud through overcharge, that the Mishnah lists, as indicated. No. 2 makes a distinction, important also in the Mishnah, between verbal and monetary fraud. Both are prohibited, but they represent different counts and are subjected each to its own sanction. Nos. 3–6 and 8 are simply lifted from the Mishnah. No. 9 continues the program of No. 8. No. 7 provides a conventional proposition of an inclusionary order.

CCL:II.1 A.   ["According to the number of years after the jubilee, you shall buy from your neighbor, and according to the number of years for crops he shall sell to you. If the years are many you shall increase the price, and if the years are few you shall diminish the price, for it is the number of the crops that he is selling to you:"]

B.   How do we know that **he who sells his field of possession, that is, one received by inheritance, at the time of the Jubilee's being in effect, is not permitted to redeem it in less than two years [Mishnah-tractate Arakhin 9:1A]?**

C.   Scripture says, "and according to the number of years for crops he shall sell to you."

D.   What about a sale made after the Jubilee or near the Jubilee or at some time-span distant from the Jubilee?

E.   Scripture says, "according to the number of years for crops he shall sell to you. If the years are many you shall increase the price, and if the years are few you shall diminish the price, for it is the number of the crops that he is selling to you."

2.   A.   "number of crops:"

B.   **if it was a year of blight or mildew or a seventh year, it does not count in the reckoning of the crop years.**

C.   **If he only broke the ground or left it fallow, it does count in the reckoning of the crop years. [R. Eleazer says, "If he sold it to him before the New Year and it was full of produce, lo, this one enjoys the usufruct from it for three crops in a period of two years"] [M. Arakhin 9:1C–E].**

D.   **R. Eleazar says, "If one left it and went forth prior to the New Year, and it is full of produce, might one suppose that he may say to him, 'Leave it before me full of fruit, just as I left it before you full of fruit?'**

E.   **"Scripture says, 'for it is the number of the crops that he is selling to you.'**

F.   **"There are times that one can enjoy the usufruct of it for three crops in a period of two years" [T. Arakhin 5:1E–H].**

The entire program is borrowed from Mishnah tractate Arakhin.

III.   Some Preliminary Observations

The blatant and definitive trait of our document is simple and everyone has known it for ages: The topical program and order derive from

Scripture. As the Mishnah defines the topical program and order for Tosefta, the Yerushalmi, and the Bavli, Scripture does so for Sifra. It follows that Sifra takes as its structure the plan and program of the written Torah, by contrast to decision of the framers or compilers of Tosefta and the two Talmuds. The implications of that fundamental decision will occupy us in successive chapters.

Not only so, but for sizable passages, the sole point of coherence for the discrete sentences or paragraphs of Sifra's authorship derives from the base verse of Scripture that is subject to commentary. Whereas the Mishnah holds thought together through propositions of various kinds, with special interest in demonstrating propositions through a well-crafted, if particular, program of logic, Sifra's authorship appeals to a different logic altogether. It is one that I have set forth as fixed-associative discourse, a term to be defined in context later on. Here it suffices to note that, time and again, our units of thought bearing Arabic numerals, which are the smallest complete units of thought, those that can be read fully and comprehensibly on their own and without reference to what is standing fore and aft, link to one another in a single way — through the base verse that joins them all, but not through the progression of thought that moves from the one to the next. That mode of joining two autonomous and completed units of thought never characterizes discourse in the Mishnah.

The third fundamental observation draws attention to the paramount position, within this restatement of the written Torah, of the oral Torah. We may say that, in a purely formal and superficial sense, a sizable proportion of our sample passage consists of the association of completed statements of the oral Torah with the exposition of the written Torah, the whole re-presenting as one whole Torah the dual Torah received by Moses at Sinai (speaking within the Torah myth). Even at the very surface we observe a simple fact. Without the Mishnah or the Tosefta, our authorship will have had virtually nothing to say about one passage after another of the written Torah. A deeper knowledge of Sifra, set forth in my complete translation, will show, furthermore, that far more often than citing the Mishnah or the Tosefta verbatim, our authorship cites principles of law or theology fundamental to the Mishnah's treatment of a given topic, even when the particular passage of the Mishnah or the Tosefta that sets forth those principles is not cited verbatim.

Therefore, even our preliminary survey highlights the three basic and definitive traits of Sifra; first, its total adherence to the topical program of the written Torah for order and plan; second, its common reliance upon the phrases or verses of the written Torah for the joining into coherent discourse of discrete thoughts (e.g., comments on, or amplifications of, words or phrases); and third, its equally profound dependence upon the oral Torah for its program of thought and, in effect, the problematic that defines the issues the authorship wishes to explore and resolve. In a simple and fundamental sense, then, Sifra joins the two Torahs into a single statement, a re-presentation of the written Torah in topic, in program, and in the logic of cogent discourse, and of the oral Torah in problematic and in substantive proposition. Here the written Torah provides the form, the oral Torah, the content. What emerges is not merely a united, dual torah, but The Torah, stated whole and complete, for the context defined by the book of Leviticus: The Torah as a proper noun, all together, all at once, and, above all, complete and utterly coherent. In successive chapters, we will explore the intellectual substrate on which our authorship has constructed its document: first, the critique of the Mishnah, then the defense of the Mishnah.

Notes

[1] So far as I know, no other reference system has been offered to compete with mine. To be sure, even now, rabbinic texts are presented, in Hebrew, German, and English, lacking any reference system beyond "chapter" and translation-page-number. But that only confirms my claim to have invented the only useful and simple reference-system.

CHAPTER FOUR

From Common Noun to Proper Noun: Sifra's Re-presentation of the Two Torahs as One

I. From Torah to "The" Torah

Sifra's relationship to Scripture may be characterized as the same as the Tosefta's or the two Talmuds' relationship to the Mishnah. Just as we can make no sense out of Tosefta without constant interchange with the Mishnah, so Sifra is unintelligible without the book of Leviticus, which supplies the document's structure, order, topic, and irreducible corpus of facts. It is at the fulcrum of Scripture, then, that our authorship undertakes to shift the Mishnah back into Scripture. That is how they restore to the common noun *torah* a single sense as a proper noun, even while exploring a broad new sense of what The Torah encompassed. The importance of the Mishnah, by contrast, is considerably diminished. Whereas we cannot have Sifra without the Mishnah, we do not interpret Sifra solely by appeal to the Mishnah.[1] The reason is that, vis-a-vis the Mishnah in particular, Sifra makes an autonomous statement in its own name. In this respect it is in a different category from Tosefta, which is unintelligible without the Mishnah, and from the two Talmuds, which likewise appeal to the Mishnah for not only structure and order, but also topic and problematic. Those documents that serve as successors and continuators of the Mishnah and impute to the Mishnah the authority, standing, or classification of *torah* in no way stand as autonomous documents.

In order to move the Mishnah back into Scripture, the authorship of Sifra undertook a systematic and multilayered critique of the Mishnah. But their focus was upon the applied and practical reason of the Mishnah. They demolished the Mishnah's autonomous standing by systematically showing its dependency, both formal and in far more profound dimensions, upon Scripture. And the form corresponded to the substance of thought. The Mishnah's authorship presented its propositions as free-

72

standing exercises of the hierarchical classification of the traits of things. Sifra's authorship demonstrated that traits of things by themselves do not sustain taxonomic inquiry. If we wish to know the classes of things and the relationship of those classes, we must turn to The Torah, that is, the written Torah, to find out how things are to be classified and, therefore, set into hierarchical relationship – on that basis alone will we derive the rules that govern diverse kinds of things. It is The Torah that tells us, for the species of things (actions, objects alike), the proper names, that is, classifications, and the rules that form of diverse species subject to a single law. When, secure in The Torah's identification of their genera and their species, we turn to the Mishnah, we find that well-ordered world, each action or object under its proper name and in its proper order of which Scripture spoke in its account of the creation of a world that is to be sanctified. In that critique of applied reason and rehabilitation of *Listenwissenschaft,* the dual Torah becomes one.

The single most penetrating critique opened the way, moreover, for the reconstruction and rehabilitation of the Mishnah as a component of the Torah. This was accomplished in an exercise conducted at the deepest layers of the Mishnah's intellectual and aesthetic foundations. Specifically, the Mishnah rested on a tripartite base made up of (1) subjects of its authorship's own choosing, explored within (2) the inner logic deemed to inhere in the several topics subject to inquiry, and analyzed through (3) a system of classification that rested upon the traits of the subjects and their taxonomy: a perfect circle. For its part, the authorship of Sifra maintained that The Torah, the written Torah, in the present case the book of Leviticus, dictated (1) the subjects to be treated, and framed its discourse through (2) a cogency defined in conformity not with an autonomous set of traits inhering in the topics under discussion but with the supplied traits of fact and order dictated by Scripture. Above all, it (3) systematically dismantled the logical un-derpinning of Mishnaic analysis and substituted a different taxonomic structure, the one defined by Scripture and by Scripture alone.

This it did in two stages. First, the authorship of Sifra showed that the traits of things viewed on their own do not provide reliable taxonomic indicators; we cannot classify things merely because we, for our part, discern that they belong in a single classification. Topics or subjects by themselves are not susceptible to final classification. Second, that same authorship demonstrated that Scripture, and only Scripture, supplies the correct classification of things. Traits imputed by Scripture, not traits found in the natural condition of things, provide the correct indicators of classification. In working out its critique of the analytical logic of the Mishnah, our authorship furthermore accomplished the rehabilitation of the principles of analytical logic to which the authorship of the Mishnah resorted. Consequently, adopting precisely the same conceptions of analytical thought and propositional discourse, our authorship both affirmed a common logical foundation with the authorship of the Mishnah and, upon that same foundation, denied to the authorship the fundamental premise of its entire ouevre: the autonomy of things distinct from Scripture. Accordingly, we will examine the traits of the Mishnah and then systematically follow the critique of those traits by the authorship of the Sifra. A clear definition of what is at stake, stage by stage, will make possible a full understanding of how the authorship of Sifra regained for the common noun *torah* the status of a proper noun: *The* Torah, not a classification, not a status, but sole source of classifications, and, it goes without saying, sole delineator of status as well.

II. [1] Choosing and Ordering Topics, [2] The Logic of Cogent Discourse, and [3] Modes of Proof of Propositions: The Mishnah's and Sifra's

To understand what was at stake, the full dimension of argument, we have now to distinguish several intellectual tasks facing any authorship in the literature at hand. First, to explain the source for my view of the decisions an authorship had to make and did make: The catalogue of tasks I now outline simply moves backward from the finished product to the decisions that are made to present things in one way, rather than some other. We undertake the reversal of the process of constructing the text, that is, in no technical sense, a simple process of deconstruction. Every document in the canon of Judaism in the formative age works out a topical program. What decisions told our authorship to take this topic, rather than that? Every document appeals to an implicit logic that makes possible intelligible discourse. What were the alternative ways of joining one sentence to another to form an intelligible paragraph or cogent thought? Every document sets forth propositions and (mostly implicitly, but occasionally explicitly) seeks general rules among diverse data that constitute those propositions and demonstrate their truth. On what basis did our authorship prove its propositions in this way, rather than in some other, appealing to one probative, self-evidently valid mode of argument, rather than some other?

Since we have in hand more than Sifra but a whole library of related writings, we know choices that other authorships explored. I have shown how this set of tasks was carried out in all of the principal documents of the dual Torah of late antiquity, from the Mishnah through the Bavli, and refer the reader to the bibliography of the Midrash studies given in the Preface. At this point I simply stipulate that every authorship worked out a policy and program to guide the writing of its document, and that every document in its own limits uniformly conforms to a topical, rhetorical, and logical program that we can readily identify.[2] On that basis I maintain the proposition that our authorship faced a repertoire of possibilities on topic, logic of cogent discourse, and principles of probative demonstration of propositions. I will now explain the documentary choices to which I have alluded.

1.   An authorship determines the choice and ordering of topics.

2.   An authorship identifies a principle of association that joins one topic to another, and that does so in one way, rather than another. I call this the logic of cogent discourse, in that the chosen logic joins one sentence or proposition to another sentence or proposition.

3.   Finally, an authorship determines a principle of the proof of proposition, allowing the demonstration, in detail, that things are one way, rather than some other, accord with one law, rather than another.

We will turn to our two great documents, the Mishnah and Sifra, and compare and contrast them on the three points just listed. After this brief statement, in the next four chapters, I will detail how our authorship has done its work of deconstruction and rehabilitation, yielding its restatement of the dual Torah in a single remarkable representation.

[1]   We do not know – and here need not speculate about – the origin of the Mishnah's choice of topics. Some topics derived from Scripture; others appeared only tangentially in Scripture; still other topics, important in the Mishnah, bear no counterpart in Scripture. Those simple facts, familiar from our review of the relationship of the Mishnah's tractates to Scripture, underline the topical autonomy of the oral Torah. As to the sequence of subject, the Mishnah's authorship orders discourse through what it conceives to be the correct *grouping* of topics (e.g., concerning agriculture, civil commerce, the family).

No topic treated in Sifra originates elsewhere than in Scripture. That simple fact rests upon my translation of the 277 chapters of Sifra.[3] An equally well-grounded fact concerns sequential treatment of topics. Our sample has shown that Sifra's authorship appeals to the topics of Scripture, however these may be grouped or ordered, and a given topic will be worked out in the order in which, in the verse that states what Scripture has to say about that topic, the words of the verse unfold. We return presently to the matter of the ordering of discourse.

[2]   The principle of cogent discourse in the Mishnah derives from the requirements of the exposition of a topic. One sentence joins to the next because of the requirement of setting forth a proposition at which discourse aims. Discourse in the Mishnah is always propositional, and, therefore, appeals to how two or more statements (e.g., facts) join together to make a single point or express (and prove) a given proposi-

tion. For its part, Sifra comprises sentences but, more often than not,[4] appeals for medium and large-scale compositions, and, commonly enough, even for joining two or more sentences into a single statement. In addition, Sifra appeals to the logic of cogent discourse provided by fixed association and deriving from the base verse of Scripture for the joining of two or more otherwise entirely incoherent sentences.

Within the context of cogent discourse, what about the ordering of topics? We may explain how each set of authors knew what came first and what then followed. Within the treatment of topics the Mishnah's authorship ordinarily allows the requirements of the exposition or logical analysis of a topic to dictate the order of argument.[5] A given subject for the Mishnah's authorship was possessed of a trait that required special attention; that authorship did not write an encyclopedia of information on a subject but worked out a particular problem that that trait generated. Therefore, I call this a generative problematic, that is, a problematic concerned with what the Mishnah's authorship wanted to know about a topic. The question, of course, concerns the topic that that authorship wanted to answer. The inner logic and problematic of a topic, the aspect of a given topic that attracts attention and special interest, the thing about which an authorship wishes to find out, ordinarily in the Mishnah explain the grouping of topics or the order of analysis of topics. Sifra's authorship, on the other hand, arranges its topics solely through appeal to Scripture's grouping (and, consequently, order) of topics. I cannot point to a single passage in Sifra at which the problematic of a topic explains the ordering of propositions concerning that topic.

[3] The Mishnah's authorship proves its points by appeal to a logic of comparison and contrast, yielding a syllogism based on hierarchization. This is expressed very simply. Things are either alike or not alike. If they are alike, they follow one rule. If they are not alike, they follow a different, and opposite, rule. Comparison and contrast, therefore, form the mode of discovering the laws that govern things. That simple logic of the derivation of propositions then rests upon classification. We must know what is like what. It furthermore yields the possibility of hierarchization. Things are not merely alike or not alike. Because they are alike, they form a classification of one kind or status within a possible sequence, and because they are not alike, they *necessarily* fall into a different pattern of hierarchization. Difference is invariably determinative – of standing or status. That is the foundation of the ubiquitous argument a fortiori: things that are alike follow one rule, things that are not alike follow a different, and (in the nature of things) more weighty rule. If, therefore, X, which falls into a lesser classification, adheres to rule Q, then Y, which falls into a higher classification, surely should adhere to rule Q.

The form for the Mishnah's syllogistic proposition and implicit demonstration will be the list, which joins like to like and, often implicitly but occasionally explicitly, generates a rule common to all the items on the list. The argument, therefore, is that like follows like: What is within a single taxon follows one rule. And, so it is deemed self-evident, what is within a different taxon (species of the same genus) follows the opposite rule. The tacit hierarchization then permits the argument a fortiori, as I just said.

Sifra's authorship accepts without demure the principle of the demonstration of propositions by showing that like things follow the same rule, unlike things, the opposite. What that authorship maintains, however, is that when we wish to know what constitutes a taxon, we must be guided by the dictates of Scripture. The classification of things derives from Scripture, not from the traits of things, viewed independent of Scripture. Therefore, Sifra's authorship makes its points in this particular way: they can be understood only when we grasp how the Mishnah's authorship carries on its intellectual tasks.[6] We will see ample exemplification of these general observations. At this point it will suffice to observe that Sifra's authorship has its own ideas about the correct principles of classification. To state the basic point with emphasis:

All flows from our authorship's critique of the generative principle of Mishnaic classification and its reconstruction of the correct identification of the origins of the correct classification of things. The critique of the Mishnah's mode of syllogistic proof derives from Sifra's authorship's insistence that Scripture, and Scripture alone, defines the right ordering and classification of things. To stress, Scripture is the sole source of the final classification of things.

Choice and ordering of topics, principles of cogent discourse that explain why one sentence joins to another sentence in making a single cogent and intelligible statement, and modes of proof or propositions form a single, entirely unified structure. We cannot explain the one trait of a given document without invoking the second, and the two together – any two – will allow us to predict or explain the third. Now to see the three indicative traits of a document as whole and one.

For Sifra, Scripture dictates the topics and their order; Scripture supplies the joining of one sentence or completed thought to another; Scripture, it follows, will dictate the classifications and the relationship between and among those classifications. That is the topical, sequential, and logical proposition of Sifra, seen all together and all at once.

For the Mishnah, an encompassing theory and perspective of social reality by contrast tells the authorship of the Mishnah what topics it wishes to discuss, as well as the order, within any given topic, of the pertinent questions and propositions. That same theory will require propositional discourse, such that two or more sentences will form cogent and meaningful statements only if and when they set forth the demonstration of a given syllogism. And the correct mode of demonstration is the classification of the traits of diverse things in such wise that we assign to the like a given rule, and to the unlike the opposite rule.

III. Conclusion

The single difference between the Bavli and Sifra is the blatant one: choice of base text, Mishnah or Scripture. We will now see that Sifra's entire critique of the Mishnah was presented as an autonomous statement and the reconstruction – the re-presentation – of The Torah rested on that simple choice. Why should the matter of form – the organizing principle for large units of discourse – dictate all else? Because, as we will see, the Mishnah's reliance on the topical organization of data derived from the logic of syllogistic proof upon which the Mishnah's authorship built all of its propositions. The authorship of Sifra systematically criticized that logic of syllogistic proof resting on free-standing reason deriving from traits of classifications of things.[7] It equally systematically rehabilited logic by showing the correct origin of classifications.[8] So one mode of taxonomic syllogism, the Mishnah's, resting on the topical ordering of discourse and definition of classifications, was subjected to the critique deriving from a different mode of taxonomic discourse altogether. And, as we now recognize, the taxa of that other system of thought derived from Scripture, to begin with, the topical program of Scripture, but at the deepest layers of thought and argument, the taxonomic data of Scripture as well. We cannot understand either the Mishnah or Sifra without knowing the relationship, therefore, between the logic of analytical thought and the logic of cogent discourse represented by the ordering of topics. Each document had its choices as to basic structure, that is, logic of cogent discourse of topics, in whatever sequence, and these choices derived from the deeper layers of the logic of syllogistic proof, which itself rested upon profound judgments as to the origin of taxa.

In Chapters Five and Six I demonstrate in detail that I have now accurately characterized the two documents as to: (1) their topical programs, in both selection and ordering and (2) their logical principles, both as to their rules for cogent discourse. In Chapter Seven I turn to (3) modes for demonstrating the propositions expressed through that discourse. There we delve into the deep structure of the logic. I investigate the traits of taxonomic proof, *Listenwissenschaft*, demonstrably affirmed by both authorships, but, in the view of Sifra's authorship, profoundly misconstrued by the Mishnah's framers. Then in Chapter Eight I show how Sifra's authorship united the dual Torah by rejoining the application of the universally self-evident principles of *Listenwissenschaft* to what they insisted was the sole source of defining classifications, Scripture. Once the structure was set upon the correct taxonomic foundation, all else followed: choice of topics and their ordering, identification of correct principles of cogent discourse, and, it goes without saying, definition of taxa and also determination of their hierarchical standing. So when we rehearse the simple fact that the authorship of Sifra selects as its definitive structure Scripture, while the Mishnah's authorship aims at a free-standing topical program, we, in fact, explain the deepest layers of thought and most profound arguments by which our authorship proposed to unite the dual Torah: *let torah be The Torah, that alone.*

Notes

[1] But, as I noted in the preceding chapter, that statement bypasses the central role of conceptions of the Mishnah in Sifra's authorship's reading of Scripture. Some of these conceptions are simply givens, facts that apparently circulated broadly within the Judaic system that come to expression here in some aspects, there in others. Among these conceptions others appear to be particular to the Mishnaic system. I am in no position methodologically to demonstrate the differences or to prove how we may know one from the other. In my translation and commentary to Sifra, however, I identify the premise of discussion, so far as the premise is imputed to Scripture from without, at every pertinent point. I am puzzled on how to know when a datum simply was in circulation as an acknowledged fact of scriptural interpretation, and when imputing to Scripture a proposition critical to the Mishnaic system accounts for the importance accorded to a halakhic principle. My point here is a simple one. Whatever the premises as to prevailing practice, we can understand the bulk of Sifra's statements without opening the Mishnah, which is subordinated and never accorded a generative position in the unfolding of a proposition. But try to understand the Yerushalmi or the Bavli without having in hand both the Mishnah and the Tosefta! That fixed relationship of relationships is what I refer to in the present context. It seems to me a nearly banal observation, but it does help us to compare and contrast the plans of the two modes of uniting the dual Torah.

[2] In the companion study to this one, *Sifra in Context,* I will demonstrate that each document can be shown to be sui generis when analyzed from a monothetic taxonomy and to form part of a larger set of books of a single classification only when viewed from a polythetic taxonomy. That is a satisfying result indeed, when, as we will see, we realize that our authorship presented as the climax of logical analysis and proof of propositions nothing other than a polythetic taxonomy.

[3] But it also rests on the tests I made at random in my commentary on my translation, when I asked whether we could account for the selection of those passages of the Mishnah that treated a given subject the authorship of Sifra adduced in its program, and those that it did not. We can account for both inclusions and exclusions of Mishnaic discussion – proposition and problem alike – by examining the exegetical problem set forth within a given verse of

Scripture. So the single blatant fact that distinguishes our document from the Mishnah also accounts for not entirely self-evident traits of our document: Why does it draw from the Mishnah upon this, but not that? It would carry us far afield to work out, in acute detail, the answer to that question, but the answer in general is entirely clear. The requirements of Scripture's treatment of a given problem guide our authorship in its selections of Mishnah pericopes for reproduction.

4   I will presently spell out what I mean by the logic of cogency supplied by the principle of fixed association. The analysis of the principles of cogent discourse of Sifra will be worked out in the companion volume, *Sifra in Context.* The sample we have already examined, however, suffices to show that the cogency imparted by fixed association is the paramount, though not exclusive, logic of cogent discourse in Sifra.

5   I demonstrated that fact for all of the tractates of the Mishnah's second through sixth divisions in my *History of the Mishnaic Law,* and my students did the same for the tractates of the first division. I stress that that is ordinarily the case; there are a few exceptions, and there are some instances in which more than a single order of analysis of a topic can be defended. But, in most tractates, we can show that the logic of a given topic dictated the order in which the analytical treatment of that topic in a given tractate would unfold. There is no need at this late stage in the process of analysis to defend propositions set forth more than a decade ago and defended in detail for sixty-two tractates (and also shown not to apply to the sixty-third tractate, tractate Avot).

6   That Sifra constitutes a response to, and a critique of, the Mishnah scarcely requires argument at this point, since no definitive trait of Sifra can be understood out of relationship with the corresponding trait of the Mishnah. That much is clear even now. A glance at the sample cited in Chapter Three shows us how much of Sifra comprises simply a restatement of Mishnaic materials. Still, the setting of this analysis is phenomenological, not historical in any narrow sense, since what I propose to set forth are positions within logic, not policies geared to vivid politics.

7   This is the theme of Chapter Seven.

8   This is the proposition of Chapter Eight.

CHAPTER FIVE

Sifra's Alternative to the Mishnah's Topical Program and Its Order

An authorship determines the choice and ordering of topics

I. The Ordering of the Mishnah's Topics

No explanation for the order of the divisions or tractates of the Mishnah can appeal to the topics treated therein, or accounts for the logic that explains why topic A has to be treated before, or after, topic B. But, then, the order of the divisions and tractates cannot be shown to be intrinsic to the plan of the framers of the document.[1] On the other hand, when we examine the unfolding of the treatment of a given topic as represented by a tractate, we ordinarily are able to explain why a given subject comes before or after another subject, or, more commonly still, why a given problem must be solved before another, and logically secondary, problem can be addressed. It would carry us far afield to demonstrate the validity of that judgment, however.[2]

II. The Topical Program of the Mishnah

The protracted account of the Mishnah's topical program shows us in great detail what it means for an authorship to define a plan of discourse on various subjects and to work out that plan within what the authorship conceives to be the problematic of the subject matter, item by item. The framers of the Mishnah know precisely what they want to find out about a given subject. That point of special interest, which, as I have explained, I call the problematic, is what they work out. Why does that fact help us to compare and contrast the Mishnah to Sifra? The reason is simple. From the viewpoint of the framers of the Mishnah, the subject matter of a given tractate, viewed autonomously in terms of its own traits, inner tensions, logical progression, contains within itself its own point of interest. The traits of the topic are, therefore, conceived on their own to precipitate thought about that topic. The importance of that simple fact is such that I will devote considerable time to defining it. When we see, as we will in the final section of this chapter, whence the authorship of Sifra discovers *its* topical assignment and, more importantly, how the authorship of Sifra defines what *it* wishes to know about a topic, we will grasp full well the importance of the Mishnah's framers' contrary plan. The authorship of Sifra opens the book of Leviticus and discovers the topics it is supposed to discuss. It finds in the book of Leviticus what it is, about those topics, that requires investigation – there, and, of course, in the Mishnah too.

The authors of the Mishnah reshaped whatever subjects or issues came into their hands. Upon close reading, the document proves sustainedly systematic and orderly as to the respective tractates, nearly always purposive and almost always well composed. The basis for that judgment is simple. Facts in most of the Mishnah tractates are formed into statements of sense and meaning. The Mishnah is no mere scrapbook of legal data, arranged merely for purposes of reference. Each topic bears its point of interest, and that is what defines what the authorship wishes to tell us about that topic.[3] That is why the topic under discussion dictates the structure of the document at that point (the tractate) and also the order of subtopics in accord with which a given topic will be set forth. The Mishnah is a systemic document that is meant to make a statement on virtually every page, a document in which the critical problematic at the center almost always exercises influence over the merely instrumental, peripheral facts, dictating how they are chosen, arranged, and utilized. Our brief survey of the relationships between the several tractates and Scripture has already shown us that Scripture in no way has dictated the topics treated in the Mishnah, let alone the order and manner in which these are set forth and analyzed.

Let us now turn to a cursory survey of the topical program of the document as a whole, which will show us how, within the six divisions of the Mishnah, the traits of a given subject form the centerpiece of interest and endow the document as a whole with its cogency.[4] The Mishnah forms a treatise on a set of subjects, not an exposition of what Scripture has said about various subjects. And, as we shall see, Sifra sets forth a devastating judgment upon what the Mishnah has to say about a given subject. My account of the topical program of the Mishnah and its inner cogency shows in complete detail that the document works out its program through undertaking a propositional, rarely exegetical, treatment of one subject after another. As a result, the authorship of the Mishnah proposed, on any given subject, to make statements of its own about that subject, in total independence from Scripture, which is reduced to a source of interesting facts. The subjects then derived from the system's larger interests, not from Scripture's repertoire of interests. The contrast to Sifra is simply stated. At no point can we find a topic treated in

Sifra that the book of Leviticus has not identified for the authorship of Sifra.

The Division of Agriculture treats two topics, first, producing crops in accord with the Scriptural rules on the subject, second, paying the required offerings and tithes to the priests, Levites, and poor. The principal point of the Division is that the Land is holy, because God has a claim both on it and upon what it produces. God's claim must be honored by setting aside a portion of the produce for those for whom God has designated it. God's ownership must be acknowledged by observing the rules God has laid down for use of the land. In sum, the Division is divided along these lines: (1) rules for producing crops in a state of holiness – tractates *Kilayim, Shebiit,* and *Orlah;* (2) rules for disposing of crops in accord with the rules of holiness – tractates *Peah, Demai, Terumot, Maaserot, Maaser Sheni, Hallah, Bikkurim,* and *Berakhot.* The division thus identifies, as the problematic of its topic, the question of how, where, and under what circumstances, God, as landowner, and the farmer, as God's partner, lay claim to, and divide, the produce of the holy land.

The Division of Appointed Times forms a system in which the advent of a holy day, like the Sabbath of creation, sanctifies the life of the Israelite village through imposing on the village rules on the model of those of the Temple. The purpose of the system, therefore, is to bring into alignment the moment of sanctification of the village and the life of the home with the moment of sanctification of the Temple on those same occasions of appointed times. The underlying and generative theory of the system is that the village is the mirror image of the Temple. If things are done in one way in the Temple, they will be done in the opposite way in the village. Together the village and the Temple on the occasion of the holy day, therefore, form a single continuum, a completed creation, thus awaiting sanctification. The subject of special occasions or appointed times is explored within the problematic of how space is transformed by the advent of special time.

The village is made like the Temple. For example, on appointed times one may not freely cross the lines distinguishing the village from the rest of the world, just as one may not freely cross the lines distinguishing the Temple from the world. But the village is a mirror image of the Temple as well. The boundary lines prevent free entry into the Temple, so they restrict free egress from the village. On the holy day what one may do in the Temple is precisely what one may not do in the village. Therefore, the advent of the holy day affects the village by bringing it into sacred symmetry so as to effect a system of opposites: Each is holy in a way precisely the opposite of the other. Because of the underlying conception of perfection attained through the union of opposites, the village is not represented as conforming to the model of the cult, but of constituting its antithesis. The world thus regains perfection when on the holy day heaven and earth are united, the whole completed and done: the heaven, the earth, and all their hosts. This moment of perfection renders the events of ordinary time, of "history," essentially irrelevant. For what really matters in time is that moment in which sacred time intervenes and effects the perfection formed of the union of heaven and earth, of Temple, in the model of the former, and Israel, its complement. It is not a return to a perfect time but a recovery of perfect being, a fulfillment of creation, which explains the essentially ahistorical character of the Mishnah's Division on Appointed Times. Sanctification constitutes an ontological category and is effected by the creator.

The contrast to Leviticus should not be missed, though it is not critical to my argument. The spatial division of Leviticus falls between the tent of meeting and the camp beyond, corresponding, in post-exilic times, to the inner sanctum of the temple and the temple courtyard. The camp of Israel, the people, is represented in Leviticus as holy, that is, corresponding to the temple space; and within the camp of Israel, the tent of meeting then is the place where God lives, corresponding to the inner sanctum of the temple space. Leviticus, therefore, knows nothing that we might identify with the village beyond, that is, a fundamentally unconsecrated space, accessible of sanctification in holy time. The authorship of Sifra, of course, takes for granted the ontological facts that form the premises of the Mishnah. But the argument I construct must deem the constrast trivial, though interesting. Let us return to the Mishnah's own address to the topics it has chosen for exposition and exploration.

The Division in its rich detail is composed of two quite distinct sets of materials. First, it addresses what one does in the sacred space of the Temple on the occasion of sacred time, as distinct from what one does in that same sacred space on ordinary, undifferentiated days. Second, the Division defines how for the occasion of the holy day one creates a corresponding space in one's own circumstance, and what one does, within that space, during sacred time. The issue of the Temple and cult on the special occasion of festivals is treated in tractates *Pesahim, Sheqalim, Yoma, Sukkah,* and *Hagigah.* Three further tractates, *Rosh Hashanah, Taanit,* and *Megillah,* are necessary to complete the discussion. The matter of the rigid definition of the outlines in the village, of a sacred space, delineated by the limits within which one may move on the Sabbath and festival, and of the specification of those things which one may not do within that space in sacred time, is in *Shabbat, Erubin, Besah,* and *Moed Qatan.* Whereas the twelve tractates of the Division appear to fall into two distinct groups, joined merely by a common theme, in fact they relate through a shared, generative metaphor. It is, as I said, the comparison, in the context of sacred time, of the spatial life of the Temple to the spatial life of the village, with activities and restrictions to be specified for each, upon the common occasion of the Sabbath or festival. The Mishnah's purpose, therefore, is to correlate the sanctity of the Temple, as defined by the holy day, with the restrictions of space and of action that make the life of the village different and holy, as defined by the holy day.

The Division of Women defines the women in the social economy of Israel's supernatural and natural reality. Women acquire definition wholly in relationship to men, who impart form to the Israelite social economy. The status of women is effected through both supernatural and natural action. What man and woman do on earth provokes a response in heaven, and the correspondences are perfect. So women are defined and secured both in heaven and here on earth, and that position is always and invariably relative to men. The principal interest for the Mishnah is the point at which a woman becomes, and ceases to be, holy to a particular man, that is, enters and leaves the marital union. These transfers of women are the dangerous and disorderly points in the relationship of woman to man, therefore, the Mishnah states, to society as well.

The formation of the marriage comes under discussion in *Qiddushin* and *Ketubot,* as well as in *Yebamot.* The rules for the duration of the marriage are scattered throughout, but derive especially from parts of *Ketubot, Nedarim,* and *Nazir,* on the one side, and the paramount unit of *Sotah,* on the other. The dissolution of the marriage is dealt with in *Gittin,* as well as in *Yebamot.* We see very clearly, therefore, that important overall are issues of the transfer of property, along with women, covered in *Ketubot* and to some measure in *Qiddushin,* and the proper documentation of the transfer of women and property, treated in *Ketubot* and *Gittin.* As such, the critical issues turn upon legal documents – writs of divorce, for example – and legal recognition of changes in the ownership of property, for example, through the collection of the settlement of a marriage contract by a widow, through the provision of a dowry, or through the disposition of the property of a woman during the period in which she is married. Within this orderly world of documentary and procedural concerns a place is made for the disorderly conception of the marriage not formed by human volition but decreed in heaven, the levirate connection. *Yebamot* states that supernature sanctifies a woman to a man (under the conditions of the levirate connection). What it says by indirection is that man sanctifies too: Man, like God, can sanctify that relationship between a man and a woman, and can also effect the cessation of the sanctity of that same relationship. Five of the seven tractates of the Division of Women are devoted to the formation and dissolution of the marital bond. Of them, three treat what is done by man here on earth, that is, formation of a marital bond through betrothal and marriage contract and dissolution through divorce and its consequences: *Qiddushin, Ketubot,* and *Gittin.* One of them is devoted to what is done by woman here on earth: *Sotah.* And *Yebamot,* greatest of the seven in size and in formal and substantive brilliance, deals with the corresponding heavenly intervention into the formation and end of a marriage: the effect of death upon both forming the marital bond and dissolving it through death. The other two tractates, *Nedarim* and *Nazir,* draw into one the two realms of reality, heaven and earth, as they work out the effects of vows, perhaps because vows taken by women and subject to the confirmation or abrogation of the father or husband make a deep impact upon the marital life of the woman who has taken them.

The Division and its system delineate the natural and supernatural character of the woman's role in the social economy framed by man: the beginning, end, and middle of the relationship. And it is these transfer points, as with property, that define the problematic for the framers of the Mishnah. What they want to know about the topic, women, is defined by the movement of woman from one domain to another. The whole constitutes a significant part of the Mishnah's encompassing system of sanctification, for the reason that heaven confirms what men do on earth. A correctly prepared writ of divorce on earth changes the status of the woman to whom it is given, so that in heaven she is available for sanctification to some other man, whereas, without that same writ, in heaven's view, should she go to to some other man, she would be liable to be put to death. The earthly deed and the heavenly perspective correlate. That is indeed very much part of larger system, which says the same thing over and over again.

The system of women thus focuses upon the two crucial stages in the transfer of women and of property from one domain to another, the leaving of the father's house in the formation of a marriage, and the return to the father's house at its dissolution through divorce or the husband's death. There is yet a third point of interest, though, as is clear, it is much less important than these first two stages: the duration of the marriage. Finally, included within the division and at a few points relevant to women in particular are rules of vows and of the special vow to be a *Nazir* (cf. Numbers 6). The former is included because, in the Scriptural treatment of the theme, the rights of the father or husband to annul the vows of a daughter or wife form the central problematic. The latter is included for no very clear reason except that it is a species of which the vow is the genus.

The Division of Damages comprises two subsystems, which fit together in a logical way. One part presents rules for the normal conduct of civil society. These cover commerce, trade, real estate, and other matters of everyday intercourse, as well as mishaps, such as damages by chattels and persons, fraud, overcharge, interest, and the like, in that same context of everyday social life. The other part describes the institutions governing the normal conduct of civil society, that is, courts of administration, and the penalties at the disposal of the government for the enforcement of the law. The two subjects form a single tight and systematic dissertation on the nature of Israelite society and its economic, social, and political relationships, as the Mishnah envisages them. The subject of the conduct of civil society and government is explored within a simple problematic: How do we sustain the unchanging division of power and scarce resources, so that no one gets richer, no one poorer, than good order requires?

The main point of the first of the two parts of the Division is expressed in the sustained unfolding of the three *Babas, Baba Qamma, Baba Mesia,* and *Baba Batra.* It is that the task of society is to maintain perfect stasis, to preserve the prevailing situation, and to secure the stability of all relationships. To this end, in the interchanges of buying and selling, giving and taking, borrowing and lending, it is important that there be an essential equality of interchange. No party in the end should have more than what he had at the outset, and none should be the victim of a sizable shift in fortune and circumstance. All parties' rights to, and in, this stable and unchanging economy of society are to be preserved. When the condition of a person is violated, so far as possible the law will secure the restoration of the antecedent status.

An appropriate appendix to the *Babas* is at *Abodah Zarah,* which deals with the orderly governance of transactions and relationships between Israelite society and the outside world, the realm of idolatry, relationships that are subject to certain special considerations. These are generated by the fact that Israelites may not derive benefit (e.g., through commercial transactions) from anything that has served in the worship of an idol. Consequently, commercial transactions suffer limitations on account of extrinsic considerations of cultic taboos. Whereas these cover both special occasions (e.g., fairs and festivals of idolatry) and general matters, that is, what Israelites may buy and sell, the main practical illustrations of the principles of the matter pertain to wine. The Mishnah supposes that gentiles routinely make use, for a libation, of a drop of any sort of wine to which they have access. Therefore, it is taken for granted that wine over which gentiles have had control is forbidden for Israelite use, and also that such wine is prohibited for Israelites to buy and sell. This other matter – ordinary everyday relationships with the gentile world, with special reference to trade and commerce – concludes what the Mishnah has to say about all those matters of civil and criminal law that together define everyday relationships within the Israelite nation and between that nation and all others in the world among whom, in Palestine as abroad, they lived side by side.

The other part of the Division describes the institutions of Israelite government and politics. This is in two main aspects, first, the description of the institutions and their jurisdiction, with reference to courts, conceived as both judicial and administrative agencies, and, second, the extensive discussion of criminal penalties. The penalties are three: death, banishment, and flogging. There are four ways by which a person convicted of a capital crime may be put to death. The Mishnah organizes a vast amount of information on what sorts of capital crimes are punishable by which of the four modes of execution. That information is alleged to derive from Scripture. But the facts are many, and the relevant verses few. What the Mishnah does contribute to this exercise is a supurb organization and elucidation of available facts. Where the facts come from we do not know. The Mishnah tractate *Sanhedrin* further describes the way in which trials are conducted in both monetary and capital cases and pays attention to the possibilities of perjury. The matter of banishment brings the Mishnah to a rather routine restatement of flogging. Application of that mode of punishment concludes the discussion.

These matters, worked out at *Sanhedrin-Makkot*, are supplemented in two tractates, *Shebuot* and *Horayot*, both emerging from Scripture. Leviticus 5 and 6 refer to various oaths that apply mainly, though not exclusively, in courts. Leviticus 4 deals with errors of judgment inadvertently made and carried out by the high priest, the ruler, and the people; the Mishnah knows that these considerations apply to Israelite courts too. What, for the editors of Leviticus, draws Chapters Four, Five and Six together is their common interest in the guilt offering, owed for violation of the rather diverse laws under discussion. Now in tractates *Shebuot* and *Horayot* the materials of Leviticus 4–6 are worked out. But here is it from the viewpoint of the oath or erroneous instruction, rather than the cultic penalty. In *Shebuot* the discussion is intellectually imaginative and thorough, in *Horayot*, routine. The relevance of both to the issues of *Sanhedrin* and *Makkot* is obvious. For the matter of oaths in the main enriches the discussion of the conduct of the courts. The possibility of error is principally in the courts and other political institutions. Therefore, the four tractates on institutions and their functioning form a remarkable unified and cogent set.

The goal of the system of civil law is the recovery of the prevailing order and balance, the preservation of the established wholeness of the social economy. This idea is powerfully expressed in the organization of the three *Babas*, which treat first abnormal and then normal transactions. The framers deal with damages done by chattels and by human beings, thefts, and other sorts of malfeasance against the property of others. The

Babas in both aspects pay closest attention to how the property and person of the injured party so far as possible are restored to their prior condition, that is, a state of normality. So attention to torts focuses upon penalties paid by the malefactor to the victim, rather than upon penalties inflicted by the court on the malefactor for what he has done. When speaking of damages, the Mishnah thus takes as its principal concern the restoration of the fortune of victims of assault or robbery. Then the framers take up the complementary and corresponding set of topics, the regulation of normal transactions. When we rapidly survey the kinds of transactions of special interest, we see from the topics selected for discussion what we have already uncovered in the deepest structure of organization and articulation of the basic theme.

The other half of this same unit of three tractates presents laws governing normal and routine transactions, many of them of the same sort as those dealt with in the first half. Bailments, for example, occur in both wings of the triple tractate, first, bailments subjected to misappropriation, or accusation thereof, by the bailiff, then, bailments transacted under normal circumstances. Under the rubric of routine transactions are those of workers and householders, that is, the purchase and sale of labor, rentals and bailments, real estate transactions, and inheritances and estates. Of the lot, that involving real estate transactions is the most fully articulated and covers the widest range of problems and topics. All together, the *Babas* thus provide a complete account of the orderly governance of balanced transactions and unchanging civil relationships within Israelite society under ordinary conditions.

The character and interests of the Division of Damages present probative evidence of the larger program of the philosophers of the Mishnah. Their intention is to create nothing less than a full-scale Israelite government, subject to the administration of sages. This government is fully supplied with a constitution and bylaws *(Sanhedrin, Makkot)*. It makes provision for a court system and procedures *(Shebuot, Sanhedrin, Makkot)*, as well as a full set of laws governing civil society *(Baba Qamma, Baba Mesia, Baba Batra)* and criminal justice *(Sanhedrin, Makkot)*. This government, moreover, mediates between its own community and the outside ("pagan") world. Through its system of laws it expresses its judgment of the others and, at the same time, defines, protects, and defends its own society and social frontiers *(Abodah Zarah)*. It even makes provision for procedures of remission, to expiate its own errors *(Horayot)*.

The (then nonexistent) Israelite government imagined by the second-century philosophers centers upon the (then nonexistent) Temple, and the (then forbidden) city, Jerusalem. For the Temple is one principal focus. There the highest court is in session; there the high priest reigns.

The penalties for law infringement are of three kinds, one of which involves sacrifice in the Temple. (The others are compensation, physical punishment, and death.) The basic conception of punishment, moreover, is that unintentional infringement of the rules of society, whether "religious" or otherwise, is not penalized but rather expiated through an offering in the Temple. If a member of the people of Israel intentionally infringes against the law, to be sure, that one must be removed from society and is put to death. And if there is a claim of one member of the people against another, that must be righted, so that the prior, prevailing status may be restored. So offerings in the Temple are given up to appease heaven and restore a whole bond between heaven and Israel, specifically on those occasions on which without malice or ill will an Israelite has disturbed the relationship. Israelite civil society without a Temple is not stable or normal, and not to be imagined. And the Mishnah is above all an act of imagination in defiance of reality.

The plan for the government involves a philosophy of society that defines the purpose of the government and ensures that its task is not merely to perpetuate its own power. What the Israelite government, within the Mishnaic fantasy, is supposed to do is to preserve that state of perfection that, within the same fantasy, the society everywhere attains and expresses. This is in at least five aspects. First, one ongoing principle of the law, expressed in one tractate after another, is that people are to follow and maintain the prevailing practice of their locale. Second, the purpose of civil penalties, as we have noted, is to restore the injured party to his prior condition, so far as this is possible, rather than merely to penalize the aggressor. Third, there is the conception of true value, meaning that a given object has an intrinsic worth, which, in the course of a transaction, must be paid. In this way the seller does not leave the transaction any richer than when he entered it, or the buyer any poorer (parallel to penalties for damages). Fourth, there can be no usury, a biblical prohibition adopted and vastly enriched in the Mishnaic thought, for money ("coins") is what it is. Any pretense that it has become more than what it was violates, in its way, the conception of true value. Fifth, when real estate is divided, it must be done with full attention to the rights of all concerned, so that, once more, one party does not gain at the expense of the other. In these and many other aspects the law expresses its obsession with the perfect stasis of Israelite society. Its paramount purpose is in preserving and ensuring that that perfection of the division of this world is kept inviolate or restored to its true status when violated.

The Division of Holy Things presents a system of sacrifice and sanctuary, matters concerning the praxis of the altar and maintenance of the sanctuary. Specifically, the praxis of the altar involves sacrifice and things set aside for sacrifice and so deemed consecrated. The topic covers these among the eleven tractates of the present Division: *Zebahim* and part of *Hullin, Menahot, Temurah, Keritot*, part of *Meilah, Tamid*, and *Qinnim*. The maintenance of the sanctuary (inclusive of the personnel) is dealt with in *Bekhorot, Arakhin*, part of *Meilah, Middot*, and part of *Hullin*. Viewed from a distance, therefore, the Mishnah's tractates divide themselves up into the following groups (in parentheses are tractates containing relevant materials): (1) rules for the altar and the praxis of the cult – *Zebahim Menahot, Hullin, Keritot, Tamid, Qinnim (Bekhorot, Meilah)*; (2) rules for the altar and the animals set aside for the cult – *Arakhin, Temurah, Meilah (Bekhorot)*; and (3) rules for the altar and support of the Temple staff and buildings – *Bekhorot, Middot (Hullin, Arakhin, Meilah, Tamid)*. In a word, this Division speaks of the sacrificial cult and the sanctuary in which the cult is conducted. The law pays special attention to the matter of the status of the property of the altar and of the sanctuary, both materials to be utilized in the actual sacrificial rites, and property the value of which supports the cult and sanctuary in general. Both are deemed to be sanctified, that is: "holy things."

The Division of Holy Things centers upon the everyday with rules always applicable to the cult: the daily whole offering, the sin offering and guilt offering that one may bring any time under ordinary circumstances; the right sequence of diverse offerings; the way in which the rites of the whole-offering, sin, and guilt offerings are carried out; what sorts of animals are acceptable; the accompanying cereal offerings; the support and provision of animals for the cult and of meat for the priesthood; and the support and material maintenance of the cult and its building. We have a system before us: the system of the cult of the Jerusalem Temple, seen as an ordinary and everyday affair, a continuing and routine operation. That is why special rules for the cult, both in respect to the altar and in regard to the maintenance of the buildings, personnel, and even the holy city, will occur elsewhere – in Appointed Times and Agriculture. But from the perspective of Holy Things, those Divisions intersect by supplying special rules and raising extraordinary (Agriculture: land-bound; Appointed Times: time-bound) considerations for the theme that Holy Things claims to set forth in its most general and unexceptional way: the cult as something permanent and everyday.

Therefore, the Division of Holy Things in a concrete way maps out the cosmology of the sanctuary and its sacrificial system, that is, the world of the Temple, which had been the cosmic center of Israelite life. A later saying states matters as follows: "Just as the navel is found at the center of a human being, so the land of Israel is found at the center of the world . . . and it is the foundation of the world. Jerusalem is at the center of the land of Israel, the Temple is at the center of Jerusalem, the Holy of Holies is at the center of the Temple, the Ark is at the center of the Holy of Holies, and the Foundation Stone is in front of the Ark, which spot is the foundation of the world." (*Tanhuma Qedoshim* 10).

The Division of Purities presents a very simple system of three principal parts: sources of uncleanness, objects and substances susceptible to uncleanness, and modes of purification from uncleanness. So it tells the story of what makes a given sort of object unclean and what makes it clean. The tractates on these several topics are as follows: (1) sources of uncleanness – *Ohalot, Negaim, Niddah, Makhshirin, Zabim,* and *Tebul Yom;* (2) objects and substances susceptible to uncleanness – *Kelim, Tohorot,* and *Uqsin;* and (3) modes of purification – *Parah, Miqvaot,* and *Yadayim.* Viewed as a whole, the Division of Purities treats the interplay of persons, food, and liquids. Dry inanimate objects or food are not susceptible to uncleanness. What is wet is susceptible – liquids activate the system. What is unclean, moreover, emerges from uncleanness through the operation of liquids, specifically, through immersion in fit water of requisite volume and in natural condition – liquids deactivate the system. Thus, water in its natural condition is what concludes the process by removing uncleanness. Water in its unnatural condition, that is, deliberately affected by human agency, is what imparts susceptibility to uncleanness to begin with. Furthermore, the uncleanness of persons is signified by body liquids or flux in the case of the menstruating woman *(Niddah)* and the *zab (Zabim).* Corpse uncleanness is conceived to be a kind of effluent, a viscous gas, that flows like liquid. Utensils receive uncleanness when they form receptacles able to contain liquid. In sum, we have a system in which the invisible flow of fluidlike substances or powers serve to put food, drink, and receptacles into the status of uncleanness and to remove those things from that status. Whether or not we call the system "metaphysical," it certainly has no material base but is conditioned upon highly abstract notions. In material terms, the effect of liquid is upon food, drink, utensils, and man. The consequence has to do with who may eat and drink what food and liquid, and what food and drink may be consumed in which pots and pans. These loci are specified by tractates on utensils *(Kelim)* and on food and drink *(Tohorot, Uqsin).*

The human being is ambivalent. Persons fall in the middle, between sources and loci of uncleanness, because they are both. They serve as sources of uncleanness and also become unclean. The zab, suffering the uncleanness described in Leviticus Chapter 15, the menstruating woman, the woman after childbirth, and the person afflicted with the skin ailment described in Leviticus Chapters 13 and 14 – all are sources of uncleanness. But being unclean, they fall within the system's loci, its program of consequences. So they make other things unclean and are subject to penalties because they are unclean. Unambiguous sources of uncleanness also never constitute loci affected by uncleanness. They always are unclean and never can become clean: the corpse, the dead creeping thing, and things like them. Inanimate sources of uncleanness and inanimate objects are affected by uncleanness. Systemically unique, man and liquids have the capacity to inaugurate the processes of uncleanness (as sources) and also are subject to those same processes (as objects of uncleanness). The Division of Purities, which presents the system just described, is not only the oldest in the Mishnah. It also is the largest and contains the most complex laws and ideas.

Overall, the topical program of the Mishnah lays stress on sanctification, understood as the correct arrangement of all things, each in its proper category, each called by its rightful name, just as at the creation: Everything having been given its proper name, God called the natural world very good and God sanctified it. For the Mishnah makes a statement of philosophy, concerning the order of the natural world in its correspondence with the supernatural world. The priests who wrote Leviticus, within the larger Priestly Code, of course make the same points. But they make them in different ways and do not deem interesting all of the topics covered by the Mishnah's framers. This brings us to ask the judgment of the authorship of Sifra on the topical plan of the Mishnah.

III. Sifra's Critique of the Mishnah: The Attack on Topical Organization

By this point in my argument, it is banal to observe that the authorship of Sifra has chosen the topics of Scripture and treated them in the order in which Scripture does. My brief sample, in Chapter Three, leaves no doubt on that fact. But how does our authorship view the topical program of the Mishnah? That is a more urgent, but also more subtle, question. The answer emerges in two simple comparisons. If we examine the exposition of a topic presented by the Mishnah with the exposition of that same topic presented by Sifra, we will see ways not taken, choices of matters to treat in the Mishnah that have been either not recognized or rejected by the authorship of Sifra.[5] Two sizable examples will suffice for that purpose. The first shows us that Sifra's authorship has picked and chosen, within the Mishnah's treatment of a topic, the passages of the Mishnah that it wishes to treat. Therefore, the first proposition is that our authorship in no way finds itself bound to follow the program of the Mishnah. The reason that fact is important lies in the contrast to Sifra's authorship's systematic and thorough address to the statements of the book of Leviticus. So, by contrast to its careful attention to each assertion of the book of Leviticus, verse by verse, it does not find itself bound to present discourses upon the entire program of the Mishnah for any given topic.

271. Parashat Behuqotai Pereq 9

CCLXXI:I.1   A.   ["If it is an animal such as men offer as an offering to the Lord, all of such that any man gives to the Lord is holy. He shall not substitute anything for it or exchange it, a good for a bad or a bad for a good; and if he, in exchanging, makes any exchange of beast for beast, then both it and that for which it is exchanged shall be holy. And if it is an unclean animal such as is not offered as an offering to the Lord, then the man shall bring the animal before the priest, and the priest shall value it as either good or bad; as you, the priest, value it, so it shall be. But if he wishes to redeem it, he shall add a fifth to the valuation" (Lev. 27:9–13)].

B.   "[If] someone said, 'The leg of this beast is a burnt offering,' might someone suppose that the whole of it is to be a burnt offering?

C.   "Scripture says, 'all of such that any man gives to the Lord is holy.'

D.   "['of such'] but the whole of it is not holy.

E.   "Then might one suppose that the beast should go forth to unconsecrated status?

F.   "Scripture says, 'is holy.'

G.   "What should he then do with the beast [of which he has spoken]?

H.   "The beast should be sold to those who are obligated [e.g., by vow] to bring a burnt offering, and the proceeds received for the beast are unconsecrated, except for the value of that leg," the words of R. Meir.

I.   R. Judah, R. Yosé, and R. Simeon say, "How do we know that even if one has said, 'The leg of this beast is a burnt offering,' the whole of the beast is deemed a burnt offering?

J.   "Scripture says, 'all of such that any man gives to the Lord is holy.'

K.   " 'is holy' serves to encompass the whole of the beast [only part of which has been consecrated]."

2.   A.   Might one suppose that even in connection with what has been consecrated for the upkeep of the house, the law of substitution should apply [so that if something has been consecrated for the upkeep of the temple buildings, and a person said, "That is substituted for this," both items are deemed consecrated, as is the case with a beast for the altar]?

B.   Scripture says, "[If it is an animal such as men offer as] an offering [to the Lord],"

C.   which then excludes what has been consecrated for the upkeep of the temple building, which does not fall into the category of an offering at all.

D.   I shall then exclude what has been consecrated for the upkeep of the temple building, which does not fall into the category of an offering at all, but I shall not exclude **what has been declared a substitute for an offering by action of the community at large [is not substituted] [M. Tem. 1:6C].**

E.   Scripture says, *"He* [shall not substitute anything for it or] exchange it."

F.   I shall exclude what has been declared a substitute for an offering by action of the community at large, but I shall not exclude **what belongs to partners [one of whom has declared the beast a substitute for an already consecrated beast] [M. Tem. 1:6C].**

G.   Scripture says, "He shall not substitute anything for it,"

H.   an individual thus effects an act of substitution, and neither the community at large nor partners can effect an act of substitution.

3.   A.   Said R. Simeon, "Now is it not the fact that tithe was covered by the law at hand, [prohibiting making substitutions]. When then was it singled out below [when Scripture says, later in this same passage, "And all the tithe of herds and flocks, every tenth animal of all that pass under the herdsman's staff, shall be holy to the Lord. A man shall not inquire whether it is good or bad, neither shall he exchange it; and if he exchanges it, then both it and that for which it is exchanged shall be holy; it shall not be redeemed"]?

B.   "It was to establish in its classification a rule that governs other items as well, specifically:

C.   "just as a beast designated as tithe is the offering of an individual, so I know that covered by the law of substitution is only the offering of an individual.

D.   "Or might one maintain that, in a matter subjected to reasoning in a single way, one might as well derive conclusions from all of the available ways that are contained therein [so we may draw further comparisons from the rules governing beasts designated as tithe, as follows:]

E.   "just as what is singular to a beast in the status as tithe is that it is consecrated for the altar, applies to the herd and to the flock, and must be eaten in a span of two days, so I encompass under the law of substitution only what bears these same indicative traits.

F.   "How do I know that the law of substitution then encompasses Most Holy Things and Lesser Holy Things that belong to an individual?

G.   "Scripture says, 'if [he makes any exchange of] beast [for beast]. . . .' "

4.   A.   "He shall not substitute anything for it:"

B.   What has been consecrated imposes the status of substitute on what has been declared to be its substitution,

C.   but what has been declared a substitute does not impose the status of substitute on yet another beast.

D.   R. Judah says, "The offspring [of a consecrated beast] effects the status of substitute [for any beast that is declared to be in place of the offspring of a consecrated beast, so that the offspring and the substitute both are equally holy]."

E.   They said to him, "What has been consecrated imposes the status of substitute on what has been declared to be its substitution, but neither the offspring of a consecrated beast nor what has been declared a substitute does not impose the status of substitute on yet another beast."

5.   A.   **"a good for a bad or a bad for a good:"**

B.   **unblemished beasts for blemished ones, blemished beasts for unblemished ones [M. Tem. 1:2D].**

C.   How do we know that "for bad" refers to a blemished beast?

D.   Scripture says, "You shall not sacrifice to the Lord your God an ox or a sheep in which is a blemish, any bad trait whatever, [for that is an abomination to the Lord your God]" [Dt. 17:1].

6.   A.   "and if he, in exchanging, makes any exchange:"

B.   the use of the duplicated verb serves to encompass a woman.

7.   A.   "and if he, in exchanging, makes any exchange:"

B.   the use of the duplicated verb serves to encompass an heir.

8.   A.   "of beast for beast:"

B.   **one for two, two for one, one for a hundred, a hundred for one.**

C.   **R. Simeon says, " 'of beast for beast' – not a beast for beasts."**

D.   **They said to him, "A single beast may be called 'beast,' but many beasts also may be called 'beast' " [M. Tem. 1:2H–J].**

9.   A.   "beast for beast:"

B.   **not beast for fowl, not fowl for beast,**

C.   **not beast for meal offerings, not meal offerings for beast,**

D.   **not beast for them [M. Tem. 1:6A].**

10.   A.   "beast for beast:"

B.   **not beast for foetuses, nor foetuses for beast,**

C. not limbs for foetuses, not foetuses for limbs,

D. not limbs for whole beasts, not whole beasts for them.

E. R. Yosé says, "An act of substitution may be effected between limbs and whole beasts, but not whole beasts for them."

F. Said R. Yosé, "Is it not the fact that, in the case of consecrated beasts, he who says, 'The leg of this beast is a burnt offering,' the whole of it is held to be a burnt offering?

G. "So here too, he who says, 'The foot of this beast in exchange for that,' –

H. "the whole of it should be held to have been declared a substitute in its stead [and therefore to have been consecrated]" [M. Tem. 1:3A–E].

11. A. "then both it and that for which it is exchanged shall be holy:"

B. [These lines find their context below.] Where does the sanctity apply to it?

C. In the house of the owner.

D. Then here too, the sanctity applies to it in the house of the owner [M. Tem. 1:1N–O].

E. [The foregoing form part of a discussion and are out of place. I supply, following M. Tem. 1:1H–O: Priests do not effect a substitution in the case either of a sin offering or of a guilt offering or of a firstling.

F. Said R. Yohanan b. Nuri, "And on what account do the priests who own firstlings not effect substitution in the case of a firstling?"

G. Said R. Aqiba, "A sin-offering and a guilt-offering are a gift to the priest, and a firstling is a gift to the priest. Just as in the case of a sin offering and a guilt offering, they do not effect a substitution, so in the case of a firstling, they should not effect a substitution."

H. Said to him R. Yohanan b. Nuri, "What difference does it make to me that one does not effect a substitution in the case of a sin offering and a guilt offering? For in the case of these, the priests have no claim to the beasts while the beasts are alive. But will you say the same in the case of the firstling, to which the priests do have a claim while the firstling is still alive?"

I. Said to him R. Aqiba, "You have responded to the argument based on comparison. But what will you say to Scripture: 'Then both it and that for which it is exchanged shall be holy' (Lev. 27:10)? At what point does sanctity descend onto it? In the house of the owner. So the substitute too becomes holy in the house of the owner. [The substitute and the animal for which it is designated are comparable. The original animal became holy in the owner's house, not in the house of a priest. The priest therefore has no power to effect a substitution for a firstling. If an Israelite exchanged a firstling, the substitute is sacred. If a priest did so, the substituted beast remains unconsecrated.]"

J.   But once the beasts have been given to a priest, neither the owner nor the priest effects an act of substitution [the former because the beast is no longer his, the latter because the beast is not yet in his domain (Hillel)].

12. A.   "so it shall be:"

B.   **That which has been sanctified has the power to effect substitution [so that if someone says that another beast is a substitute for a beast that has been sanctified, the other beast is in the status of the sanctified beast and so is holy],**

C.   **but a beast that has attained sanctification merely by being declared a substitute for a sanctified beast does not transmit its status to yet another beast [M. Tem. 1:5E].**

D.   Is not the opposite of that proposition a matter of reason?

E.   If a sanctified beast, which is not deemed to be holy if it is blemished with a permanent blemish, effects the status of sanctification for the beast declared to be its substitute,

F.   a beast declared to be a substitute for a sanctified beast, which is deemed to be sanctified even though it bears a permanent blemish, surely should have the power to effect substitution [so that if someone says that another beast is a substitute for a beast that has been sanctified as a substitute, the other beast is in the status of the substituted, now sanctified beast and so it too is holy].

G.   Scripture says, "so it shall be:"

H.   That which has been sanctified has the power to effect substitution [so that if someone says that another beast is a substitute for a beast that has been sanctified, the other beast is in the status of the sanctified beast and so is holy], but a beast that has attained sanctification merely by being declared a substitute for a sanctified beast does not transmit its status to yet another beast.

13. A.   "shall be holy:"

B.   **This teaches that sanctified applies to a beast declared a substitute even though it bears a permanent blemish. [M. Tem. 1:2, 2:33F].**

C.   But is not the opposite of that proposition not a matter of logic?

D.   if the beast that is sanctified, which effects substitution in the case of another beast declared holy in its stead, cannot be sanctified if it bears a permanent blemish,

E. a beast that has been declared a substitute, which does not have the power of effecting substitution should yet another beast be declared a substitute for it, surely should not be deemed sanctified if it bears a permanent blemish!

F. Scripture says, "shall be holy:"

G. This teaches that sanctified applies to a beast declared a substitute even though it bears a permanent blemish.

I. R. Yosé says, " 'shall be holy' serves to indicate that the act of substitution is equally valid when performed inadvertently as when performed deliberately."

As I see it, our exposition of provides little more than a reprise of the language and positions of the parts of the Mishnah's treatment of the same subject. That is the case, clearly, for Nos. 2, 5, and 8–13. A closer look at the propositions, as distinct from the language, would show that the same correspondence is exhibited by the entire exposition before us. Still, even a brief glance at Mishnah-tractate Temurah shows us how much our authorship has *not* attempted to replicate or associate with passages of Scripture. And that is the important point. The authorship of Sifra has not seen itself as bound to the Mishnah's treatment of the topic at hand.

Only a few of the many important principles of the Mishnah tractate are drawn upon, and the reason for what is chosen, explaining also what is omitted, then is clear. Our authorship has no task of demonstrating the correspondence of every rule in the Mishnah to a verse of Scripture, because that authorship deems the Mishnah to be a valid source of law on its own; but where our authorship can show that a rule of the Mishnah relates to, or summarizes, or rests upon a statement of Scripture, it will do so. What it tacitly affirms is the validity of the Mishnah's own, enormously rich and speculative reading of the topical program at hand. What is equally interesting is that the established program of our authorship – exclusion, inclusion, for instance – scarcely makes its appearance.

The second abstract allows us to compare the Mishnah's treatment of a topic with Sifra's authorship's disposition of the same topic. We will compare the whole of Sifra's treatment of a topic with the whole of the Mishnah's treatment of the same topic.

241. Parashat Emor Pereq 18

CCXLI:I.1 A. ["And you shall take fine flour and bake it into twelve loaves of it; two tenths of an ephah shall be in each loaf. And you shall set them in two rows, six in a row, upon the table of pure gold. And you shall put pure frankincense with each row, that it may go with the bread as a memorial portion to be offered by fire to the Lord. Every

Sabbath day Aaron shall set it in order before the Lord continually on behalf of the people of Israel as a covenant for ever. And it shall be for Aaron and his sons, and they shall eat it in a holy place, since it is for him a most holy portion out of the offerings by fire to the Lord, a perpetual due" (Lev. 24:5–9).]

B. "fine flour and bake it:"

C. How do we know that one may also take wheat [for baking the twelve loaves of bread under discussion here]?

D. Scripture says, "You shall take fine flour."

E. Might one suppose that other meal offerings also may derive from wheat [not barley, the usual grain for that purpose]?

F. Scripture says, "it."

G. This derives from wheat, but other meal offerings do not derive from wheat.

2. A. "twelve cakes of it:"

B. they are to be equal to one another.

3. A. "two tenths of an ephah shall be [in each cake]:"

B. that they should be equal in volume.

4. A. "in each cake:"

B. **Every act of kneading and cutting of the dough [of the Twelve Loaves of show bread] should be done for each loaf by itself [M. Men. 11:1B].**

C. How do we know that in the case of the Two Loaves, the acts of kneading and cutting the dough should be done for each loaf by itself?

D. Scripture says, ". . . shall be in each cake."

E. Then how do we know that **the [the twelve loaves] are to be put down into the oven two by two [M. Men. 11:1B]**?

F. Scripture says, "And you shall set them."

G. Might one suppose that the Two Loaves also should be put down into the oven two by two?

H. Scripture says, ". . . them . . . :"

I. this offering is baked two by two, but **the Two Loaves are baked each by itself [M. Men. 11:1A].**

5. A. "And you shall set them:"

B. into the mould.

C. **There were three molds there [in line with M. Men. 11:1C–D]. One was for the bread in the oven, one was for the dough, and one was for when one took the bread out of the oven.**

D. **And one puts the dough into the mould so that they will not spoil the bread [T. Men. 11:3A–B].**

6. A. "[And you shall set them] in two rows, [six in a row,]:"

B. Might one suppose that **one puts eight loaves in one row and four in the other [T. Men. 11:4:C: if one has put eight in one and four in the other or made three rows of four loaves, he has done nothing]**?

C. Scripture says, "six in a row."

D. If there are to be six in a row, might one suppose it is six, six, and six?

E. Scripture says, "twelve loaves."

F. Then if there are to be twelve loaves, might one suppose that one may make **three rows of four loaves [T. Men. 11:14:C]**?

G. Scripture says, "in two rows, six in a row."

H. Lo, unless three verses had made the point clear, [we do not know the correct arrangement], and had the verses not done so, we should have been unable to derive the law.

7. A. "upon the table of pure gold:"

B. on the clean area of the table [which is the surface].

C. This is so that the props should not hold the bread above the surface of the table.

D. In this connection sages have said:

E. **Four golden props were there, at the corners of the table, with their heads shaped into branches like a Y, with which they would support the loaves of bread, two props for this row of bread, and two for that row.**

F. **And there were, inserted into the propers, twenty-eight golden rods, each shaped like half of a hollow reed, fourteen for this row, and fourteen for that row [M. Men. 11:6A–D].**

8. A. "And you shall put [pure frankincense with each row]:"

B. might one suppose that we speak of [putting incense with] a single row?

C. Lo, I argue as follows:

D. Here we find reference to "row," and elsewhere we find reference to "row" ["and set the bread in order on it before the Lord" (Lev. 40:23)].

E. Just as the reference to "setting . . . in rows" stated elsewhere involves a mold of two rows, so "setting in rows" stated here involves a mold of two rows [on both of which frankincense is to be placed].

9. A. "pure frankincense [with each row]:"

B. the frankincense should be clear.

10. A. "that it may go with the bread [as a memorial portion to be offered by fire to the Lord]:"

B. [frankincense] is obligatory for the bread.

11. A. "that it may go with the bread [as a memorial portion to be offered by fire to the Lord]:"

B. This teaches that the frankincense was essential to the bread offering, had the capacity to impart the status of refuse to the bread, and had the capacity to invalidate the bread.

12. A. "that it may go with the bread:"

B. It is not put on top of the bread.

C. But one puts it into two dishes which have sides and one puts the two dishes on the table [not on top of the bread] in such a way that they will not break the bread loaves.

13. A. "as a memorial portion to be offered by fire to the Lord:"

B. R. Simeon says, "Here we find reference to 'a memorial portion,' and elsewhere we find reference to 'a memorial portion' [in connection with the meal offering of an individual, 'And he shall take from it a handful of the fine flour and oil . . . as its memorial portion . . .' (Lev. 2:2)].

C. "Just as 'memorial portion' in the latter passage refers to a handful, so 'memorial portion' in the present passage refers to a handful.

D. "This teaches that the rite requires taking up of two handfuls [of frankincense], a handful for this row, and a handful for that row."

14. A. "Every Sabbath day:"

B. On the Sabbath one sets forth the fresh bread, and on the Sabbath one burns up the old.

15. A. "[Aaron] shall set it in order [before the Lord continually]:"

B. One did not set forth the props with it on the Sabbath,

C. but one enters on the eve of the Sabbath, draws them out, and places them parallel to the length of the table. All the utensils which were in the sanctuary are laid out lengthwise, parallel to the length of the temple [east to west] [M. Men. 11:6F–G],

D. except for the ark.

E. After the Sabbath one would enter and arrange three rods under each one and two under the middle one, since there is no weight on top of it [T. Men. 11:16B–F, with somewhat different wording].

16. A. "on behalf of the people of Israel:"

B. at the pleasure of the people of Israel.

17. A. "as a covenant for ever:"

B. with the one whose is the covenant.

18. A. "And it shall be for Aaron and his sons, and they shall eat it in a holy place:"

B. this teaches that the bread is eaten in the holy place.

C. I know only that eating them is to be done in a holy place.

D. How do I know that also kneading them and cutting them out are to be done in a holy place?

E.   Scripture says, "it shall be."

F.   Might one suppose that the same rule applies to the Two Loaves, that kneading them and cutting out the dough are to be done in a holy place?

G.   Scripture says, "a most holy portion."

H.   R. Judah says, "All acts of prearing them are done inside [that is, both the Two Loaves and the twelve loaves of the show bread]."

I.   R. Simeon says, "One should always be accustomed to state the rule as follows: 'The Two Loaves and the show bread are valid if made in the courtyard of the temple and are valid if made in Bethphage' " [M. Men. 11:2D–E].

19. A.   "And it [shall be for Aaron and his sons]:"

B.   if one of them was split in half, all of the bread is invalid [cf. T. Men. 11:16I].

20. A.   "for Aaron:"

B.   might one suppose for him alone [meaning, for the high priest only]?

C.   Scripture says, "and his sons."

D.   If "for his sons," might one suppose that it is for them and not for him?

E.   Scripture says, "for Aaron."

F.   How so?

G.   It is for Aaron without an act of dividing up the bread by lot, and it is for his sons through an act of dividing up the bread by lot.

H.   Just as Aaron, who was high priest, derives his share without an act of division by lot, so his sons, high priests, derive their share without an act of division by lot.

21. A.   "out of the offerings by fire:"

B.   the priests' claim is effective only after the gift to the altar fires has been made.

22. A.   "a perpetual due:"

B.   for the eternal house.

Overall, the program at hand links some of the rules of the Mishnah and the Tosefta with Scripture. But that is not an exercise carried on in a polemical spirit. The intrusion of passages from the Mishnah or the Tosefta is routine and unexceptional. Our authorship knows a set of rules not contained within Scripture and proposes to discover them in Scripture, mainly by the process of "this, not that" or "this, and also that." The later comes into play at No. 1, which involves both wheat and barley here, but not elsewhere. Nos. 2 and 3 impose a familiar consideration; the loaves are to be in equal weight and dimension. Nos. 4–7 draw us into the orbit of the Mishnah. No. 8 attempts an argument from analogy, and contains no refutation; either the argument then is deemed valid, or the text is flawed. Nos. 9–12 simply gloss phrases. No. 13 permits an argument from analogy to do its work, which suggests that the earlier argument also should be deemed a valid one. Why no objection? Because Scripture itself dictates the shared genus of the two species in both instances. The remainder is routine and presents no surprises.

If we now turn back to Mishnah-tractate Menahot Chapter Eleven, we are able to compare the program of the Mishnah for the topic before us with the program of our authorship. I follow the outline of my *History of the Mishnaic Law of Holy Things. II. Menahot. Translation and Explanation* (Leiden, 1978: E. J. Brill), pp. 6–7. I set in italics those *topics* that are covered in both the Mishnah and Sifra.

11:1–2: *Two loaves of bread and of Pentecost and the twelve loaves of the show bread: how they are kneaded and baked*

11:3: Baked cakes of a high priest: kneading and rolling them out.

11:4–5: Dimensions of the two loaves and the show bread. Dimensions of the table on which they are displayed.

11:6 *The appurtenances on the table used for displaying the show bread.*

11:7 The tables on which the bread is displayed. The way in which the priests take the fresh bread in and remove the bread of the preceding week.

11:8 If one set out the bread on the Sabbath but the dishes of frankincense after the Sabbath. Rules on the week-long display of the two together.

11:9 The two loaves are eaten neither earlier than two days nor later than three after being baked, and the show bread is eaten neither less than nine nor more than eleven days after it is baked.

The upshot is clear. We omit Mishnah-tractate Menahot 11:3, because that is not covered by our verses of Scripture, M. 11:4–5 because the passage at hand does not attend to the table. We include M. 11:6 because the display of the bread is at issue in our base verse. The really interesting omissions come at M. 11:7–9, however.

Can we account, in the comparison with the Mishnah's discussion of precisely the same subject, for the order and topical program of Sifra? Indeed so. What our authorship does not cover at all is, first, the actual conduct of the rite, and, second, those components of a casuistical exposition that yield stunning generalizations about the conduct of affairs. Specifically, I refer to the interstitial cases, those matters of unclarity, the excluded middle, that the authorship of the Mishnah so lovingly dwells upon, all of which generate vast generalizations, governing rules and principles, an account of possibilites (e.g., neither before . . . nor later . . ., and the like. Indeed, a comparison of the rules concerning menstruation in Leviticus 15 and those about the woman in her menstrual period in Mishnah tractate *Niddah* will yield the same result: intersection at some points of detail, but, for the authorship of the Mishnah, a fundamentally different generative logic altogether. And if Sifra's authorship avoids that Mishnaic obsession with the intermediate and the interstitial, it is because our authorship conceives that problem to be less important than those to which it devotes attention. In its judgment, the work of category formation, classification and taxonomy overall, has been so well construed that the issues of the muddled middle and interstitial cases scarcely require attention. The source for that confidence in the available taxonomy of nature and supernature is our authorship's identification of what is primary and definitive, which is Scripture: its categories, its classifications of things, its encompassing taxonomy, within the topic at hand. I have again moved far ahead in my argument, but the point is becoming increasingly self-evident.

For Sifra's authorship has a clear definition of what it finds and what it does not find of interest and in the topics treated in the book of Leviticus, and that definition in no way conforms to the Mishnah's. Accordingly, Sifra's authorship rejects not only the Mishnah's principle of topical organization, but also the program of analysis of the topics that are presented. Here, therefore, we do see ways not taken, choices of matters to treat in the Mishnah that have been either not recognized or rejected by the authorship of Sifra. When, as I claim, an authorship determines the choice and ordering of topics, that is a considerable matter indeed. Sifra's authorship finds in Scripture not only the topics it will treat and the order in which it will address them, but also the definition of what it wants to know about those topics, and what it does not want to know. And, as we have seen just now, the authorship of Sifra in no way finds urgent that obsessive interest in interstitial problems, the excluded middle, problems of doubt, the nature of mixtures, and the like, that forms the generative problematic of the Mishnah, viewed all together and whole. However, the differences between the two sets of writers, those of the Mishnah and those of Sifra, extend not only to the selection and treatment of topics, but also to the deeper matter of the way in which intelligible discourse will be conducted: modes of cogent composition.

Notes

[1] It seems self-evident that the tractates are ordered by length, longer then shorter. As to the ordering of the divisions – Seeds, Seasons, Women, Damages, Holy Things, Purities – I know no evidence internal to the Mishnah that suggests the divisions were set forth in that and in no other order. But the sequence in which the propositions concerning a given topic, treated in a single tractate, are worked out is easily explained and can be shown to be intrinsic to the plan of the authorship of tractates. When we consider the propositions concerning a topic and set forth not only how they are now ordered, but how they might otherwise be ordered, we can nearly always account for the present arrangement. That again forms an aspect of deconstruction, the identification of choices facing an authorship, and reconstruction and (for logic) rehabilitation. The next note indicates where I have done this work for all the divisions of the second through the sixth divisions.

[2] I have done so in each of the volumes of my *History of the Mishnaic Law* for the tractates of the second through the sixth divisions of the Mishnah.

[3] That is somewhat of an overstatement, since not all tractates can be shown to develop a generative problematic concerning their topics. But most can.

[4] I review conclusions first presented in my *Judaism: The Evidence of the Mishnah* (Second printing, augmented: Atlanta, 1988: Scholars Press for Brown Judaic Studies).

[5] I see "not recognized" in the supposition that the framers of Sifra never saw the Mishnah, or ignored, in the supposition that they did. I obviously take the latter view, but for phenomenological argument, matters have to be framed outside the framework of temporal order. All the reader has to concede is that, within a given subject and its logic, inhered the issues discerned by the framers of the Mishnah. Then the authorship of Sifra, addressing the same issue, in which inhered the same logic, can have asked the same questions as did the framers of the Mishnah. But they did not do so. Hence I justify using the language, "not recognized," alongside the more reasonable "rejected."

CHAPTER SIX

Sifra's Alternative to the Mishnah's Logic of Cogent Discourse

An authorship identifies a principle of association that joins one topic to another, and that does so in one way, rather than another. I call this the logic of cogent discourse, in that the chosen logic joins one sentence or proposition to another sentence or proposition.

I. The Four Logics of Cogent Discourse in the Canon of the Dual Torah

The logic of cogent discourse explains how an authorship joins one sentence to another and groups of sentences together into cogent statements (e.g., paragraphs, propositions).[1] That is to say, I ask about the way in which people add up two and two to make four. In cogent discourse there is always the appeal to the *and*, and to the *equal*, which is to say, the conclusion yielded by the *and*. There are four ways in which an authorship in the canon of the dual Torah may join one sentence to another. One is familiar to us as philosophical logic. Philosophical discourse is built out of propositions and arguments from facts and reason. The second is equally familiar as what I call teleological logic, namely, cogent discourse attained through narrative. These two are logics of a propositional order. The third logic is not propositional, and, as a matter of fact, also is not ordinarily familiar to us at all. It is a mode of joining two or more statements – sentences – not on the foundation of meaning or sense or proposition but on foundations of a different order altogether. The fourth, distinct from the prior three, is a mode of establishing connections at the most abstract and profound level of discourse, the level of methodical analysis of many things in a single way, which forms the most commonplace building block of thought in our document. It is, as a matter of fact, stunning in its logical power. But, in a limited sense, it also is not propositional, though it yields its encompassing truths of order, proportion, structure, and self-evidence. These third and fourth modes of establishing connections between sentences, that is, logics of cogent discourse, predominate in Sifra; the first in Scripture, the second in the Mishnah.

Let us dwell on the Mishnah's logic of cogent discourse, which establishes propositions that rest upon philosophical bases, for example, through the proposal of a thesis and the composition of a list of facts that prove the thesis. This – to us entirely familiar, – mode of scientific expression through the classification of data that, in a simple way, we may call the science of making lists *(Listenwissenschaft)*, as we will see in Chapter Seven, is exemplified by the Mishnah. The issue at hand is one of connection, that is, not of fact (such as is conveyed by the statement of the meaning of a verse or a clause of a verse) but of the relationship between one fact and another. That relationship is shown in a conclusion, different from the established facts of two or more sentences, that we propose to draw when we set up in sequence two or more facts and claim out of that sequence a proposition different from, and transcending, the facts at hand. We demonstrate propositions in a variety of ways, appealing to both a repertoire of probative facts and also a set of accepted modes of argument. In this way we engage in a kind of discourse that gains its logic from what, in general, we may call philosophy: the rigorous analysis and testing of propositions against the canons of an accepted reason.

Philosophy accomplishes the making of the whole more – or less – than the sum of the parts, that is, in the simple language we have used up to now, showing the connections between fact 1 and fact 2, in such wise as to yield proposition A. We begin with the irrefutable fact; our issue is not how facts gain their facticity, rather, how, from givens, people construct propositions or make statements that are deemed sense and not nonsense or gibberish. Therefore, the problem is to explain the connections between and among facts, accounting for the conclusions people draw, on the one side, or the acceptable associations people tolerate, on the other, in the exchange of language and thought. When, in the next chapter, we return to this mode of cogent discourse, we will consider its logical foundations in the science of classification, that is, making lists or *Listenwissenschaft.*

When we appeal to narrative as a mode of making connections and presenting conclusions, we link fact to fact and also prove (ordinarily implicit) propositions by appeal to teleology. A proposition (whether or not it is stated explicitly) may be set forth and demonstrated by showing through the telling of a tale (of a variety of kinds, e.g., historical, fictional, parabolic, and the like) that a sequence of events, real or imagined, shows the ineluctable truth of a given proposition. The logic of connection demonstrated through narrative, rather than philosophy, is simply stated. It is connection attained and explained by invoking some mode of narrative in which a sequence of events, first this, then that, is understood to yield a proposition, first this, then that – *because of this.* That manufactured sequence both states *and also establishes* a proposition in a way different from the philosophical and argumentative mode of propositional discourse. Whether or not the generalization is stated in so many words rarely matters, because the power of well-crafted narrative is to make unnecessary the explicit drawing of the moral. Narrative sees cogency in the purpose, the necessary order of events understood as causative. That is then a logic or intelligibility of connection that is attained through teleology: the claim of purpose and cause in the garb of a story of what happened because it had to happen. Narrative conveys a proposition through the setting forth of happenings in a framework of inevitability, in a sequence that makes a point, for example, establishes not merely the facts of what happens, but the teleology that explains those facts. As a result we speak not only of events – our naked facts – but of their relationship. We claim to account for that relationship teleologically, in the purposive sequence and necessary order of happenings.

Along with cogency attained through methodical analysis of many things in a single way, the third logic (i.e., the cogency of fixed associative logic) is paramount in Sifra. The logic of fixed association simply does not yield a proposition. The mere sequence that links in one composition sentence 1, then sentence 2, then sentence 3, within this logic of cogent discourse is deemed to form of the three unrelated sentences a single composition, even though there is no propositional connection between 1 and 2 or 2 and 3. Clearly, this logic rests upon principles of intelligibility practically unknown to us. In a discourse that finds large-scale cogency in fixed association, therefore, we have a sequence of absolutely unrelated sentences (that is, facts), made up in each instance of a clause of a verse, followed by a phrase of amplification. Nothing links one sentence (completed thought or fact) to the ones fore or aft. Yet the compositors have presented us with sequences of episodic sentences that they represent side by side with sentences that do form large propositional compositions, that is, that are linked one to the next by connections that we can readily discern.[2] It follows that episodic sentences or facts have formed into a composite, even while lacking a shared proposition or making a point all together. Before proceeding, let me give an example of what I mean by the logic of fixed associations, since this mode of forming intelligible discourse is unfamiliar in our world.

101. Parashat Shemini Pereq 1

CI:II.1   A.   "Take the cereal offering:"

    B.   [Since on the day on which the altar was dedicated, which coincided with the eighth day of the consecration of the priests, the princes began to make their presentation, and that on the first day was Nachshon, so Num. 7:12, including basins "full of fine flour mixed with oil for a cereal offering,"] this refers to the meal offering brought by Nachshon.

    C.   "that remains:"

    D.   this is the meal offering of the eighth day.

    E.   "of the offerings by fire to the Lord:" the priests have their claim to the residue only after the rest has been offered up by fire.

2.   A.   "and eat it unleavened:"

    B.   What is the point of Scripture here?

    C.   Since it was for the occasion at hand that the meal offering of the community was offered, a meal offering of unleavened cakes, and an equivalent offering is not presented in the coming generations, [there was no clear rule on how to consume it, and] therefore Scripture says, "and eat it unleavened."

3.   A.   "beside the altar:"

    B.   not in the holy place [outside of the Holy of Holies], nor on the altar.

    C.   I know only that the rule applies to the case at hand. How do I know that it encompasses all food in the status of Most Holy Things?

    D.   Scripture says, "for it is most holy."

4.   A.   The language "it" in the nominative and accusative serves as exclusionary,

    B.   thus omitting from the rule the thanksgiving offering and the bread that accompanies it, the ram brought by the Nazirite and the bread that accompanies it, and the ram of consecration and the bread that accompanies it.

5.   A.   "You shall eat it in a holy place:"

    B.   What is the purpose of Scripture?

    C.   Since Scripture says, "beside the altar," I know only that one may eat the food near the altar itself.

    D.   How do I know that as to the rooms that are built on unconsecrated ground but open into holy ground, [one may eat the food there as well]?

    E.   Scripture says, "You shall eat in a holy place."

6.   A.   "because it is your due and your sons' due:"

    B.   It is the due of the sons, and it is the due of the daughters.

7.   A.   "from the offerings by fire to the Lord:"

    B.   You have a right to the food only after the sacrificial portions have been placed on the altar fires.

8.   A.   "for so I am commanded:"

    B.   Just as I have been commanded, so the Lord has commanded.

9.   A.   "for so I am commanded:"

B. "to tell you that at the time even that one has suffered a bereavement [as with Nadab and Abihu] and not yet buried his dead, the priest may eat it."

10. A. "for so I am commanded:"

B. at the time of the event itself.

11. A. "as the Lord has commanded:"

B. "And it is not on my own authority that I speak to you."

12. A. "But the breast:" this refers to the breast.

B. "that is waved: this refers to the waving of the basket.

C. "and the thigh: this refers to the thigh.

D. "that is offered:" this refers to the offering of the thanksgiving offering.

13. A. "you shall eat in any clean place:"

B. Said R. Nehemiah, "Now were the items mentioned earlier not to be eaten in a clean place?

C. "But this refers to a kind of cleannesss that is not subject to uncleannesss, that is, that does not have to be rendered clean of the uncleanness of the one afflicted by the skin ailment.

D. "The point is that the items under discussion now may be eaten anywhere in Jerusalem [where those afflicted by the skin disease are not permitted to enter]"

14. A. "you and your sons and your daughters with you:"

B. "you and your sons:" by a properly conducted division [i.e., through the chance division of lots, not through human intervention].

C. "your daughters with you:" through a division by gift [from the father, that is, through human intervention].

D. Or might one suppose that "you and your sons and your daughters with you" means that all should be done by a properly conducted division?

E. When Scripture says, "and it shall be yours and your sons' with you, as a due for ever," it excludes a due for the daughters [and hence the procedure for dividing the food will differ for the daughters and not conform to the priestly rite of division].

F. How then am I to interpret the phrase, "you and your sons and your daughters with you"

G. "you and your sons:" by a properly conducted division.

H. "your daughters with you:" through a division by gift.

15. A. "for they are given . . . from the sacrifices of the peace offerings of the people of Israel:"

B. this serves to encompass the sacrifices of peace offerings of the community at large,

C. indicating that on that day they should be there as well.

D. For it is said, "He killed the ox also and the ram, the sacrifice of peace offerings for the people" (Lev. 9:18).

16. A. "The thigh that is offered and the breast that is waved they shall bring with the offerings by fire of the fat to wave for a wave offering before the Lord:"

B. This teaches that the sacrificial fat is placed below [when the whole is waved].

The phrase-by-phrase amplification follows the program of the verses at hand and, so far as I can see, draws little from some intellectual plan other than that of the verses under discussion. It is an excellent example of the power of the logic of fixed association to join together utterly discrete sentences into what is, to our authorship and its readers, a perfectly cogent composition. The third logic, therefore, rests upon this premise: *An established sequence of words joins whatever is attached to those words into a set of cogent statements, even though it does not form of those statements propositions of any kind, implicit or explicit.*

The established sequence of words may be made up of names always associated with one another. It may be made up of a received text, with deep meanings of its own, for example, a verse or a clause of Scripture. It may be made up of the sequence of holy days or synagogue lections, which are assumed to be known by everyone and so to connect on their own. The fixed association of these words, whether names, whether formula such as verses of Scripture, whether lists of facts, serves to link otherwise unrelated statements to one another and to form of them all not a proposition but, nonetheless, *an entirely intelligible sequence of connected or related sentences.*

Our fourth logic of intelligible discourse involves sustained and highly cogent discourse in which one analytical method applies to many sentences, with the result that many, discrete and diverse sentences are shown to constitute a single intellectual structure. This logic of joining sentence to sentence into proposition works at two levels, which is why I call it metapropositional. A variety of explanations and amplifications, topically and propositionally unrelated, will be joined in such a way, which is very common in our document, as to make a point beyond themselves and applicable to them all. Here we have a fixed way of connecting diverse things, showing that many things really conform to a single pattern or structure. Methodologically coherent analysis imposes upon a variety of data a structure that is external to all of the data, yet that imposes connection between and among facts or sentences, a connection consisting in the order and balance and meaning of them all, seen in the aggregate.

This is the other paramount logic of cogent discourse in Sifra. One of the most common modes of intelligible discourse in our document is to ask the same question to many things and to produce a single result, wherever that question is asked: methodical analysis of many things showing pattern and, therefore, order where, on the surface, none exists. Another metapropositional exercise will ask about the limitations and restrictions or broad applicability of a rule, everywhere raising the same question: Does the detail of a scriptural case serve to restrict the rule to a case precisely in conformity with the detail, or does the detail of the scriptural case mean to exemplify a classification or type? In my commentary on Sifra, I point to countless instances in which a fixed program of exclusion and inclusion tells our authorship what it wishes to know about a given topic. That is the single most common example of recurrent methodical analysis or metapropositional cogency in our document.

In fact, that methodical analysis imposes stunning cogency on otherwise unrelated facts or sentences that themselves have been formed into sizable compositions, showing one thing out of many things. For unity of thought and discourse derives not only from what is said, or even from a set of fixed associations. It may be imposed by addressing a set of fixed questions, imposing a sequence of stable procedures, to a vast variety of data. Such a method will yield not a proposition, nor even a sequence of facts formerly unconnected but now connected, but a different mode of cogency, one that derives from showing that many things follow a single rule or may be interpreted in a single way. It is the intelligible proposition that is general and not particular, that imposes upon the whole a sense of understanding and comprehension, even though the parts of the whole do not join together. What happens, in this mode of discourse, is that we turn the particular into the general, the case into a rule, and if we had to point to one purpose of our authorship overall, it is to turn the cases of the book of Deuteronomy into rules that conform, overall, to the way in which the Mishnah presents its rules: logically, topically, a set of philosophically defensible generalizations. With these four logics in mind, let us turn to the Mishnah's choices and Sifra's authorship's judgments upon those choices.

II. Scripture's and the Mishnah's Logics of Cogent Discourse

While addressing the book of Leviticus and commonly inserting sizable abstracts of the Mishnah, Sifra's authorship has appealed neither to Scripture nor to the Mishnah for its logic of cogent discourse. Rather, its principles of cogent discourse are, in the main, two: fixed association or methodical analysis. Neither principle plays a considerable role in the Mishnah. I cannot point to a single passage in the Mishnah in which a sequence of sentences is joined together on wholly formal, a priori, and nonpropositional grounds. Methodical analysis takes a minor role in the Mishnah. The principal and dominent logic of cogent discourse derives from philosophical logic of propositions and their proof. What about the comparison of Sifra's and Scripture's (i.e., Leviticus's) modes of attaining intelligibility between and among sequential sentences? The Pentateuch tells a story and weaves all rules into that story. Its logic of cogent discourse is fundamentally teleological, and into that logic all its rules are fit.

The Mishnah presents rules and treats stories (inclusive of history) as incidental and of merely taxonomic interest. Its logic is propositional, and its intellect does its work through a vast labor of classification, comparison and contrast generating governing rules and generalizations. The Pentateuch provides an account of how things were in order to explain how things are and set forth how they should be, with the tabernacle in the wilderness the model for (and modeled after) the temple in Jerusalem continuously being built. The Mishnah speaks in a continuing present tense, saying only how things are, indifferent to the *were* and the *will be.* The Pentateuch focuses upon self-conscious "Israel," saying who they were and what they must become to overcome how they now are. The Mishnah understands by "Israel" as much the individual as the nation and identifies as its principal actors, the heroes of its narrative, not the family become a nation, but the priest and the householder, the woman and the slave, the adult and the child, and other castes and categories of person within an inward-looking, established, fully landed community. Given the Mishnah's authorship's interest in classifications and categories, therefore, in systematic hierarchization of an orderly world, one can hardly find odd that (re)definition of the subject matter and problematic of the systemic social entity.

Let us dwell on this matter of difference in the prevailing logic. Whereas the Pentateuch appeals to teleology to draw together and make sense of facts, so making connections by appeal to the end and drawing conclusions concerning the purpose of things, the Mishnah's authorship knows only the philosophical logic of syllogism, the rule-making logic of lists. The Pentateuchal logic reached concrete expression in narrative, which served to point to the direction and goal of matters, hence, in the nature of things, of history. Accordingly, those authors, when putting together diverse materials, so shaped everything as to form of it as continuous a narrative as they could construct, and through that "history" that they made up, they delivered their message and also portrayed that message as cogent and compelling. If the Pentateuchal writers were theologians of history, the Mishnah's aimed at composing a natural philosophy for supernatural, holy Israel. Like good Aristotelians, they would uncover the components of the rules by comparison and contrast, showing the rule for one thing by finding out how it compared with like things and contrasted with the unlike.[3] Then, in their view, the unknown would become known, conforming to the rule of the like thing, also to the opposite of the rule governing the unlike thing.

That purpose is accomplished, in particular, though list making, which places on display the data of the like and the unlike and implicitly (ordinarily, not explicitly) then conveys the role. That is why, in exposing the interior logic of its authorship's intellect, the Mishnah had to be a book of lists, with the implicit order, the nomothetic traits, dictating the ordinarily unstated general and encompassing rule. But why? It is in order to make a single statement, endless times over, and to repeat in a mass of tangled detail precisely the same fundamental judgment. The Mishnah in its way is as blatantly repetitious in its fundamental statement as is the Pentateuch. But the power of the Pentateuchal authorship, denied to that of the Mishnah, lies in their capacity always to be heard, to create sound by resonance of the surface of things. The Pentateuch is a fundamentally popular and accessible piece of writing. By contrast, the Mishnah's writers spoke into the depths, anticipating a more acute hearing than they ever would receive. So the repetitions of Scripture reenforce the message, whereas the endlessly repeated paradigm of the Mishnah sits too deep in the structure of the system to gain hearing from the ear that lacks acuity or to attain visibility to the untutored eye. So much for the logic. What of the systemic message? Given the subtlety of intellect of the Mishnah's authorship, we cannot find surprising that the message speaks not only in what is said, but in what is omitted.

III. Sifra's Critique of the Mishnah: Sifra's Paramount Logics of Fixed Associative Discourse and Methodical Analysis

Methodical analysis repeatedly asks a single question of a vast range of diverse material. The net effect is to impart to a diverse text, covering many topics, a coherent character. Asking the same question of many things and producing answers of the same sort, utilizing rhetoric of a single pattern, thus turns discrete sentences into a cogent whole, even while not appealing to a common sense or a common proposition for that purpose. Let me give a single instance of a methodical analytical pattern, and the reader will in other examples given elsewhere in this book find its counterparts, sometimes formally, always intellectually, and logic, everywhere. The operative rhetoric here is "I know only this . . . how about that . . .?"

CLXIV:I.1   A.   "And whoever sits on anything on which he who has the discharge has sat will be unclean [shall wash his clothes and bathe himself in water and be unclean until the evening]" (Lev. 15:6).

B.   I know only that this is the case if he sits on it and [actually] touches it. [That is to say, if the Zab is in direct contact with the chair, then he imparts uncleanness to it.]

C.   How do I know that [if the Zab sits on] ten chairs, one on the other, and even [if he sits] on top of a heavy stone, [what is underneath is clean]? [If the chair bears the weight of the Zab, even though the Zab is not touching the chair, the chair is made unclean.]

D.   Scripture says, "And he who sits on the utensil on which the Zab has sat will be unclean" –

E.   In any place in which the Zab sits and imparts uncleanness, the clean person sits and becomes unclean.

F.   I know only that when the Zab sits on it, and the Zab is there [that it is unclean]. How do I know that I should treat the empty as the full one?

G.   Scripture says, "Utensil" – to treat the empty like the full.

H.   I know only that this [rule concerning transmission of the Zab's uncleanness merely through applying the burden of his weight, even without his actually being in contact with the object] applies to the chair. How do I know that it applies to the saddle?

I.   And it is logical:

J.   If we have found that Scripture does not distinguish between the one who carries and the one who is carried in respect to sitting, so we should not distinguish between the one who is carried and the one who carries with respect to the saddle.

K.   But what difference does it make to me that Scripture did not distinguish between carrying and being carried in respect to the chair?

L.   For it did not distinguish touching it and carrying it.

M.   Should we not distinguish between carrying and being carried with reference to the saddle,

N.   for lo, it has indeed distinguished touching it from carrying it?

O.   Scripture [accordingly is required] to state, "A utensil" – to encompass even the saddle.

The inclusionary method will utilize diverse rhetoric, but it always is characterized by the intent to encompass within a single law a variety of cases. The intent is the same as that of the Mishnah, namely, to show the rule governing diverse cases. The contrary exercise, the one that excludes examples from a rule, is to be stipulated. That, of course, is also what the framers of the Mishnah propose through their making of lists of like and unlike things and determination of the rule that governs them all. When the framers of the Mishnah appeal to the making of lists, they do no more, and no less, than is accomplished by our authorship in its exegetical exercises of exclusion and inclusion. Here our authorship demonstrates the possibility of doing, through rewriting the written Torah, precisely what the oral Torah is meant to do. The judgment on modes of cogent discourse operative in the Mishnah is tacitly negative; we do things this way because this is the way to do them, that is to say, through appeal to, and amplification of, the written Torah – not through appeal to, and ordering of, traits of things sorted out independently of the written Torah.

A single example will suffice to show the principles of cogency on which our authorship depends. For that purpose, we turn to a sizable sample chapter. I present the chapter complete, then ask how sentences are joined into sense units, and, more important, how each unit is set into place side by side with others.

10. Parashat Vayyiqra Dibura Denedabah. Parashah 5

X:I.1   A.   "If [his offering for a burnt offering is from the flock, of sheep or of goats, he shall make his offering a male without blemish. It shall be slaughtered before the Lord on the north side of the altar, and Aaron's sons, the priests, shall dash its blood against all sides of the altar. When it has been cut up into sections, the priest shall lay them out, with the head and the suet, on the wood that is on the fire upon the altar. The entrails and the legs shall be washed with water; the priest shall offer up and turn the whole into smoke on the altar. It is a burnt offering, an offering by fire, of pleasing odor to the Lord" (Lev. 1:10–13)]:

B.   Lo, this matter adds to the earlier one. [That is to say, rules governing the burnt offering made of an animal from the herd apply to the burnt offering made of an animal from the flock and vice versa.]

C.   Then what purpose was there in setting forth free-standing statements [such as those that commence without reference to speaking or saying]?

D.   It was so as to give Moses a pause to collect his thoughts between the statement of one passage and the next, between the presentation of one topic and the next.

E.   And lo, that yields an argument *a fortiori:*

F.   If one who was listening to words from the mouth of the Holy One, and who was speaking by the inspiration of the Holy Spirit, nonetheless had to pause to collect his thoughts between one passage and the next, between one topic and the next,

G.   all the more so an ordinary person in discourse with other common folk [must speak with all due deliberation].

The same question raised earlier recurs, underlining the methodical inquiry that is imposed throughout.

X:II.1   A.   "[If his offering for a burnt offering is] from the flock, of sheep or of goats:"

B.   These specifications ["of sheep, or of goats" after "of the flock"] serve as exclusionary statements, omitting from the list of acceptable types of animal offering a beast that is superannuated, sick, or filthy.

2.   A.   ". . . his offering . . .:"

B.   the reference to the personal pronoun excludes the possibility of using a stolen beast.

3.   A.   "of sheep or of goats:"

B.   this excludes hybrids.

4.   A.   "Now you maintain that these several exclusionary specifications serve solely for the stated purpose.

B.   "But perhaps the intent is solely to exclude those beasts that have been the medium for committing a transgression, or that have threshed with an ox and an ass together while they were consecrated, or produce that has grown as mixed seeds in a vineyard, or produce of the seventh year, or produce that has been worked on the intermediate days of the festival, the Day of Atonement, the Sabbath, [and the like]?

C.   "[After specifying 'flock, which encompasses both sheep and goats',] Scripture says, '. . . sheep . . . for a burnt offering . . ., or goats . . . for a burnt offering.'

D.   "This [additional specification serves as a generalizing rule, thus] encompassing all these cases [and not solely the ones listed above]," the words of R. Judah.

Nos. 1–3 go over several exclusions implicit in the specifications. Then, at No. 4, Judah wishes to extend the catalogue of prohibited classifications, and this he does by an exegetical device that treats the specified items as exemplary of a general rule. The rest follows. The fixed association is imposed by the base-verse; no proposition joins one unit to the next. Methodical analysis directs the presentation of a fixed program of questions. In our document these commonly concern the exclusion or inclusion of items not covered. The exclusionary, then inclusionary inquiry dominates above. It is certainly the most common methodical analysis available to our authorship. When one covers a fair part of Sifra as a whole, that recurrent set of questions joins discrete parts to one another and imparts to the whole a fine sense of composition and order.

X:III.1   A.   R. Simeon says, "Scripture says, . . . sheep . . . for a burnt offering . . ., or goats . . . for a burnt offering.'

B.   "This serves to encompass within the rule a beast that has been substituted for a burnt offering [which, in accord with Lev. 27:10, takes on the status of the animal that was originally consecrated, so that both of them then have to be offered]."

C. But is this proposition not to be proven merely on the basis of logic?

D. If animals designated as substitutes for those in the status of peace offerings, for which purpose fowl cannot be designated, themselves nonetheless are suitable to be offered up, the substitute designated in place of an animal consecrated as a burnt offering, for which purpose a fowl *may* be designated, surely *should* be validly consecrated [which is the proposition of B].

E. [But the two types of sacrificial protocol, peace offerings and whole offerings, are not comparable, so the argument of D is null, for] if you have stated the rule for peace offerings, which may validly derive from either female or male beasts, will you apply the same rule to animals designated for burnt offerings, which may derive only from male but not from female beasts. Since a burnt offering may not derive from a female but only from a male beast, [there should be other pertinent restrictions as well, with the consequence] that a beast that has been designated as its substitute should not be deemed valid for offering.

F. That is why it was necessary for Scripture to make this point:

G. Scripture says, ". . . sheep . . . for a burnt offering . . ., or goats . . . for a burnt offering."

H. This serves to encompass within the rule a beast that has been substituted for a burnt offering [which, in accord with Lev. 27:10, takes on the status of the animal that was originally consecrated, so that both of them then have to be offered]."

We find ourselves on the familiar turf of proving that Scripture serves as the sole source of appropriate rules, because exercises of comparison and contrast prove invariably flawed. Here we have two methodical inquiries, first, B, the inclusionary question, second, C, the recurrent and paramount issue of the source of correct classification for purposes of hierarchical logic.

X:IV.1 A. R. Eleazar says, "Why does Scripture say, '. . . sheep . . . for a burnt offering . . ., or goats . . . for a burnt offering'?

B. "One might have reasoned as follows:

C. "I know only that a beast should be offered up as a burnt offering if it is purchased from the excess of funds contributed to begin with for the provision of beasts for the burnt offering.

D. "How do I know that the excess of funds contributed for the purchase of animals for use as sin offerings, the excess of funds contributed for purchase of animals used as guilt offerings, for the purchase of the tenth-ephah of fine flour, for the purchase of birds for use in the purification rites of Zab-males and Zab-females and women after childbirth, the excess of funds contributed for the purchase of offerings for the rites of the Nazir and the leper to be purified,

E.   "[and further:] one who consecrates his possessions, among which were things that were suitable for use on the altar, for example, wine, oil, and fowl –

F.   "how do we know that they are to be sold for the purposes of that same species [e.g., to pilgrims who require wine or oil or fowl for an offering], and with the proceeds animals to be designated for us as burnt offerings are to be purchased?

G.   "Scripture says, '. . . sheep . . . for a burnt offering . . ., or goats . . . for a burnt offering,'

H.   "which serves to encompass all these cases."

I.   And sages say, "Let the proceeds fall to a fund for the purpose of purchasing free will offerings."

J.   But is it not the fact that beasts that are offered as free will offerings fall into the classification of burnt offerings? So what is at issue between R. Eleazar and sages?

K.   The difference is this: when a burnt offering is brought in fulfillment of an obligation, the person who brings it relies upon the beast for that purpose in carrying out his obligation, brings in its regard drink offerings, and the drink offerings are paid for by the one who benefits from the offering, and if he was a priest, the right of preparing the beast and the hide belong to him.

L.   But when a burnt offering is brought as a free will offering, the one who brings it may not rely upon it in fulfillment of an obligation, and he does not bring the drink offerings in its connection, and the cost of the drink offerings derives from communal funds, and even though the donor may be a priest, the right of preparing the beast and the hide go not to him in particular but to the members of the priestly watch of that particular week.

The exercise has no bearing upon any other passage in our context, and it concerns issues entirely abstracted from the details at hand. The purpose is to distinguish the burnt offering brought as a free will offering, which is the subject of the scriptural passage at hand, and the burnt offering brought in fulfillment of an individual's obligation, which is the next major subject. We stand too far from the unit beyond to propose that we deal with a transitional exercise. The reason for including the passage here, then, is solely the fact that Eleazar appeals to our text to prove his point. Otherwise the passage hardly fits. But the key language is the question of D, which introduces the inclusionary issue and generates the remaining discussion. Once more we see that the whole holds together through process of thought, rather than through proposition.

X:V.1 A.   "It shall be slaughtered [before the Lord on the north side of the altar]:"

B.   That particular offering is slaughtered at the north side of the altar, but fowl brought as a burnt offering are not slaughtered at the north side of the altar.

C.   But is the opposite of that proposition not a matter of logic?

D.   If a beast deriving from the flock, for which a priest in particular is not assigned the task, the location of the rite at the north of the altar is established as a requirement, a fowl, for which a priest in particular is assigned the task of slaughter, surely should be assigned a place at the north of the altar as well?

E.   Because of the possibility of reaching that false conclusion, [it was necessary for] Scripture to state explicitly, "*It* shall be slaughtered [before the Lord on the north side of the altar]" –

F.   That particular offering is slaughtered at the north side of the altar, but fowl brought as a burnt offering are not slaughtered at the north side of the altar.

2.   A.   R. Eliezer b. Jacob says, " '*It* shall be slaughtered [before the Lord on the north side of the altar]' – that particular offering is slaughtered at the north side of the altar, but a beast that is designated a Passover offering is not slaughtered at the north side of the altar."

B.   But is the contrary not logical? If a burnt offering, which is not assigned a particular time for its slaughter, is assigned a particular place of slaughter,

C.   a beast designated as a Passover offering, which is assigned a particular time for its slaughter, surely should be assigned a particular place for slaughter.

D.   Because of the possibility of reaching that false conclusion, [it was necessary for] Scripture to state explicitly, "*It* shall be slaughtered before the Lord on the north side of the altar]" –

E.   That particular offering is slaughtered at the north side of the altar, but fowl brought as a burnt offering are not slaughtered at the north side of the altar.

3.   A.   R. Hiyya says, " '*It* shall be slaughtered [before the Lord] on the north side of the altar,' but the one who does the slaughtering does not have to be standing at the north side of the altar.

B.   "Now we know as fact that the one who receives the blood does have to be standing at the north side of the altar and does have to receive the blood at the north side of the altar. If he stood at the south side of the altar and received the blood at the north side of the altar, he has invalidated the offering.

C.   "Might one think that the same rule applies to the one who slaughters the beast?

D.   "Scripture says, '*It* shall be slaughtered [before the Lord] on the north side of the altar,' but the one who does the slaughtering does not have to be standing at the north side of the altar."

No. 1 explains in a negative way why the proof from Scripture is required for the proposition at hand. No. 2 goes over the same exercise, with the result that the differentiating indicators among the diverse types of offerings are laid forth. The implicit proposition hardly requires specification. No. 3 entertains yet another false proposition, this time classifying two actions as one and then showing that the single classification does not fit – because of Scripture's own decree. It is the counterpart to the argument of Nos. 1 and 2. Here is another methodical inquiry, of the sort that will occupy us again in Chapters Seven and Eight. Its formal character as a recurrent pattern of thought, and its function of holding the document together – providing a uniformity over and above a mere formal joining of discrete bits and pieces of exegesis – should not be missed.

X:VI.1   A.   "[It shall be slaughtered before the Lord] on the north side of the altar:"

B.   For the actual side of the altar stands at the northern limits of the altar. [The altar is not bisected, with half assigned to the south, the other half to the north, but the northern side of the altar is at the very dividing point between north and south vis-a-vis the altar itself.]

C.   And where is the face of the altar? It is at the south. Thus we learn that the ramp is at the southern side of the altar.

D.   R. Judah says, " 'And the ramp shall face east' (Ezek. 43:17), so that the person who goes up on it turns to his right, which is eastward. Lo, we learn therefore that the ramp is at the southern side of the altar."

2.   A.   "[It shall be slaughtered before the Lord] on the north side of the altar:"

B.   **"For the whole altar is deemed north, [T. Zeb. 7:1A]**, so that if one has slaughtered Most Holy Things at the head of it, they are deemed valid," **the words of R. Yosé.**

C.   **R. Yosé b. R. Judah says, "From the midway point of the altar and to the north is deemed north, and from the midway point and outward is deemed south"** [M. Zeb. 6:1C].

We have at B–C and D two proofs for the same proposition. It seems to me the passage is included only because of the intersection with the detail referring to the north side of the altar. No. 2 is tacked on for obvious reasons. Here we cannot point to elements of thought or expression or inquiry that join the passage to what has gone before.

What holds one sentence together with another, or one set of sentences together with another set? To state the simple fact, we have two principles of cogent discourse in play here.[4] First, within each unit of thought bearing an Arabic numeral, the (to us) normal philosophical principle governs. What that means is that propositions are proven, syllogistic argument undertaken, and, in all, we have an argument leading to a desired conclusion, and that is what holds the whole together. No. 1 adduces the fact at hand to prove the proposition of the argument a fortiori at 1.F–G: people should speak with deliberation. A deeper logic is at hand, of course, since the methodical inquiry (not set forth here) into connections between one passage and another recurs throughout. We recall in this context the opening question of the lection for *Behar*: what has this to do with that? The workings of a methodical–analytical logic are more difficult to discern; and they affect the formation of the document at a more encompassing level of discourse. We cannot miss them.

When we come to No. 1, we see a sequence of sentences that do not form a paragraph, that is, No. 1 has nothing to do with No. 2, No. 2 with No. 3, and so on. For the whole to form some sort of sense, we must appeal to the logic of fixed association, here represented by the base verse: "If his offering for a burnt offering is from the flock, of sheep or of goats." That is what links sentence to sentence, each sentence represented by an Arabic numeral. Then there is that further link (methodical analytical) that occurs at No. 4 and holds the whole together in yet another way. The one thing we do not find is the sort of propositional cogency to which, in normal discourse, we are accustomed to. **X:III** proves a point and also carries on a sustained methodical analysis, as we will see in the next chapter. The point or proposition occurs at **X:III.1B**. The methodical analysis is at Cff., where we show that logic unsustained by Scripture (for reasons I will clarify in Chapter Seven) will not serve. The same cogency holds together the lettered components of **X:IV** as well as **X:V**. **X:VI** brings us back to a sequence of unrelated and episodic, miscellaneous thoughts. What holds the several components together is only the constant reference to the base verse. So much for the cogency of the parts. But what holds the whole together? One thing, and one thing alone: the sequence of clauses of the verses of Scripture that are under discussion.

The chapter of Sifra represents the whole of Sifra. Whatever the inner cogency of a given paragraph – a completed unit of thought – the sequence, order, and cogency of paragraphs depend wholly upon the base verses of the book of Leviticus, one after another. We could set in a different sequence altogether, that is, reorder, any set of paragraphs of Sifra with no loss – or gain! – of meaning, since the paragraphs hold together as poorly or as well in any order. Only Scripture holds them together in their present position. This is why the logic of fixed association, and that alone, accounts for the cogency of the document as a whole. The contrast to the Mishnah hardly needs to be drawn. The Mishnah is cogent not only in the order and sequence of its sentences, whether episodic and miscellaneous or sustained and protracted in proposition and discourse. The Mishnah-tractates are cogent, beginning, middle, and end, from one sentence to the next, and that is because the cogency derives, whole and not only in part, from the exposition of the topic at hand, – that and one other thing: from the proposition concerning that topic that the framers of the Mishnah wish to lay forth. Simply, Sifra's authorship resorted to diverse logics for the joining of one sentence to another, one paragraph to another. The Mishnah's authorship appealed to only a single logic of cogent discourse, and that was the same logic that served for the presentation and demonstration of propositions: a philosophical logic of a syllogistic character. It is to the exposition of that logic and the critique of Sifra's authorship that we now turn.

Notes

[1] I here review the results of my *Making of the Mind of Judaism* (Atlanta, 1987: Scholars Press for Brown Judaic Studies), pp. 39–58.

[2] That seems to me to indicate that our authorship conceives one mode of connecting sentences to form a counterpart to another. The alternative is to try to imagine that Sifré to Deuteronomy (and similar documents) originated in absolutely unrelated fragments of this and that, only later on formed into a conglomeration, a scrapbook lacking all order, sense, or purpose. But that characterization of the document is false on the fact of it, as my study has shown, *Sifré to Deuteronomy. An Introduction to the Rhetorical, Logical, and Topical Program* (Atlanta, 1987: Scholars Press for Brown Judaic Studies).

[3] Compare G. E. R. Lloyd, *Polarity and Analogy. Two Types of Argumentation in Early Greek Thought* (Cambridge, 1966: Cambridge University Press). But the core logic of *Listenwissenschaft* extends back to Sumerian times.

[4] The same is the fact for the two Talmuds, as I show in my *The Formation of the Jewish Intellect* (in press). I do not claim that the mixed logics of cogent discourse mark Sifra apart from all other documents; that is not the case. But the resort to two logics that are uncommon in the Mishnah and dominant in Sifra is a definitive indicator of difference between choices made by one authorship and those selected by another.

CHAPTER SEVEN

Sifra's Alternative to the Mishnah's Proof of Propositions Through Taxonomic Classification and Hierarchization

An authorship determines a principle of the proof of proposition, allowing the demonstration, in detail, that things are one way, rather than some other, accord with one law, rather than another. . . . It is the argument of Sifra's authorship that without the revelation of the Torah, we are not able to effect any classification at all, we are left, that is to say, only with species, but no genus, only with cases, but no rules

I. The Importance of Classification in the System of the Mishnah

The system of philosophy expressed through concrete and detailed law presented by the Mishnah consists of a coherent logic and topic, a cogent world view, and comprehensive way of living. It is a world view that speaks of transcendent things, a way of life in response to the supernatural meaning of what is done, a heightened and deepened perception of the sanctification of Israel in deed and in deliberation. That paramount concern accounts for the centrality of classification, the appeal of the logic of hierarchical classification in the demonstration of comparisons and contrasts, and in the formation of the thought of the document. For sanctification in the Mishnah's system means establishing the stability, order, regularity, predictability, and reliability of Israel in the world of nature and supernature particularly at moments and in contexts of danger. It is through assigning to all things their rightful name, setting of all things in their proper position, that we discover the laws of stability, order, regularity, and predictability. Danger means instability, disorder, irregularity, uncertainty, and betrayal. Each topic of the system as a whole takes up a critical and indispensable moment or context of social

125

being. Through what is said in regard to each of the Mishnah's principal topics, what the system as a whole wishes to declare is fully expressed. Yet if the parts severally and jointly give the message of the whole, the whole cannot exist without all of the parts, so carefully joined and crafted are they all.

What this means for the requirements of logical demonstration is obvious. To show something to be true, one has to demonstrate that, in logic, it conforms to the regularity and order that form the guarantee of truth. Analysis is meant to discover order: the rule that covers diverse, by nature disorderly, things, the shared trait, the general and prevailing principle of regularity. To discover the prevailing rule, one has to know how to classify things that seem to be each sui generis, how to find the rule that governs diverse things. This need, in the system of the Mishnah, explains the centrality of its classification of things. However, at issue between the framers of the Mishnah and the authorship of Sifra is the correct sources of classification. The framers of the Mishnah effect their taxonomy through the traits of things. The authorship of Sifra insists that the source of classificaton is Scripture. We will now see two expressions of this considerable debate. In this chapter we will show how Sifra's authorship time and again demonstrates that classification without Scripture's data cannot be carried out without that data, and, it must follow, hierarchical arguments based on extrascriptural taxa always fail. In Chapter Eight we will follow Sifra's authorship's rehabilitation of demonstration of propositions through classification and (necessarily consequent) hierarchical argument, showing what they conceive to be the right way of demonstrating the truth of propositions.

II.   Sifra's Critique of Designating Classifications Without Scriptural Definition: A Preliminary View

Let us begin with a sustained example of how Sifra's authorship rejects the principles of the logic of hierarchical classification *as these are worked out by the framers of the Mishnah.* I emphasize that the critique applies to the way in which a shared logic is worked out by the other authorship. For it is not the principle that like things follow the same rule, unlike things, the opposite rule, that is at stake. Nor is the principle of hierarchical classification embodied in the argument a fortiori at issue. What our authorship disputes is that we can classify things on our own by appeal to the traits or indicative characteristics, that is, utterly without reference to Scripture. The argument is simple. On our own, we cannot classify species into genera. Everything is different from everything else in some way. But Scripture tells us what things are like what other things for what purposes, hence Scripture imposes on things the definitive classification, that and not traits we discern in the things themselves. When we see the nature of the critique, we will have a clear picture of what is at stake when we examine, in some detail, precisely how the Mishnah's logic does its work. That is why at the outset I present a complete composition in which Sifra's authorship tests the modes of classification characteristic of the Mishnah, resting as they do on the traits of things viewed out of context of Scripture's categories of things.

5. Parashat Vayyiqra Dibura Denedabah Parashah 3

V:I.1 A. "[If his offering is] a burnt offering [from the herd, he shall offer a male without blemish; he shall offer it at the door of the tent of meeting, that he may be accepted before the Lord; he shall lay his hand upon the head of the burnt offering, and it shall be accepted for him to make atonement for him]" (Lev. 1:2):

B. Why does Scripture refer to a burnt offering in particular?

C. For one might have taken the view that all of the specified grounds for the invalidation of an offering should apply only to the burnt offering that is brought as a free will offering.

D. But how should we know that the same grounds for invalidation apply also to a burnt offering that is brought in fulfillment of an obligation [for instance, the burnt offering that is brought for a leper who is going through a rite of purification [Lev. 14], or the bird brought by a woman who has given birth as part of her purification rite, Lev. 12]?

E. It is a matter of logic.

F. Bringing a burnt offering as a free will offering and bringing a burnt offering in fulfillment of an obligation [are parallel to one another and fall into the same classification].

G. Just as a burnt offering that is brought as a free will offering is subject to all of the specified grounds for invalidation, so to a burnt offering brought in fulfillment of an obligation, all the same grounds for invalidation should apply.

H. No, [that reasoning is not compelling. For the two species of the genus, burnt offering, are not wholly identical and can be distinguished, on which basis we may also maintain that the grounds for invalidation that pertain to the one do not necessarily apply to the other. Specifically:] if you have taken that position with respect to the burnt offering brought as a free will offering, for which there is no equivalent, will you take the same position with regard to the burnt offering brought in fulfillment of an obligation, for which there is an equivalent? [For if one is obligated to bring a burnt offering by reason of obligation and cannot afford a beast, one may bring birds, as at Lev.

14:22, but if one is bringing a free will offering, a less expensive form of the offering may not serve.]

I. Accordingly, since there is the possiblity in the case of the burnt offering brought in fulfillment of an obligation, in which case there is an acceptable equivalent [to the more expensive beast, through the less expensive birds], all of the specified grounds for invalidation [which apply to the, in any case, more expensive burnt offering brought as a free will offering] should not apply at all.

J. That is why in the present passage, Scripture refers simply to "burnt offering," [and without further specification, the meaning is then simple:] all the same are the burnt offerings brought in fulfillment of an obligation and a burnt offering brought as a free will offering in that all of the same grounds for invalidation of the beast that pertain to the one pertain also to the other.

2. A. And how do we know that the same rules of invalidation of a blemished beast apply also in the case of a beast that is designated in substitution of a beast sanctified for an offering [in line with Lev. 27:10, so that, if one states that a given, unconsecrated beast is to take the place of a beast that has already been consecrated, the already consecrated beast remains in its holy status, and the beast to which reference is made also becomes consecrated]?

B. The matter of bringing a burnt offering and the matter of bringing a substituted beast fall into the same classification [since both are offerings that in the present instance will be consumed upon the altar, and, consequently, they fall under the same rule as to invalidating blemishes].

C. Just as the entire protocol of blemishes apply to the one, so in the case of the beast that is designated as a substitute, the same invalidating blemishes pertain.

D. No, if you have invoked that rule in the case of the burnt offering, in which case no status of sanctification applies should the beast that is designated as a burnt offering be blemished in some permanent way, will you make the same statement in the case of a beast that is designated as a substitute? For in the case of a substituted beast, the status of sanctification applies even though the beast bears a permanent blemish! [So the two do not fall into the same classification after all, since to begin with one cannot sanctify a permanently blemished beast, which beast can never enter the status of sanctification, but through an act of substitution, a permanent blemished beast can be placed into the status of sanctification.]

E. Since the status of sanctification applies [to a substituted beast] even though the beast bears a permanent blemish, all of the specified grounds for invalidation as a matter of logic should not apply to it.

F. That is why in the present passage, Scripture refers simply to "burnt offering," [and without further specification, the meaning is then simple:] all the same are the burnt offerings brought in fulfillment of an obligation and a burnt offering brought as a substitute for an animal designated as holy, in that all of the same grounds for invalidation of the beast that pertain to the one pertain also to the other.

3. A. And how do we know [that the protocol of blemishes that apply to the burnt offering brought as a free will offering apply also to] animals that are subject to the rule of a sacrifice as a peace offering?

B. It is a matter of logic. The matter of bringing a burnt offering and the matter of bringing animals that are subject to the rule of a sacrifice as a peace offering fall into the same classification [since both are offerings and, consequently, under the same rule as to invalidating blemishes].

C. Just as the entire protocol of blemishes apply to the one, so in the case of animals that are subject to the rule of a sacrifice as a peace offering, the same invalidating blemishes pertain.

D. And it is furthermore a matter of an argument a fortiori, as follows:

E. If a burnt offering is valid when in the form of a bird, [which is inexpensive], the protocol of invalidating blemishes apply, to peace offerings, which are not valid when brought in the form of a bird, surely the same protocol of invalidating blemishes should also apply!

F. No, if you have applied that rule to a burnt offering, in which case females are not valid for the offering as male beasts are, will you say the same of peace offerings? For female beasts as much as male beasts may be brought for sacrifice in the status of the peace offering. [The two species may be distinguished from one another].

G. Since it is the case that female beasts as much as male beasts may be brought for sacrifice in the status of the peace offering, the protocol of invalidating blemishes should not apply to a beast designated for use as peace offerings.

H. That is why in the present passage, Scripture refers simply to "burnt offering," [and without further specification, the meaning is then simple:] all the same are the burnt offerings brought in fulfillment of an obligation and an animal designated under the rule of peace offerings, in that all of the same grounds for invalidation of the beast that pertain to the one pertain also to the other.

The systematic exercise proves for beasts that serve in three classifications of offerings – burnt offerings, substitutes, and peace offerings – that the same rules of invalidation apply throughout. The comparison of the two kinds of burnt offerings, voluntary and obligatory, shows that they are sufficiently different from one another so that, as a matter of logic, what pertains to the one need not apply to the other. Then come the differences between an animal that is consecrated and one that is designated as a substitute for one that is consecrated. Finally, we distinguish between the applicable rules of the sacrifice: A burnt offering yields no meat for the person in behalf of whom the offering is made, whereas one sacrificed under the rule of peace offering does. What is satisfying, therefore, is that we run the changes on three fundamentally different differences and show that, in each case, the differences between like things are greater than the similarities. I cannot imagine a more perfect exercise in the applied and practical logic of comparison and contrast.

V:II.1   A.   "[If his offering is a burnt offering] from the herd, [he shall offer a male without blemish:"

B.   The reference to "from the herd" serves to eliminate from consideration a beast that has been torn [and suffers a terminal ailment].

The exposition of the verse is not expanded with the anticipated logical argument, which follows.

V:III.1   A.   "Male:"

B.   And not a female.

2.   A.   When further on, Scripture once more refers to a male, it is only to exclude a beast with undefined sexual characteristics or with the sexual traits of both genders.

B.   But is that not a matter of logic?

C.   If animals designated for use as peace offerings, which are valid whether male or female, or not valid, should they come with undefined sexual characteristics or with the sexual traits of both genders.

D.   a burnt offering [under discussion in our base verse], which is not equally valid whether male or female [but only male, as specified], surely should not be valid in the case of an animal with undefined sexual characteristics or with the sexual traits of both genders!

E.   No, if you have invoked that rule in the case of an animal designated for use as peace offerings, in which instance fowl may not serve, will you invoke that same rule in the case of an animal that is to serve as a burnt offering, in which case fowl may not be used? [So the two are not comparable in the relationship a fortiori such as is proposed at D.]

F.   A beast designated for use as a sin offering will prove the contrary, for it may come in the form of fowl, but it may not be valid in the case of an animal with undefined sexual characteristics or with the sexual traits of both genders. [The argument of E is not valid, and the proposition of D stands.]

G. No, [the animal designated for use as a sin offering is not pertinent in context], for it cannot be brought from any species of male beast [but must be a sheep], while a burnt offering may be either cattle or sheep. [Accordingly, special rules apply, which distinguish the animal designated for use as a sin offering from an animal designated for use as a burnt offering. Will you therefore invoke the same rule for a burnt offering, which is valid in the case of any appropriate male beast.]

H. The firstling will prove to the contrary, for it may derive from a male beast of any species, but it is not suitable in the case of an animal with undefined sexual chacteristics or with the sexual traits of both genders.

J. No, if you have presented the case of the firstling, to which the status of sanctification applies from birth [so that an act of consecration is not required on the part of the farmer], will you say the same for a beast designated as a burnt offering, in which case the status of sanctification does not apply from the womb [but must be invoked on the beast by an explicit statement on the part of the farmer].

K. An animal designated as a tithe of the herd will prove to the contrary, for such a beast is not held to be sanctified from birth, and yet it is not valid in the case of an animal with undefined sexual characteristics or with the sexual traits of both genders.

L. No, that is not probative. For if you invoke the rule in the case of a beast designated as a tithe of the herd, which is one out of ten, will you declare valid a beast designated as a burnt offering, which, by definition, is simply one out of one [namely, the beast specifically chosen by the farmer]? Since it is one out of one, it should be valid in the case of an animal with undefined sexual characteristics or with the sexual traits of both genders.

M. "Male:"

N. And not a female.

O. When further on, Scripture once more refers to a male, it is only to exclude a beast with undefined sexual characteristics or with the sexual traits of both genders.

What we accomplished at V:I is now repeated on a still broader scale. We show that each species of sacrifice or sanctified beast is sui generis for one reason or another. On that basis we can construct neither analogies, so that a rule that applies to one applies to the other, nor arguments a fortiori, with the same consequence. This is the power of polemic that unites and imparts acute interest to what is otherwise simply a set of pointless contrasts.

V:IV.1   A.   ". . . [he shall offer a male] without blemish:"
B.   Just as, if it is not unblemished, it is not pleasing, so if it does not accord with other rules in context [and is blemished in some other manner], it also is not pleasing.
2.   A.   ". . . he shall offer a male without blemish:"
B.   The farmer is to sanctify the beast only if it is unblemished [and it is a violation of the law to sanctify a beast that is blemished, even though no further act of sacrifice applies to that beast (Finkelstein)].
C.   R. Yosé says, " '. . . [he shall offer a male] without blemish:" the officiating priest must examine the beast and offer it up."
D.   Said R. Yosé, "I have heard the rule applying to one who slaughters a beast as an obligatory daily whole offering on the Sabbath, that if the beast is not correctly inspected, the priest is liable for a sin offering and must bring another beast as an obligatory daily whole offering."

We have a phrase by phrase exposition of the base verse, yielding the rules as specified.

V:V.1   A.   ". . . he shall offer it at the door of the tent of meeting:"
B.   The farmer must take care of the beast and bring it to the tent of meeting.
2.   A.   Why does Scripture repeatedly state, ". . . he shall offer it . . ."?
B.   How on the basis of Scripture do we know that if an animal designated as a burnt offering is confused with another animal designated as a burnt offering, or an animal designated as a burnt offering is confused with an animal that has been designated as a substitute [for a sacrificial beast, and so takes on the status of that specified beast, in line with Lev. 27:10], or an animal designated as a burnt offering with an unconsecrated beast, the farmer must offer it up?
C.   Scripture repeatedly states, ". . . he shall offer *it* . . ."
3.   A.   Might one suppose that if a sanctified beast was confused with blemished animals, [the same rule applies, and one should offer up also the blemished beasts]?
B.   Scripture says, ". . . he shall offer *it* . . .," meaning to exclude the case in which a consecrated beast has become confused with invalid beasts not suitable for being offered up.
4.   A.   How do we know that even if a beast was confused with animals that elsewhere, but not in the present context, are designated as sin offerings [the beasts are to be sacrificed]?

B.   Indeed I shall exclude [from the present rule, e.g., the bullock of the priest who is to be anointed, or the bullock brought because of a communal transgression that is concealed or a goat that is brought by the prince] those that are confused with animals designated in other contexts as sin offerings, for the blood of these is tossed above the red line around the altar, while the blood of the others is tossed below [so a single rite of sacrifice does not apply to both categories of beasts, and therefore they cannot be sacrificed together].

C.   But how then do I know that even if such a beast has become confused with animals designated in the present context as sin offerings, [the animals should not be sacrificed altogether]?

D.   Indeed I shall exclude [from the present rule] a confusion of beasts designated as sin offerings in the present context, for these are to be offered within, while the others [animals designated as sin offerings for individuals, as distinct from those that serve communal purposes or officials] are to be sacrificed on the outer altar.

E.   But then how do I know that even if there is a confusion between an animal designated as a firstling, an animal designated as tithe of the herd, and an animal designated as a Passover offering, [the rule applies, that all three should be sacrificed together]?

F.   Indeed I shall exclude from the present rule an animal designated as a firstling, an animal designated as tithe of the herd, and an animal designated as a Passover offering, for in the case of the one, there are four acts of tossing the blood, while in the case of the other, only a single act.

G.   And how then do I know that even if there is a confusion between animals designated for sacrifice under the rule of a peace offering and animals designated under the rule of sacrifice of a thanksgiving offering, [the rule applies, that all should be sacrificed together]?

H.   I shall indeed exclude the case of confusion between animals designated for sacrifice under the rule of a peace offering and animals designated under the rule of sacrifice of a thanksgiving offering, for the one is in the classification of Most Holy Things, while the other is in the classification of Lesser Holy Things.

I.   Might I maintain, then, that even if there is a confusion of some other beast with a beast designated as a guilt offering [which must be a ram, in the status of Most Holy Things, such as a burnt offering, and its blood is tossed below the red line, in two acts of tossing which yield four, also like a burnt offering, the one important difference being that a burnt offering is wholly consumed on the altar fire, while the meat of a guilt offering is eaten by the priests]?

J.   Scripture says of that particular case, ". . . he will offer *it* . . .," meaning that alone is to be offered, but not in the case of a mixture of the beast designated as a burnt offering given as a free will offering and beasts designated for any other purpose.

4. A. Why have you then limited the rule to the case of the confusing of a burnt offering confused with another burnt offering, which constitutes a single classification in any event?

B. If it is an animal designated as a burnt offering confused with a beast that has been substituted, the rule also applies, for the beast that has been substituted is offered in the classification of a burnt offering.

C. If it is an animal designated as a burnt offering confused with unconsecrated beasts, the same rule should apply, for the farmer can consecreate the unconsecrated beasts and treat the entire lot as burnt offerings.

The exposition of the base verse in terms of its own language now takes over with a sequence of ad hoc rules. We accomplish an exercise of reason at Nos. 2 and 3, however, for what we achieve here is to establish that a variety of species of sacrificial beast fall under a single rule, but then we eliminate one species of beast from the same rule. In No. 3 we systematically show why diverse types of sacrifice are distinct from one another, specifying the particular distinction in a systematic way. Then No. 4 identifies some categories that may be treated in common, that is, under the rule governing the burnt offering, and we explain why that is the case. What is important is that no effort to prove on the basis of logic that the same rule applies across the board is even undertaken here. The polemic is quite the opposite. Now we show why the use of mere logic cannot have worked to begin with, namely, the diversity of genera, and the grounds for that diversity. No. 4 gives back only a small portion of what No. 3 has taken away, and then for reasons extrinsic to the issue altogether! That, therefore, strengthens the basic polemic.

The upshot is simple. The authorship of Sifra concurs in the fundamental principle that sanctification consists in calling things by their rightful name, or, in philosophical language, discovering the classification of things and determining the rule that governs diverse things. Where that authorship differs from the view of the Mishnah's concerns is in (my emphasis) *the origins of taxa:* how we know what diverse things form a single classification of things. Taxa originate in Scripture. Accordingly, at stake in the critique of the Mishnah is not the principles of logic necessary for understanding the construction and inner structure of creation. All parties among sages concurred that the inner structure set forth by a logic of classification alone could sustain the system of ordering all things in proper place and under the proper rule. The like belongs with the like and conforms to the rule governing the like, the unlike goes over to the opposite and conforms to the opposite rule. When we make lists of the like, we also know the rule governing all the items on those lists, respectively. We know that and one other thing, namely, the opposite rule, governing all items sufficiently like to belong on those lists, but sufficiently unlike to be placed on other lists. That rigorously philosophical logic of analysis, comparison and contrast, served because it was the only logic that could serve a system that proposed to make the statement concerning order and right array. Let us first show how the logic of proving propositions worked, then review Sifra's authorship's systematic critique of the way in which the Mishnah's framers applied that logic, specifically, proposed to identify classifications.

III. The Logical Principles of Classification of the Mishnah: Comparison, Contrast, and *Listenwissenschaft* as the Mishnah's Mode of Syllogistic Proof

Now let us turn back to the Mishnah and see what mode of probative logic has been subjected to the sustained, coherent critique we have followed. This will tell us in a concrete way precisely what is at stake in the debate. It is not *Listenwissenschaft* as such, but the way in which that scientific inquiry is to proceed. As I have made clear, the frames of the Mishnah appeal solely to the traits of things. The authorship of Sifra insists that, by themselves, the traits of things do not settle anything. Only Scripture designates classifications that serve. When we understand the logical basis of *Listenwissenschaft*, we will understand the issue in a clear way.

Listenwissenschaft defines a way of proving propositions through classification, that is, establishing a set of shared traits that form a rule that compels us to reach a given conclusion. Probative facts derive from the classification of data, all of which point in one direction and not in another. A catalogue of facts, for example, may be so composed that, through the regularities and indicative traits of the entries, the catalogue yields a proposition. A list of parallel items all together point to a simple conclusion; the conclusion may or may not be given at the end of the catalogue, but the catalogue – by definition – is pointed. All the catalogued facts are taken to bear self-evident connections to one another, etablished by those pertinent shared traits implicit in the composition of the list. Therefore, they also bear meaning and point to an inescapable conclusion. The discrete facts then join together because of some trait common to them all. This is a mode of classification of facts that leads to an identification of what the facts have in common and, it goes without saying, to an explanation of their meaning. These and other modes of philosophical argument are entirely familiar to us all. In calling all of them "philosophical," I mean only to distinguish them from the other three logics we will presently examine. Now we see how fundamental to thought was Sifra's authorship's insistence that Scripture, not things viewed on their own, dictates the classification of things.

The diverse topical program of the Mishnah, time and again making the same points on the centrality of order, works itself out in a single logic of cogent discourse, one which seeks the rule that governs diverse cases. And, as we now see, that logic states within its interior structure the fundamental point of the document as a whole. The correspondence of logic to system here, as in the Penateuch viewed overall, hardly presents surprises. Seeing how the logic does its work within the document, therefore, need not detain us for long. Let us take up two pericopes of the Mishnah and determine the logic that joins fact to fact, sentence to sentence, in a cogent proposition, that is, in our terms, a paragraph that makes a statement. To see how this intellect does its work, we turn first to Mishnah-tractate *Berakhot*, Chapter Eight, to see list making in its simplest form, and then to Mishnah-tractate *Sanhedrin*, Chapter Two, to see the more subtle way in which list making yields a powerfully argued philosophical theorem.

IV.   Two Examples of Mishnah's Classification of Things

In the first of our two abstracts we have a list, carefully formulated, in which the announcement at the outset tells us what is catalogued, and in which careful mnemonic devices so arrange matters that we may readily remember the conflicting opinions. In formal terms, then, we have a list that means to facilitate memorization. But in substantive terms, the purpose of the list and its message(s) are not set forth, and only ample exegesis will succeed in spelling out what is at stake. Here is an instance of a Mishnah passage that demands an exegesis not supplied by the Mishnah's authorship.

Mishnah-Tractate Berakhot Chapter Eight

8:1.   A.   These are the things which are between the House of Shammai and the House of Hillel in [regard to] the meal:

[1]   B.   The House of Shammai say, "One blesses over the day, and afterward one blesses over the wine."

And the House of Hillel say, "One blesses over the wine, and afterward one blesses over the day."

[2]   8.2.   A.   The House of Shammai say, "They wash the hands and afterward mix the cup."

And the House of Hillel say, "They mix the cup and afterward wash the hands."

[3]   8.3.   A.   The House of Shammai say, "He dries his hands on the cloth and lays in on the table."

And the House of Hillel say, "On the pillow."

[4] 8:4. A. The House of Shammai say, "They clean the house, and afterward they wash the hands."

And the House of Hillel say, "They wash the hands, and afterward they clean the house."

[5] 8:5. A. The House of Shammai say, "Light, and food, and spices, and *Havdalah.*"

And the House of Hillel say, "Light, and spices, and food, and *Havdalah.*"

[6] B. The House of Shammai say, "Who created the light of the fire."

And the House of Hillel say, "Who creates the lights of the fire."

The mnemonic serving the list does its work by the simple reversal of items. If authority A has the order 1, 2, then authority B will give 2, 1. Only entry [3] breaks that pattern. What is at stake in the making of the list is hardly transparent, and why day/wine versus wine/day, with a parallel (e.g., clean/wash versus wash/clean) yields a general principle the authorship does not indicate. All we know at this point, therefore, is that we deal with list makers. But how lists work to communicate principles awaits exemplification.

The next abstract allows us much more explicitly to identify the *and* and the *equal* of Mishnaic discourse, showing us through the making of connections and the drawing of conclusions the propositional and essentially philosophical mind that animates the Mishnah. In the following passage, drawn from Mishnah-tractate *Sanhedrin* Chapter Two, the authorship wishes to say that Israel has two heads, one of state, the other of cult, the king and the high priest, respectively, and that these two offices are nearly wholly congruent with one another, with a few differences based on the particular traits of each. Broadly speaking, therefore, our exercise is one of setting forth the genus and the species. The genus is head of holy Israel. The species are king and high priest. Here are the traits in common and those not shared, and the exercise is fully exposed for what it is, an inquiry into the rules that govern, the points of regularity and order, in this minor matter, of political structure. My outline, imposed in bold face, makes the point important in this setting.

Mishnah-Tractate Sanhedrin Chapter Two

1. The rules of the high priest: subject to the law, marital rites, conduct in bereavement

2:1 A. A high priest judges, and [others] judge him;

B. gives testimony, and [others] give testimony about him;

C. performs the rite of removing the shoe [Deut. 25:7–9], and [others] perform the rite of removing the shoe with his wife.

D. [Others] enter levirate marriage with his wife, but he does not enter into levirate marriage,

E. because he is prohibited to marry a widow.

F. [If] he suffers a death [in his family], he does not follow the bier.

G. "But when [the bearers of the bier] are not visible, he is visible; when they are visible, he is not.

H. "And he goes with them to the city gate," the words of R. Meir.

I. R. Judah says, "He never leaves the sanctuary,

J. "since it says, '*Nor shall he go out of the sanctuary*' (Lev. 21:12)."

K. And when he gives comfort to others

L. the accepted practice is for all the people to pass one after another, and the appointed [prefect of the priests] stands between him and the people.

M. And when he receives consolation from others,

N. all the people say to him, "Let us be your atonement."

O. And he says to them, "May you be blessed by Heaven."

P. And when they provide him with the funeral meal,

Q. all the people sit on the ground, while he sits on a stool.

2. The rules of the king: not subject to the law, marital rites, conduct in bereavement

2:2   A.   The king does not judge, and [others] do not judge him;

B. does not give testimony, and [others] do not give testimony about him;

C. does not perform the rite of removing the shoe, and others do not perform the rite of removing the shoe with his wife;

D. does not enter into levirate marriage, nor [does his brother] enter levirate marriage with his wife.

E. R. Judah says, "If he wanted to perform the rite of removing the shoe or to enter into levirate marriage, his memory is a blessing."

F. They said to him, "They pay no attention to him [if he expressed the wish to do so]."

G. [Others] do not marry his widow.

H. R. Judah says, "A king may marry the widow of a king.

I. "For so we find in the case of David, that he married the widow of Saul,

J. "For it is said, '*And I gave you your master's house and your master's wives into your embrace*' (II. Sam. 12:8)."

2:3   A.   [If] [the king] suffers a death in his family, he does not leave the gate of his palace.

B.   R. Judah says, "If he wants to go out after the bier, he goes out,

C.   "for thus we find in the case of David, that he went out after the bier of Abner,

D.   "since it is said, '*And King David followed the bier*' (2 Sam. 3:31)."

E.   They said to him, "This action was only to appease the people."

F.   And when they provide him with the funeral meal, all the people sit on the ground, while he sits on a couch.

3.   Special rules pertinent to the king because of his calling

2:4   A.   [The king] calls out [the army to wage] a war fought by choice on the instructions of a court of seventy-one.

B.   He [may exercise the right to] open a road for himself, and [others] may not stop him.

C.   The royal road has no required measure.

D.   All the people plunder and lay before him [what they have grabbed], and he takes the first portion.

E.   *"He should not multiply wives to himself"* (Deut. 17:17) – only eighteen.

F.   R. Judah says, "He may have as many as he wants, so long as they *do not entice him* [to abandon the Lord (Deut. 7:4)]."

G.   R. Simeon says, "Even if there is only one who entices him [to abandon the Lord] – lo, this one should not marry her."

H.   If so, why is it said, "He should not multiply wives to himself"?

I.   Even though they should be like Abigail [1 Sam. 25:3].

J.   *"He should not multiply horses to himself"* (Deut. 17:16) – only enough for his chariot.

K.   *"Neither shall he greatly multiply to himself silver and gold"* (Deut. 17:16) – only enough to pay his army.

L.   *"And he writes out a scroll of the Torah for himself"* (Deut. 17:17)

M.   When he goes to war, he takes it out with him; when he comes back, he brings it back with him; when he is in session in court, it is with him; when he is reclining, it is before him.

N.   as it is said, *"And it shall be with him, and he shall read in it all the days of his life"* (Deut. 17:19).

2:5   A.   [Others may] not ride on his horse, sit on his throne, handle his sceptre.

B.   And [others may] not watch him while he is getting a haircut, or while he is nude, or in the bath-house.

C. since it is said, *"You shall surely set him as king over you"* (Deut. 17:15) – that reverence for him will be upon you.

The subordination of Scripture to the classification scheme is self-evident. Scripture supplies facts. The traits of things – kings, high priests – dictate classification categories on their own, without Scripture's dictate.

The philosophical cast of mind is amply revealed in this essay, which in concrete terms effects a taxonomy, a study of genus, national leader, and its two species, (1) king, (2) high priest: how are they alike, how are they not alike, and what accounts for the differences. The premise is that national leaders are alike and follow the same rule, except where they differ and follow the opposite rule from one another. But that premise also is subject to the proof effected by the survey of the data consisting of concrete rules, those systemically inert facts that here come to life for the purposes of establishing a proposition. By itself, the fact that, for example, others may not ride on his horse, bears the burden of no systemic proposition. In the context of an argument constructed for nomothetic and taxonomic purposes, the same fact is active and weighty. The whole depends upon three premises: (1) the importance of comparison and contrast, with the supposition that (2) like follows the like, and the unlike follows the opposite, rule; and (3) when we classify, we also hierarchize, which yields the argument from hierarchical classification: if this, which is the lesser, follows rule X, then that, which is the greater, surely should follow rule X. And that is the whole sum and substance of the logic of *Listenwissenschaft* as the Mishnah applies that logic in a practical way.

No natural historian can find this discourse and mode of thought unfamiliar; it forms the foundation of all disposition of data in quest of meaning. For if I had to specify a single mode of thought that established connections between one fact and another, it is in the search for points in common and, therefore, also points of contrast. We seek connection between fact and fact, sentence and sentence, in the subtle and balanced rhetoric of the Mishnah, by comparing and contrasting two things that are like and not alike. At the logical level, too, the Mishnah falls into the category of familiar philosophical thought. Once we seek regularities, we propose rules. What is like another thing falls under its rule, and what is not like the other falls under the opposite rule. Accordingly, as to the species of the genus, so far as they are alike, they share the same rule. So far as they are not alike, each follows a rule contrary to that governing the other. The work of analysis is what produces connection, and, therefore, the drawing of conclusions derives from comparison and contrast: the *and,* the *equal.* The proposition then that forms the conclusion concerns the essential likeness of the two offices, except where they are different, but the subterranean premise is that we can explain both likeness and difference by appeal to a principle of fundamental order and unity. To make these observations concrete, we turn to the case at hand. The important contrast comes at the outset. The high priest and king fall into a single genus, but speciation, based on traits particular to the king, then distinguishes the one from the other. All of this exercise is conducted independently of Scripture; the classifications derive from the system, are viewed as autonomous constructs; traits of things define classifications and dictate what is like and what is unlike. Let us now see how the authorship of Sifra judges that mode of category formation.

V.   Sifra's Critique of the Mishnah: The Taxonomic Attack on Taxonomic Logic

As is now clear, the source of classification proves decisive. No one denies the principle of hierarchical classification. That is an established fact, a self-evident trait of mind. The argument of Sifra's authorship is that, by themselves, things do not possess traits that permit us finally to classify species into a common genus. There always are traits distinctive to a classification. Accordingly, it is the argument of Sifra's authorship that without the revelation of the Torah, we are not able to effect any classification at all, are left, that is to say, only with species, no genus, only with cases, no rules. We will now review a series of specific statements in that general position. Then, in the following chapter, we will see the way in which, in the view of Sifra's authorship, we correctly carry out our scientific inquiry, through *Listenwissenscahft*, into the rules that govern. It is an inquiry in which Scripture dictates the taxa: first the negative, then, in Chapter Eight, the affirmative statement. For our authorship not only presents a negative critique of taxonomic logic as applied by the Mishnah's framers, it also proposes to rehabilitate that same logic by showing how it is to apply.

The first example allows us to see the interplay of classification and hierarchization; the purpose of the former is to make possible the latter, and the two processes of analysis together are supposed to yield rules.

3. Parashat Vayyiqra Dibura Denedabah Parashah 2

III.I.1.   A.   "Speak to the Israelite people [and say to them, 'When any [Hebrew: Adam] of you presents an offering of cattle to the Lord, he shall choose his offering from the herd or from the flock. If his offering is a burnt offering from the herd, he shall offer a male without blemish; he shall offer it at the door of the tent of meeting, that he may be accepted before the Lord;] he shall lay [his hand upon the head of the burnt offering, and it shall be accepted to him to make atonement for him]' " (Lev. 1:2):

B. "He shall lay his hand:" Israelites lay on hands, gentiles do not lay on hands.

C. [But is it necessary to prove that proposition on the basis of the cited verse? Is it not to be proven merely by an argument of a logical order, which is now presented?] Now which measure [covering the applicability of a rite] is more abundant, the measure of wavings or the measure of laying on of hands?

The important point here is the unproven supposition that wavings and layings on of hands are comparable, that is, species of a single genus. That immediately yields a problem of hierarchization: which is the more weighty? The weightier will dictate the rule governing the less weighty of the same classification, a fortiori:

D. The measure of waving [the beast] is greater than the measure of laying on of hands.

E. For waving [the sacrifice] is done to both something that is animate and something that is not animate, while the laying on of hands applies only to something that is animate.

F. If gentiles are excluded from the rite of waving the sacrifice, which applies to a variety of sacrifices, should they not be excluded from the rite of laying on of hands, which pertains to fewer sacrifices? [Accordingly, I prove on the basis of reason the rule that is derived at A–B from the verse of Scripture.]

The entire argument now rests on the premise that the two species of the single genus are arranged in the specified hierarchy. But what if the relationship is the opposite of what has been supposed?

G. [I shall now show that the premise of the foregoing argument is false:] [You have constructed your argument] from the angle that yields waving as more common and laying on of hands as less common.

H. But take the other angle, which yields laying on of hands as the more common and waving as the less common.

I. For the laying on of hands, applies to all partners in the ownership of a beast [each one of whom is required to lay hands on the beast before it is slaughtered in behalf of the partnership in ownership of the beast as a whole],

J. but the waving of a sacrifice is not a requirement that applies to all partners in the ownership of a beast.

K. Now if I eliminate [gentiles' laying on of hands] in the case of the waving of a beast, which is a requirement applying to fewer cases, should I eliminate them from the requirement of laying on of hands, which applies to a larger number of cases?

The upshot is that the two taxa cannot be compared with one another, because they do not form a hierarchy at all. As a result, the species are sui generis and beyond comparison. How then can we determine the rule? It is only through Scripture's dictation.

L. Lo, since a rule pertains to the waving of the sacrifice that does not apply to the laying on of hands, and a rule pertains to the laying on of hands that does not apply to the waving of the sacrifice, it is necessary for Scripture to make the statement that it does, specifically:

M. "He shall lay his hand:" Israelites lay on hands, gentiles do not lay on hands.

The basic premise is that when two comparable actions differ, then the more commonly performed one imposes its rule upon further actions, the rule governing which is unknown. If then we show that action A is more commonly performed than action B, other actions of the same classification will follow the rule governing A, not the rule governing B. Then the correct route to overturn such an argument is to show that each of the actions, the rule governing which is known, differs from the other in such a way that neither the one nor the other can be shown to be the more commonly performed. Then the rule governing the further actions is not to be derived from the one governing the two known actions. The powerful instrument of analytical and comparative reasoning proves that diverse traits pertain to the two stages of the rite of sacrifice, the waving, the laying on of hands, which means that a rule pertaining to the one does not necessarily apply to the other. On account of that difference we must evoke the specific ruling of Scripture. We proceed, in the same context, to the demonstration of the right way, which is to allow Scripture to dictate categories and their hierarchization. We ask explicitly why we treat one category in one way, another in a different way.

III:III.1 A. "[Speak to the Israelite people and say to them, 'When] any man [Hebrew: Adam] of you [presents an offering of cattle to the Lord, he shall choose his offering from the herd or from the flock]:' "
B. "Adam" encompasses within the rule proselytes as well.
C. ". . . of you" excludes from the rule apostates.

D.   Why have you determined so to read matters that "Adam" encompasses within the rule proselytes as well, while "of you" excludes from the rule apostates? [You could have proven that fact solely on the basis of a principle of logic, spelled out as follows:]

E.   Scripture has first of all imposed an inclusionary statement, in saying "the sons of Israel."

F.   Just as the sons of Israel are those who have accepted the covenant, so proselytes have accepted the covenant.

We establish the shared classification of the two species, which then, quite logically, excludes a species that does not share the traits in common with the two species.

G.   Accordingly, excluded are apostates, who do not accept the covenant.

H.   [But that reading competes with another, namely] just as Israelites are the sons of those who accept the covenant, so apostates remain sons of those who accept the covenant, then excluding proselytes who by definition are not sons of those who accept the covenant. [So reason by itself can lead to contradictory conclusions.]

The proposed argument does not work, since the shared traits of the two species thought to form a single genus do not, in fact, exhaust the available indicative traits. There is only one solution:

I.   Scripture states, ". . . of you."

J.   Now lo, state matters only as follows: just as Israelites are those who accept the covenant, so proselytes are included within the rule, since they accept the covenant, and apostates are excluded, for they do not accept the covenant.

K.   Lo, Scripture says, "The sacrifice of the wicked is an abomination; how much more when he brings it with evil intent" (Prov. 21:27).

The upshot is that appeal to the principle invoked at D–G fails. Hence the claim that a fixed principle of logic, even one that itself invokes exegetical considerations, is rejected. Rather, we have to rely solely upon exegesis and cannot skip any step in the exegetical process. We note the premise that Adam stands only for Israelite.

In the next instance, we ask why *din*, which I translate as logic, does not suffice to prove a point. We then turn to the argument from hierarchical classification, that is to say, classifying species into a single genus, then determining which of the classified species bears the greater probative weight or standings higher in the hierarchical structure than the other.

III:VII.1   A.   ". . . of cattle:"

B.   That statement serves to exclude a beast that has had sexual relations with a human being, or one that has been used for an act of bestiality.

C.   But is the proposition not merely a matter of logic [in which case a verse of Scripture hardly is required to make the matter explicit]?

D.   If a blemished beast, which has not served for the commission of a transgression, is invalid for use on the alter, a beast that has had sexual relations with a human being, or one that has been used for an act of bestiality, with which a transgression indeed has been committed, surely should be deemed invalid for use on the altar!

E.   Lo, [to the contrary], a beast that has threshed with an ass [which should not be done by reason of the prohibition against ploughing with beasts of different species] [will prove the contrary], for with such a beast a transgression has been committed, yet, nonetheless, that beast is permitted for use on the altar.

F.   No, if you have invoked the rule concerning a beast that has threshed with an ass, on which account the beast involved does not incur liability to the death penalty, will you say the same in the case of a beast that has had sexual relations with a human being, or one that has been used for an act of bestiality, in which case the death penalty is invoked [for the beast involved in the act]!

We have two possible analogies and have to determine the indicative trait that indicates which analogy is operative. Then we know what is like what, and that will tell us the paramount rule.

G.   Now [the case at hand bears traits distinctive to itself, as we shall now see, so you must] examine the very case that you yourself have introduced [for it is not so pertinent as you maintain, specifically:]

H.   The rule would apply in the case of a beast with which a transgression has been committed, in a case in which there are two valid witnesses to the act.

I.   But how would you derive the rule governing a case in which a transgression has been committed with a beast, in a circumstance in which there is only a single valid witness, or in which only the owner of the beast himself serves as the witness?

J.   R. Ishmael said, "Lo, I reason as follows:

K.   "If a blemished beast, in which case it is not necessary for two witnesses to come and testify so that it should be rendered impermissible for eating [there being no rules of testimony pertinent to the certification of a disqualifying blemish], if a single witness should testify [as to an invalidating blemish], the beast would be invalidated for use for an offering, in the case of a beast that has had sexual relations with a human being, or one that has been used for an act of bestiality, in which instance two witnesses to the fact indeed are required to render such a beast invalid for ordinary consumption, is it not reasonable that the testimony of only a single witness should invalidate such a beast for use on the altar?" [We have now met the objection of F–H by showing, I–K, that a separate process of reasoning covers the objection spelled out at H.]

L.   Said to him R. Aqiba, "No, if you have invoked such a rule in the case of a blemished beast, when the blemish is discernible to the naked eye, will you make the same statement in the case of a beast that has had sexual relations with a human being, or one that has been used for an act of bestiality, in which case the blemish is not immediately visible [for only if there are witnesses can we prove that such an action has in fact taken place]?

M.   "Since the blemish pertaining to a beast that has had sexual relations with a human being, or one that has been used for an act of bestiality is not visible to the naked eye, perhaps the rule should be that they should not be deemed invalid for use on the altar!

N.   "[Accordingly it is necessary for a verse of Scripture to make the rule clear, namely:] '. . . of cattle:' that statement serves to exclude a beast that has had sexual relations with a human being, or one that has been used for an act of bestiality."

The somewhat meandering argument ends precisely where C wishes to lead it, namely, to proof that a verse of Scripture is the sole source of a valid rule. Reason unaided by Scripture bears no reliable evidence as to the law. When we follow discourse to the end of its exposition, we appreciate the elegance of the composition as a whole:

III:VIII.1   A.   ". . . from the herd [or from the flock]:"

B.   This reference serves to exclude [from use on the altar] a beast that has been worshipped.

C.   Is that not a matter of mere logic [to prove, so that an explicit statement by Scripture is hardly required, specifically:]

D.   if the covering of a beast given in exchange for the services of a whore or for the price of a dog is permitted for use [by a common person], even though such a beast is forbidden for use on the altar, a beast that has been worshipped, the covering of which is forbidden [for use by an ordinary person, but must be destroyed along with the beast], surely should be unfit for use on the altar!

E.   But matters may be turned around as follows:

F.   if the covering of a beast given in exchange for the services of a whore or for the price of a dog, which may not be used on the altar, may itself be used by a common person, the covering of a beast that has been worshipped, which is [for the sake of argument] permitted, surely itself should be permitted?

G.   [By way of reply, I shall show that the premise of your proposed argument is wrong:] Lo, by this argument you have nullified the rule, "You shall not covet the silver and gold that is upon them and take it for yourself" (Dt. 7:25).

H.   Not at all, for I shall carry out the requirement of the rule, "You shall not covet the silver and gold that is upon them and take it for yourself" (Dt. 7:25) by applying it only to something that is not animate. But as to something that is animate, since such a thing itself [again, for the purposes of the proposed argument] is permitted, its covering also is permitted!

I.   [The proposed agument leads in contradictory directions, so only Scripture can settle matters, as it does in the following way:] ". . . from the herd [or from the flock]:" this reference serves to exclude [from use on the altar] a beast that has been worshipped.

The exercise presents no surprises. We now review an established protocol of items, the beast used for bestiality, the beast that has been worshiped, and, in what follows, the beast suffering a terminal ailment, the beast designated for, but not yet used in, idolatry, and the like. The protocol yields the same argument time after time.

III:IX.1   A.   When Scripture states, ". . . from the herd," it serves an exclusionary purpose, namely to exclude a beast suffering a terminal ailment. [Such a beast may not be offered on the altar.]

B.   Is that not a matter of a logical inference?

C.   Namely, If a blemished beast, which is permitted for use for ordinary food, is unfit for use on the altar, a beast suffering a terminal ailment, which is forbidden for use for ordinary food, surely should be unfit for use on the altar.

D.   [No, that reasoning does not apply at all, for lo:] forbidden fat and blood will prove to the contrary, for they are forbidden for use as ordinary food, but they are most certainly valid for use on the altar [where they are to be burned up]!

E.   No, if you have stated that rule in the case of forbidden fat and blood, which derive from something that, under ordinary circumstances, is permitted [for use as food, for one may eat fat and make use of blood of a valid beast], will you say the same of the beast suffering from a terminal ailment, the whole of which is forbidden for use on the altar? [So the logical demonstration is a good one, and a verse of Scripture is needless to make the point.]

F.   A fowl that has been strangled [as an offering] will prove to the contrary, for the whole of it is forbidden [for ordinary food] yet [by definition] is valid for use on the altar.

G.   No, if you have invoked the case of fowl that has been strangled, it is the very fact that it has been sanctified that renders it forbidden for ordinary use.

H.   But will you say the same of a beast suffering a terminal ailment, which is not forbidden by reason of its having been sanctified? Since it is prohibited for reasons other than its having been sanctified, it should not be declared unfit for use on the altar!

I.   Lo, there is your answer to the proof [and there is no argument a fortiori to be made].

J.   Thus when Scripture states, ". . . from the herd," it serves an exclusionary purpose, namely to exclude a beast suffering a terminal ailment [Such a beast may not be offered on the altar.]

The sense of J is not self-evident, but we need not be detained by the obvious fact that the argument of F stands. The basic intention is consistent throughout.

III:X.1   A.   ". . . from the flock:"

B.   The specification serves to exclude from use on the altar a beast that has been designed for use for idolatrous worship [even though no act of service has taken place with it].

2.   A.   ". . . from the flock:"

B.   This serves to exclude a violent beast [one wont to gore]

3.   A.   Said R. Simeon, "A rule pertains to a beast that has had sexual relations with a human being that does not apply to a beast that is wont to gore, and one pertains to a beast that is wont to gore that does not apply to a beast that has committed an act of sexual relations with a human being.

B.   "In the case of a beast that has had sexual relations with a human being, the law has treated in one and the same way the beast that acts under constraint and the one that performs the act willingly.

C.   "But as to a beast that is wont to gore, the law does not treat in one and the same way the beast that acts under constraint and the one that performs the act willingly.

D.   "As to a beast that is wont to gore, the owner has to pay a ransom even after the death of the beast.

E.   "But in the case of a beast that has committed an act of sexual relations with a human being, the owner does not pay a ransom after death.

F. "A rule pertains to a beast that has had sexual relations with a human being that does not apply to a beast that has been worshipped for an idolatrous purpose, and a rule pertains to a beast that has been worshipped for an idolatrous purpose that does not apply to a beast that has had sexual relations with a human being.

G. "The same prohibition applies to a beast that has had sexual relations with a human being whether it belongs to the person who has done the deed or whether it belongs to some other person,

H. "while in the case of a beast that has been used for idolatrous purposes, if it belongs to the person who has used the beast in such a way, then it is forbidden, but if the beast belongs to some other person than the one who has used it for idolatrous purposes, it is permitted [since the idolworshipper had no right to use the beast in that way and no control over the status of the beast].

I. "Further, the covering of a beast that has had sexual relations with a human being is permitted, while the covering of a beast that has been worshipped for an idolatrous purpose is forbidden."

J. Therefore it was necessary for Scripture to make explicit the rule covering all of these cases [since each of them is differentiated from all the others in one way or another].

This splendid passage shows the power of the mode of thought characteristic of our authorship. What they have done is cover all possible categories or classifications and place each into relationship with all others. So the arugment is not only a negative one, against *Listenwissenschaft* and pursued without the correct source of taxonomical definition, Scripture. It also is a positive and constructive one, in favor of the workings of *Listenwissenschaft* upon the proper foundation of Scripture's taxa. And the taxa are encompassing and all of them are susceptible to the single, sustained process at hand.

That is why I find the concluding component of the composition a triumph, since it completes our examination of the conventional list of forbidden beasts, and shows that it is only through Scripture's explicit reference to each of them that we know the rule. The several items on the protocol are sui generis, on which account each has its own rule, and Scripture, and Scripture alone, can inform us of that rule. The polemic in favor of Scripture, uniting all of the components of this chapter into a single coherent argument, then insists that there really is no such thing as a genus at all, and Scripture's rules and regulations serve a long list of items, each of them sui generis, for discovering rules by the logic of analogy and contrast is simply not possible.

Lest the reader suppose that I have taken the one case and claimed it as exemplary, I now place on display yet another example among the countless instances in Sifra in which the authorship encompasses all possibilities in a given context, places them all into hierarchical relationship, demonstrates that each taxon has unique traits exclusive to itself, and then shows how, nonetheless, Scripture makes possible the logically sound procedure of comparison and contrast. But only through Scripture can we find out what species fall into a single classification, since the traits of things, by themselves, prove too diverse and complex. In the end, it is God, through the revelation of The Torah, who has organized and classified all things, each in its proper place and under its correct name. The power of what follows is its capacious capacity to encompass and place into a single rule and relationship a broad selection of taxa of a single genus.

4. Parashat Vayyiqra Dibura Denedabah Pereq 3

IV:I.1 A. ". . . you shall bring your offering [of cattle from the herd or from the flock]" (Lev. 1:2)[RSV]:

B. [The use of the plural, you,] teaches that such an offering may be given as a free will offering on the part of two persons.

C. But does not logic bring us to the same conclusion?

D. The burnt offering made of a bird may be brought either in fulfillment of a vow or as a free will offering, and the burnt offering made of a beast may be brought either in fulfillment of a vow or as a free will offering. [So the two are analogous.]

E. Just as the rule governing a burnt offering made of a bird, which may be brought either in fulfillment of a vow or as a free will offering, is that, lo, it may be offered as the free will offering of two persons, so too the burnt offering made of a beast, which may be brought either in fulfillment of a vow or as a free will offering, also should be permitted as a free will offering of two persons. [Hence since the two fall into the same classification, namely, both bird and beast may be given in fulfillment of a vow or as a free will offering, so too the rule governing the bird pertains also to the beast. The bird may be brought by a partnership, and the same is so of the beast.]

F. Or take this route:

G. A meal offering may be given either in fulfillment of a vow or as a free will offering, and so too, a burnt offering made of a beast may be given either in fulfillment of a vow or as a free will offering.

H. Just as a meal offering, which may be given either in fulfillment of a vow or as a free will offering, may be given not as a free will offering of two persons [but only by a single individual], so too the burnt offering of a beast may be given either in fulfillment of a vow or as a free will offering, also cannot derive from two persons [but only from one].

I. Let us then see which analogy applies, [that is, the bird made as an offering or the meal made as an offering].

J. We should draw an analogy from something the whole of which is burned up on the altar fire to something the whole of which also is burned up on the altar fire [thus the bird and the beast presented as a burnt offering],

K. and let us not derive an analogy from the meal offering, the whole of which is not burned up on the altar fire [but only a handful thereof].

L. Or take this route:

M. Let us derive an analogy from something that is brought in fulfillment of an obligatory offering owed by the entire community for something that also may be brought in fulfillment of an obligatory offering owed by the entire community,

N. but let a burnt offering made of a bird prove the case, for it may not be offered in fulfillment of an obligatory offering owed by the entire community.

O. [Since the proposed analogies yield no final solution, it was necessary for the rule to be derived from Scripture, namely:] ". . . you shall bring your offering of cattle from the herd or from the flock" (Lev. 1:2) [RSV]: [The use of the plural, you,] teaches that such an offering may be given as a freewill offering on the part of two persons.

The free will offerings under discussion here may be made of fowl, meal, or cattle. May two or more persons bring such an offering in partnership? Indeed so, two or more persons may join in the making of a sacrifice in the classification of free will offering, such as is under discussion at Leviticus 1:1ff. That is the proposition. But the generative problematic derives from the mode by which we prove that proposition. The mode of argument is classic and shows the range of doubt affecting argument by classification, namely, analogy and contrast.

IV.II.1 A. ". . . your offering:"

B. This teaches that such an offering made of cattle may serve as a free will offering of the entire community.

C. But can [the opposite of] that proposition not be proved solely from logic? [And if we can disprove the opposite of that proposition through the same logic, we can also prove the proposition at hand solely through logic and do not require an exegesis to tell us the law.]

D. Specifically, a meal offering is brought in fulfillment of a vow or as a free will offering, and a burnt offering made of a beast may be brought in fulfillment of a vow or as a free will offering.

E. Just as a meal offering, which may be brought in fulfillment of a vow or as a free will offering, may not be brought as a free will offering of the entire community [but only on individual initiative], so the burnt offering made of a beast, which is brought in fulfillment of a vow or as a free will offering, should not be permitted to be offered as the free will offering of a community [but only as one of an individual].

F.   No, if you have stated that rule in the case of the meal offering, it is because such an offering may not be brought as a free will offering in behalf of two persons in partnership. But will you apply the same rule to the burnt offering made of a beast, which indeed may be given as a free will offering of two persons in partnership. [The two are not analogous at all.]

G.   The burnt offering made of a bird will prove the case, then, for it indeed may be given as a free will offering in behalf of two persons, but it may not be offered as a free will offering in behalf of the community at large.

H.   No, if you have stated that rule in the case of the burnt offering made of a bird, which cannot serve in fulfillment of an obligatory offering owed by the entire community, will you apply the rule to the quite different category of a beast, which indeed may be offered in fulfillment of an obligatory offering owed by the entire community?

I.   Sacrifices under the rule governing peace offerings will prove the contrary, for they indeed may be brought in fulfillment of an obligatory offering owed by the entire community, but quite to the contrary, they may not be offered as a free will offering in behalf of the entire community. [That is to say, the free will offering made in behalf of the entire community may not be subjected to the rule governing offerings in the classification of peace offerings. The community's free will offering is governed by the rule that applies to burnt offerings; the whole is burned up on the altar, and no parts are yielded for eating.]

J.   You therefore should not find remarkable the case of the burnt offering made of a beast, that, even though it may serve in fulfillment of an obligatory offering owed by the community, it may nonetheless not serve as a free will offering given by the entire community.

K.   [The several possible analogies yield no firm conclusion, on which account we require the information of Scripture:] ". . . you shall bring your offering of cattle from the herd or from the flock" (Lev. 1:2). [The use of the plural, you,] teaches that such an offering may be given as a free will offering on the part of two persons.

2.   A.   Another mode of reasoning to yield the same conclusion:

B.   If in the case of an individual, who may not bring an obligatory burnt offering every single day, may bring a burnt offering made of a beast as a free will offering [every single day, without limit], the community at large, which indeed does bring an obligatory burnt offering [namely, the daily whole offering, of course] every single day, logically should be able to bring a burnt offering made of a beast as a free will offering [every single day, without limit].

C.   No, if you have invoked the rule for the individual, who may bring a meal offering as a free will offering, will you say the same of the community at large, in behalf of which a meal offering may not serve as a free will offering?

D.   Partners will prove the matter, who may not bring a meal offering together as a free will offering, but who may bring a burnt offering of a beast as a free will offering.

E.   But the distinctive trait governing the case of partners, who may bring as a free will offering a burnt offering made of a beast, is that they also may bring as a free will offering a burnt offering made of a bird. But will you say the same, namely, that the community may bring as a free will offering a burnt offering made of a beast, even though the community at large may not bring as a free will offering a burnt offering made of a bird?

F.   But the distinguishing trait governing the community, which may not bring a burnt offering made of a bird as a free will offering, is that it may not bring such an offering in fulfillment of an obligation at all [for the community must offer up something considerably more costly than a mere bird, and cannot carry out its obligation by offering a pigeon].

G.   But will you still maintain that the community may not offer as a free will offering a burnt offering of a beast, for the community may indeed bring such a thing in fulfillment of its obligation.

H.   Since the community may indeed bring such a thing in fulfillment of its obligation, it should also be permitted to bring it, also, as a free will offering.

I.   But a meal offering will prove the contrary [and distinguish the two cases]. For the community indeed may bring a meal offering in fulfillment of an obligation, but it may not bring a meal offering as a free will offering.

J.   So you should not find remarkable the fact that in the case of a burnt offering made of a beast, even though the community brings it as an obligatory offering, it may not bring it as a free will offering. [We remain in confusion, since argument leads to contradictory results.]

K.   [The several possible analogies yield no firm conclusion, on which account we require the information of Scripture:] ". . . you shall bring your offering of cattle from the herd or from the flock" (Lev. 1:2). [The use of the plural, you,] teaches that such an offering may be given as a free will offering on the part of the community at large.

The problem governing offering cattle as a free will offering for two or more persons, that is, a partnership, is worked out in respect to the community as well, and that is what holds Nos. 1 and 2 so close together. No. 1 compares the burnt offering of a bird and the burnt offering of a beast. The complicating analogy derives from the meal offering. We cannot settle the question of the appropriate analogy; each item is sui generis. The same reasoning is worked out at No. 2, with a parallel exegetical, and substantive, result.

IV.III.1 A. Another statement concerning ". . . your offering:"
B. From the same source from which an individual derives his offering, the community derives its offering [that is, the community's beast, offered in fulfillment of its daily obligation, must be one that would be valid were an individual to designate as his offering that same beast].

The point in common between the individual's and the community's offering has now to be specified, and we remove from the range of possibilities all but the simplest consideration: The same rules of invalidation of a beast by reason of a blemish pertain to the beast designated by the individual and one designated for use by the community.

VI. The Fundamental Critique: The Limitations of Monothetic Classification

The cases at hand seen all together show us the thrust of Sifra's authorship's attack on the Mishnah's taxonomic logic. Time and again things have so many and such diverse and contradictory indicative traits that, comparing one thing to something else, we can always distinguish one species from another. Even though we find something in common, we also can discern some other trait characteristic of one thing and not the other. Consequently, we also can show that the hierarchical logic on which we rely, the argument *a fortiori* or *qol vehomer,* will not serve. For if on the basis of one set of traits that yield a given classification, we place into hierarchical order two or more items, on the basis of a different set of traits, we have either a different classification altogether, or, much more commonly, simply a different hierarchy. So the attack on the way in which the Mishnah's authorship has done its work appeals to not merely the limitations of classification solely on the basis of traits of things. The more telling argument addresses what is, to *Listenwissenschaft,* the source of power and compelling proof: hierarchization. That is why, throughout, we must designate the Mishnah's mode of *Listenwissenschaft* a logic of hierarchical classification. Things are not merely like or unlike, therefore, following one rule or its opposite. Things also are weightier or less weighty, and that particular point of likeness or difference generates the logical force of *Listenwissenschaft.*

Time and again Sifra's authorship demonstrates that the formation of classifications based on monothetic taxonomy, that is to say, traits that are not only common to both items but that are shared throughout both items subject to comparison and contrast, simply will not serve. For at every point at which someone alleges uniform, that is to say, monothetic likeness, Sifra's authorship will demonstrate difference. Then how to proceed? Appeal to some shared traits as a basis for classification: this is not like that, and that is not like this, but the indicative trait that both exhibit is such and so, that is to say, polythetic taxonomy. The self-evident problem in accepting differences among things and insisting, nonetheless, on their monomorphic character for purposes of comparison and contrast cannot be set aside. That is, if I can adduce in evidence for a shared classification of things only a few traits among many characteristic of each thing, then what stops me from treating all things alike?

Polythetic taxonomy opens the way to an unlimited exercise in finding what diverse things have in common and imposing, for that reason, one rule on everything. Then the very working of *Listenwissenschaft* as a tool of analysis, differentiation, comparison, contrast, and the descriptive determination of rules yields the opposite of what is desired. Chaos, not order, a mass of exceptions, no rules, a world of examples, each subject to its own regulation, instead of a world of order and proportion, composition and stability, will result.

VII.   Why Leviticus in Particular?

And that, finally, explains the appeal to Scripture, and, in our case, to Leviticus. God made the world. God through Adam called all things by their rightful names, placing each in its correct place in relationship to all others. We have the power to place all things into relationship with all others of the same genus because Scripture has endowed us with that power. The foundations of all scientific knowledge, achieved through the analytical processes of comparison and contrast, classification and differentiation, yielding the rule for the like, the opposite rule for the unlike, rest upon Scripture. That is why, quite by the way, the Mishnah cannot make its statement independent of Scripture – but can make its statement within the framework of Scripture. We now see how, through the reform of practical reason, our authorship united the dual Torah and uncovered the single, uniform foundations for the multiform and polythetic realm of creation, inclusive of the celebration of creation in the cult that the book of Leviticus sets forth. Having said that, I may conclude with the obvious fact that only though attending to the book of Leviticus, read as the priestly authorship of the Priestly Code wanted it read, in relationship with Genesis 1:1–2:4, and no other book of the Pentateuch, can our authorship have made the point that it wished to make. It was, in an odd way, a generalization particular to its example. But the example encompassed the very structure of creation and the foundation of all nature – and supernature.

CHAPTER EIGHT

Re-presenting the Torah:
Sifra's Rehabilitation of Taxonomic Logic

I. How Sifra Affirms Taxonomic Logic

We turn directly to the positive side to my argument. First, we will observe a sequence of cases in which Sifra's authorship demonstrates that *Listenwissenschaft* is a self-evidently valid mode of demonstrating the truth of propositions. Second, we will note, in the same cases, that *the* source of the correct classification of things is Scripture and only Scripture. Without Scripture's intervention into the taxonomy of the world, we should have no knowledge at all of which things fall into which classifications and, therefore, are governed by which rules. Let us begin with a sustained example of the right way of doing things. Appropriately, the opening composition of Sifra shows us the contrast between relying on Scripture's classification, and the traits imputed by Scripture to the taxa it identifies, and appealing to categories not defined and endowed with indicative traits by Scripture.

1. Parashat Vayyiqra Dibura Denedabah Parashah 1

I:I.1.   A.   "The Lord called [to Moses] and spoke [to him from the tent of meeting, saying, 'Speak to the Israelite people and say to them']" (Lev. 1:1):

B.   He gave priority to the calling over the speaking.

C.   That is in line with the usage of Scripture.

D.   Here there is an act of speaking, and in connection with the encounter at the bush [Ex. 3:4: "God called to him out of the bush, 'Moses, Moses'"], there is an act of speaking.

E.   Just as in the latter occasion, the act of calling is given priority over the act of speaking [even though the actual word, "speaking" does not occur, it is implicit in the framing of the verse], so here, with

157

respect to the act of speaking, the the act of calling is given priority over the act of speaking.

2.	A.	No [you cannot generalize on the basis of that case,] for if you invoke the case of the act of speaking at the bush, which is the first in the sequence of acts of speech [on which account, there had to be a call prior to entry into discourse],

	B.	will you say the same of the act of speech in the tent of meeting, which assuredly is not the first in a sequence of acts of speech [so there was no need for a preliminary entry into discourse through a call]?

	C.	The act of speech at Mount Sinai [Ex. 19:3] will prove to the contrary, for it is assuredly not the first in a sequence of acts of speech, yet, in that case, there was an act of calling prior to the act of speech.

3.	A.	No, [the exception proves nothing,] for if you invoke in evidence the act of speech at Mount Sinai, which pertained to all the Israelites, will you represent it as parallel to the act of speech in the tent of meeting, which is not pertinent to all Israel?

	B.	Lo, you may sort matters out by appeal to comparison and contrast, specifically:

	C.	The act of speech at the bush, which is the first of the acts of speech, is not of the same classification as the act of speech at Sinai, which is not the first act of speech.

	D.	And the act of speech at Sinai, which is addressed to all Israel, is not in the same classification as the act of speech at the bush, which is not addressed to all Israel.

4.	A.	What they have in common, however, is that both of them are acts of speech, deriving from the mouth of the Holy One, addressed to Moses, in which case, the act of calling comes prior to the act of speech,

	B.	so that, by way of generalization, we may maintain that every act of speech which comes from the mouth of the Holy One to Moses will be preceded by an act of calling.

5.	A.	Now if what the several occasions have in common is that all involve an act of speech, accompanied by fire, from the mouth of the Holy One, addressed to Moses, so that the act of calling was given priority over the act of speaking, then in every case in which there is an act of speech, involving fire, from the mouth of the Holy One, addressed to Moses, should involve an act of calling prior to the act of speech.

	B.	But then an exception is presented by the act of speech at the tent of meeting, in which there was no fire.

	C.	[That is why it was necessary for Scripture on this occasion to state explicitly,] "The Lord called [to Moses and spoke to him from the

tent of meeting, saying, 'Speak to the Israelite people and say to them']"
(Lev. 1:1).

D.   That explicit statement shows that, on the occasion at hand,
priority was given to the act of calling over the act of speaking.

I:II.1.   A.   ["The Lord called to Moses and spoke to him from the
tent of meeting, saying, 'Speak to the Israelite people and say to them' "
(Lev. 1:1)]: Might one suppose that the act of calling applied only to
this act of speaking alone?

B.   And how on the basis of Scripture do we know that on the
occasion of all acts of speaking that are mentioned in the Torah, [there
was a prior act of calling]?

C.   Scripture specifies, "from the tent of meeting,"

D.   which bears the sense that on every occasion on which it was
an act of speaking from the tent of meeting, there was an act of calling
prior to the act of speaking.

2.   A.   Might one suppose that there was an act of calling only prior
to the acts of speech alone?

B.   How on the basis of Scripture do I know that the same
practice accompanied acts of saying and also acts of commanding?

C.   Said R. Simeon, "Scripture says not only, '. . . spoke, . . . ,' but '. . .
and he spoke,' [with the inclusion of the *and*] meant to encompass also
acts of telling and also acts of commanding."

The exercise of generalization addresses the character of God's meeting
with Moses. The point of special interest is the comparison of the
meeting at the bush and the meeting at the tent of meeting. At stake is
asking whether all acts of God's calling and talking with, or speaking to,
the prophet are the same, or whether some of these acts are of a different
classification from others. In point of fact, we are able to come to a
generalization, worked out at I:I.5.A., that permits us to explain why
there is a different usage at Leviticus 1:1 from what characterizes parallel
cases. I:II.1–2 proceeds to generalize from the case at hand to other
usages entirely, a very satisfying conclusion to the whole. I separate **I:II**
from **I:I** because had **I:I** ended at 5, it could have stood complete and on
its own. Therefore, I see **I:II** as a brief appendix. The interest for my
argument should not be missed. We seek generalizations, governing
rules, that are supposed to emerge by the comparison and contrast of
categories or of classifications. The way to do this is to follow the usage
of Scripture, that alone. And the right way of doing things is then
illustrated.

I.III.1   A.   Might one maintain that is also the case for free-standing
statements [which do not commence with a reference either to speak-

ing or to saying, as at Lev. 1:10, which opens, simply, "If his offering . . ."]?

B.   Scripture says, ". . . spoke . . .," meaning that on an occasion of an act of speech there was also an act of calling, but there was no act of calling prior to the setting forth of a free-standing statement.

2.   A.   What purpose was there in setting forth free-standing statements [such as those that commence without reference to speaking or saying]?

B.   It was so as to give Moses a pause to collect his thoughts between the statement of one passage and the next, between the presentation of one topic and the next.

3.   A.   And lo, that yields an argument a fortiori:

B.   If one who was listening to words from the mouth of the Holy One, and who was speaking by the inspiration of the Holy Spirit, nonetheless had to pause to collect his thoughts between one passage and the next, between one topic and the next,

C.   all the more so an ordinary person in discourse with other common folk [must speak with all due deliberation].

We proceed to a quite separate matter, at No. 1, asking about passages that do not begin with "and he called, and he spoke," of which the writing before us contains a great many. The fact that there are such is worked out at No. 1, and these are explained at No. 2. No. 3 then provides a rule applicable to ordinary folk. Again to revert to our point of interest, we see that the traits of things viewed on their own, not in the context of Scripture, prove null. Now we seek rules that emerge from Scripture's classification.

I.IV.1   A.   How on the basis of Scripture do we know that every act of speech involved the call to Moses, Moses [two times]?

B.   Scripture says, "God called to him out of the bush, 'Moses, Moses' " (Ex. 3:4).

C.   Now when Scripture says, "And he said," it teaches that every act of calling involved the call to Moses, Moses [two times].

2.   A.   And how on the basis of Scripture do we know, furthermore, that at each act of calling, he responded, "Here I am"?

B.   Scripture says, "God called to him out of the bush, 'Moses, Moses,' and he said, 'Here I am' " (Ex. 3:4).

C.   Now when Scripture says, "And he said," it teaches that in response to each act of calling, he said, "Here I am."

3.   A.   "Moses, Moses" (Ex. 3:4), "Abraham, Abraham" (Gen. 22:11), "Jacob, Jacob" (Gen. 46:2), Samuel, Samuel" (1 Sam. 3:10).

B.   This language expresses affection and also means to move to prompt response.

4. A. Another interpretation of "Moses, Moses:"

B. This was the very same Moses both before he had been spoken with [by God] and also afterward.

The final unit completes the work of generalization that began with the opening passage. The point throughout is that there are acts of calling and speech, and a general rule pertains to them all. No. 3 and No. 4 conclude with an observation outside of the besought generalization. The first of the two interprets the repetition of a name, the second, a conclusion particular to Moses personally. However, these seem merely tacked on.

The first lesson in the rehabilitation of taxonomic logic is then clear. Scripture[1] provides reliable taxa and dictates the indicative characteristics of those taxa. The next step in the argument is to maintain that Scripture alone can set forth the proper names of things: classifications and their hierarchical order.

II. Scripture as the Sole Source of Valid Classification of Species

How then do we appeal to Scripture to designate the operative classifications? Here is a simple example of the alternative mode of classification, one that does not appeal to the traits of things but to the utilization of names by Scripture. What we see is how by naming things in one way, rather than in another, Scripture orders all things, classifying and, in the nature of things, also hierarchizing them.

7. Parashat Vayyiqra Dibura Denedabah Parashah 4

VII:V.1 A. ". . . and Aaron's sons the priests shall present the blood and throw the blood [round about against the altar that is at the door of the tent of meeting]:"

B. Why does Scripture make use of the word "blood" twice [instead of using a pronoun]?

C. [It is for the following purpose:] How on the basis of Scripture do you know that if blood deriving from one burnt offering was confused with blood deriving from another burnt offering, blood deriving from one burnt offering with blood deriving from a beast that has been substituted, therefore, blood deriving from a burnt offering with blood deriving from an unconsecrated beast, the mixture should nonetheless be presented?

D. It is because Scripture makes use of the word "blood" twice [instead of using a pronoun].

2. A. If blood derives from beasts in the specified classifications, it

is to be presented, for the simple reason that if the several beasts while alive had been confused with one another, they might be offered up.

B.   But how do we know that even if the blood of a burnt offering were confused with that of a beast killed as a guilt offering, [it is to be offered up]

C.   I shall concede the case of the mixture of the blood of a burnt offering confused with that of a beast killed as a guilt offering, it is to be presented, for both this one and that one fall into the classification of Most Holy Things.

D.   But how do I know that if the blood of a burnt offering were confused with the blood of a beast slaughtered in the classification of peace offerings or of a thanksgiving offering, [it is to be presented]?

E.   I shall concede the case of the mixture of the blood of a burnt offering confused with that of a beast slaughtered in the classification of peace offerings or of a thanksgiving offering, [it is to be presented], because the beasts in both classifications produce blood that has to be sprinkled four times.

F.   But how do I know that if the blood of a burnt offering were confused with the blood of a beast slaughtered in the classification of a firstling or a beast that was counted as tenth or of a beast designated as a passover, [it is to be presented]?

G.   I shall concede the case of the mixture of the blood of a burnt offering confused with that of a beast slaughtered in the classification of firstling or a beast that was counted as tenth or of a beast designated as a passover, [it is to be presented], because Scripture uses the word "blood" two times.

H.   Then while I may make that concession, might I also suppose that if the blood of a burnt offering was confused with the blood of beasts that had suffered an invalidation, it also may be offered up?

I.   Scripture says, ". . . its blood," [thus excluding such a case].

J.   Then I shall concede the case of a mixture of the blood of a valid burnt offering with the blood of beasts that had suffered an invalidation, which blood is not valid to be presented at all.

K.   But how do I know that if such blood were mixed with the blood deriving from beasts set aside as sin offerings to be offered on the inner altar, [it is not to be offered up]?

L.   I can concede that the blood of a burnt offering that has been mixed with with the blood deriving from beasts set aside as sin offerings to be offered on the inner altar is not to be offered up, for the one is offered on the inner altar, and the other on the outer altar [the burnt offering brought as a free will offering, under discussion here, is slaughtered at the altar ". . . that is at the door of the tent of meeting," not at the inner altar].

M. But how do I know that even if the blood of a burnt offering was confused with the blood of sin offerings that are to be slaughtered at the outer altar, it is not to be offered up?

N. Scripture says, ". . . its blood," [thus excluding such a case].

In place of the rejecting of arguments that classify species into a common genus, we now demonstrate how classification really is to be carried on. It is through the imposition upon data of the categories dictated by Scripture: Scripture's use of language. That is the force of this powerful exercise. No. 1 sets the stage by pointing out that the use of the word "blood" twice encompasses a case in which blood in two distinct classifications is somehow confused in the process of the conduct of the cult. It is quite proper here to pour out the mixture of blood deriving from distinct sources, for example, beasts that have served different, but comparable purposes. We then systematically work out the limits of that rule, showing how comparability works, then pointing to cases in which comparability is set aside. Throughout the exposition, at the crucial point we invoke the formulation of Scripture, subordinating logic or, in our instance, the process of classification of like species to the dictation of Scripture. I cannot imagine a more successful demonstration of what the framers wish to say. Let us now consider the remainder of the discussion, to see how, in context, the appeal to Scripture's taxa does its work.

VII:VI.1 A. ". . . and throw the blood [round about against the altar that is at the door of the tent of meeting]:"

B. Might one suppose that this is done in a single act of throwing?

C. Scripture says, "round about against the altar," [meaning an act of tossing that yields drops on both sides of the corner of the altar].

D. If it must be "round about against the altar," might one suppose that the blood should circumambulate the altar like a thread?

E. Scripture says, ". . . and throw."

F. How so? One concludes with four acts of tossing."

2. A. ". . . round about [against the altar that is at the door of the tent of meeting]:"

B. R. Ishmael says, "The word 'round about' occurs here and elsewhere as well [at Lev. 8:15]. Just as when the word is used elsewhere, the sense is that it suffices with four acts of tossing the blood,

C. "so when the word is used here, the sense is that it suffices with four acts of tossing the blood."

VII:VII.1 A. ". . . and Aaron's sons the priests shall present the blood and throw [the blood round about against the altar that is at the door of the tent of meeting]:"

B.   Why does Scripture use the word "blood" once again?

C.   On what basis do you rule that if the blood spilled from the vessel onto the pavement and the priest gathers it up, the blood remains valid?

D.   It is because Scripture uses the word "blood" once again.

E.   Or might one suppose that even if the blood spilled directly from the neck of the beast [where the cut was made, and was not collected in a utensil, but] poured directly onto the pavement, one may go and collect it and deem it valid blood?

F.   Scripture says, ". . . the blood," meaning, blood that has been collected in a utensil.

We notice once again that the order of the words in the verse does not dictate the sequence of exegeses or amplifications. Just as above, we present two distinct theorems and show one valid, the other invalid, even though the two form a single classification, namely, spilled blood. Were we to have argued, "just as blood spilled, from the utensil . . ., so blood spilled, from the neck . . .," we should have reached the false conclusion that the mere spilling has formed a single classification out of what are, in fact, two distinct categories of blood. What we do not find, therefore, specifies the implicit polemic.

Now what about the Mishnah? In the following component of the composition, we see how the framers encompass the Mishnah's pertinent paragraph within their larger statement. This is integral to the program of the document as a whole, namely, the demonstration not merely that rules of the Mishnah derive from Scripture, which was accomplished in more than the way taken here, but also that the correct location of the Mishnah's rules is in the united dual Torah set forth as The Torah.

VII:VIII.1   A.   [". . . and Aaron's sons the priests shall present the blood and throw the blood round about against the altar that is at the door of the tent of meeting:"]

B.   ". . . the blood . . . against the altar . . .:"

C.   but the one who tosses the blood is not standing against the altar, [but on the pavement]. [The rule for the disposition of the blood of a beast in the classification of a sin offering is different. In that case the one who tosses the blood goes up to the altar to sprinkle the blood on the corners of the altar.]

2.   A.   Another rule: ". . . the blood . . . against the altar . . .:"

B.   **even though there is no valid meat [deriving from that offering. That is, if the meat got lost or was made unclean, nonetheless the blood is tossed on the altar. The operative criterion is the validity of the blood.]**

C. How then shall interpret the verse [which equates the blood and the meat, hence if the one is invalidated, the other should also not be acceptable,] "And you shall offer your burnt offerings, the flesh and the blood" (Dt. 12:27)?

D. Scripture joins the flesh to the blood. Just as blood is offered by being tossed on the altar, so flesh is offered by being tossed on the altar.

E. Might one think that one tosses the flesh but neatly piles up the meat on the altar?

F. Scripture says, "And the priest shall arrange them" (Lev. 1:12), meaning, he tosses and arranges them, but he does not toss them and pile them up on the altar [T. Zeb. 4:2: Eliezer].

No. 1 supplies an important clarification and also eliminates the classification of all acts of tossing the blood in a single genus by maintaining that some acts of tossing the blood require remaining down below, others require the priests' ascending up the ramp and standing at the corner of the altar. No. 2 simply tacks on a fragment of a discussion of the base verse in another context altogether. That it hardly belongs is shown by the simple fact that the issue important at No.2 is not raised anywhere in the present exposition. But the motive in including the passage of the Mishnah is self-evident.

III.   The Reason for Scripture's Unique Power of Classification: the Possibility of Polythetic Classification

From this simple account of the paramount position of Scripture in the labor of classification, let us turn to the specific way in which, because of Scripture's provision of taxa, we are able to undertake the science of *Listenwissenschaft,* including hierarchical classification, in the right way. What can we do because we appeal to Scripture, which we cannot do if we do not rely on Scripture? It is to establish the possibility of polythetic classification. We can appeal to shared traits of otherwise distinct taxa and so transform species into a common genus for a given purpose. Only Scripture makes that initiative feasible, so our authorship maintains. What is at stake? It is the possibility of doing precisely what the framers of the Mishnah wish to do: to join together masses of diverse data into a single, encompassing statement, to show the rule that inheres in diverse cases.

In what follows, we will see an enormous, coherent, and beautifully articulated exercise in the comparison and contrast of many things of a single genus. The whole holds together because Scripture makes possible the statement of all things within a single rule. That is, as we have noted, precisely what the framers of the Mishnah proposed to accomplish. Our authorship maintains that only by appeal to The Torah is this fete of learning possible. If, then, we wish to understand all things all together and all at once under a single encompassing rule, we had best revert to The Torah, with its account of the rightful names, positions, and order, imputed to all things.

22. Parashat Vayyiqra Dibura Denedabah Parashah 11

XXII:I.1   A.   [With reference to M. Men. 5:5:] There are those [offerings which require bringing near but do not require waving, waving but not bringing near, waving and bringing near, neither waving nor bringing near: These are offerings which require bringing near but do not require waving: the meal offering of fine flour and the meal offering prepared in the baking pan and the meal offering prepared in the frying pan, and the meal offering of cakes and the meal offering of wafers, and the meal offering of priests, and the meal offering of an anointed priest, and the meal offering of gentiles, and the meal offering of women, and the meal offering of a sinner. R. Simeon says, "The meal offering of priests and of the anointed priest – bringing near does not apply to them, because the taking of a handful does not apply to them. And whatever is not subject to the taking of a handful is not subject to bringing near,"] [Scripture] says, "When you present to the Lord a meal offering that is made in any of these ways, it shall be brought [to the priest who shall take it up to the altar]:"

B.   What requires bringing near is only the handful alone. How do I know that I should encompass under the rule of bringing near the meal offering?

C.   Scripture says explicitly, "meal offering."

D.   How do I know that I should encompass all meal offerings?

E.   Scripture says, using the accusative particle, "the meal offering."

2.   A.   I might propose that what requires bringing near is solely the meal offering brought as a free will offering.

B.   How do I know that the rule encompasses an obligatory meal offering?

C.   It is a matter of logic.

D.   Bringing a meal offering as a free will offering and bringing a meal offering as a matter of obligation form a single classification. Just as a meal offering presented as a free will offering requires bringing near, so the same rule applies to a meal offering of a sinner [brought as a matter of obligation], which should likewise require bringing near.

E.   No, if you have stated that rule governing bringing near in the case of a free will offering, on which oil and frankincense have to be added, will you say the same of the meal offering of a sinner [Lev. 5:11], which does not require oil and frankincense?

F.   The meal offering brought by a wife accused of adultery will prove to the contrary, for it does not require oil and frankincense, but it does require bringing near [as is stated explicitly at Num. 5:15].

G.   No, if you have applied the requirement of bringing near to the meal offering brought by a wife accused of adultery, which also requires waving, will you say the same of the meal offering of a sinner, which does not have to be waved?

H.   Lo, you must therefore reason by appeal to a polythetic analogy [in which not all traits pertain to all components of the category, but some traits apply to them all in common]:

I.   the meal offering brought as a free will offering, which requires oil and frankincense, does not in all respects conform to the traits of the meal offering of a wife accused of adultery, which does not require oil and frankincense, and the meal offering of the wife accused of adultery, which requires waving, does not in all respects conform to the traits of a meal offering brought as a free will offering, which does not require waving.

J.   But what they have in common is that they are alike in requiring the taking up of a handful and they are also alike in that they require bringing near.

K.   I shall then introduce into the same classification the meal offering of a sinner, which is equivalent to them as to the matter of the taking up of a handful, and also should be equivalent to them as to the requirement of being drawn near.

L.   But might one not argue that the trait that all have in common is that all of them may be brought equally by a rich and a poor person and require drawing near, which then excludes from the common classification the meal offering of a sinner, which does not conform to the rule that it may be brought equally by a rich and a poor person, [but may be brought only by a poor person,] and such an offering also should not require being brought near!

M.   [The fact that the polythetic classification yields indeterminate results means failure once more, and, accordingly,] Scripture states, "meal offering,"

N.   with this meaning: all the same are the meal offerings brought as a free will offering and the meal offering of a sinner, both this and that require being brought near.

The elegant exercise draws together the various types of meal offerings and shows that they cannot form a classification of either a monothetic or a polythetic character. Consequently, Scripture must be invoked to supply the proof for the classification of the discrete items. The important language is at H–J: these differ from those, and those from these, but what they have in common is. . . . Then we demonstrate, with our appeal to Scripture, the sole valid source of polythetic classification, M. And this is constant throughout Sifra.

XXII:II.1   A.   R. Simeon says, " '[When you present to the Lord a meal offering that is made in any of these ways,] *it shall be brought* [to the priest who shall take it up to the altar]' – that statement serves to encompass under the rule of waving also the sheaf of first grain,

B.   "for it is said, 'When you come into the land which I give you and reap its harvest, *you shall bring* the sheaf of the first fruits of your harvest to the priest, [and he shall wave the sheaf before the Lord, that you may find acceptance]' (Lev. 23:10).

C.   " '. . . who shall take it up to the altar' serves to encompass the meal offering of the wife accused of adultery, that that too requires being brought near: 'who shall take it up to the altar' [parallel to Num. 5:25].

This discussion continues in the immediately following pericope, continuous with Chapter 22.

23. Parashat Vayyiqra Dibura Denedabah Pereq 13

XXIII:I.1   A.   [Continuing the foregoing: R. Simeon says, " 'When you present to the Lord a meal offering that is made in any of these ways, *it shall be brought*] to the priest who shall take it up to the altar' – that statement serves to encompass under the rule of waving also the sheaf of first grain, for it is said, 'When you come into the land which I give you and reap its harvest, *you shall bring* the sheaf of the first fruits of your harvest to the priest, [and he shall wave the sheaf before the Lord, that you may find acceptance]' (Lev. 23:10), '. . . who shall take it up to the altar' serves to encompass the meal offering of the wife accused of adultery, that that too requires being brought near: 'who shall take it up to the altar' (parallel to Num. 5:25)]:"

B.   is that proposition not a matter of logic?

C.   If the meal offering brought by a sinner, which does not require waving, does require drawing near, the meal offering of a wife accused of adultery, which does require waving, surely should require drawing near.

D.   No, if you have invoked that rule in the case of the sinner's meal offering, which derives from wheat, will you invoke the same rule in the case of the meal offering of an accused wife, which does not derive from wheat [but from barley, and therefore falls into a different genus]?

E. The meal offering of the sheaf of first grain will prove the contrary, for it too does not derive from wheat [but rather from barley] and yet it does require being brought near!

F. No, if you have invoked that rule in the case of the meal offering of the sheaf of first grain, which requires also oil and frankincense, will you place into that same category and subject to that same rule the meal offering of an accused wife, which does not require oil and frankincense?

G. Lo, you must therefore reason by appeal to a polythetic analogy [in which not all traits pertain to all components of the category, but some traits apply to them all in common]:

H. The sinner's meal offering, which derives from wheat, is not in all respects equivalent to the meal offering of the sheaf of first grain, which after all does not derive from wheat, nor is the meal offering of the sheaf of first grain, which requires oil and frankincense, equivalent in all respects to the meal offering of the sinner, which does not require oil and frankincense. But the common trait that pertains to them both is that they both require the taking up of a handful, and, furthermore, they both require being brought near.

I. So I shall invoke the case of the meal offering of an accused wife, which is equivalent to them in that the taking up of a handful is required. It should also be equivalent to them in being brought near.

J. Or perhaps what they have in common is that they are not valid if they derive from coarse meal and they require drawing near. Then that would exclude the meal offering of the accused wife, which indeed is valid when it derives from coarse meal, and which, therefore, should not require drawing near.

K. [Accordingly, Scripture is required to settle the matter, which it does when it states,] ". . . who shall take it up to the altar,"

L. which then serves to encompass the meal offering of the wife accused of adultery, and indicates that that too requires being brought near.

Precisely the same mode of argument worked out in **XXII:I** now applies to Simeon's proposition, with the same satisfactory result.

XXIII:II.1 A. R. Judah says, " 'When you present [to the Lord a meal offering that is made in any of these ways, it shall be brought to the priest who shall take it up to the altar]:

B. "That phrase serves to encompass also the meal offering of an accused wife, indicating that it too requires being brought near, as it is said, 'And he will present her offering in her behalf' (Num. 5:15)."

2. A. But perhaps when Scripture says, "When you present . . .," the implication is only to mean that an individual is permitted to present as a free will offering a variety of meal offering other than those that are listed in the present context?

B. And that is a matter of logic:

C. The community at large presents a meal offering deriving from wheat and brought as a matter of obligation, and the individual may present a meal offering deriving from wheat and brought as a free will offering.

D. If the community, which presents a meal offering deriving from wheat and brought as a matter of obligation, also may present a meal offering deriving from barley and brought as a matter of obligation, so the individual, who may bring a meal offering deriving from wheat and brought as a matter of a free will offering, also may present as a free will offering a meal offering deriving from barley.

E. [That incorrect conclusion is forestalled by Scripture, when it says,] "[When you present to the Lord a meal offering that is made in any of] these [ways, it shall be brought to the priest who shall take it up to the altar],"

F. you have the possibility of bringing only these.

3. A. Or perhaps the sense of "these" is only as follows:

B. One who says, "Lo, incumbent on me is a meal offering" must bring all five types?

C. Scripture says, "*of* these ways,"

D. there is he who brings only one of the types, and there is he who brings all five types. [If someone made explicit which one he has in mind, he brings that one, but if he does not remember what he did specify the type of meal offering, then he may bring all five types.]

I see no close tie between No. 1, which can stand fully worked out on its own, and No. 2. The issue of No. 2, complemented by No. 3, serves to show that the logic of classification leads to false results.

XXIII:III.1 A. R. Simeon says, " '[When you present to the Lord a meal offering [that is made in any of these ways,] *it shall be brought* to the priest who shall take it up to the altar' – that statement serves to encompass all meal offerings under the rule of bringing near."

B. Might one suppose that that requirement pertains to the two loaves of bread and the show bread?

C. Scripture says, "[When you present to the Lord a meal offering that is made] in any of these ways" [which then excludes the specified bread].

2.   A.   Why then have you encompassed under the rule of being brought near all manner of meal offerings but then excluded from the rule the two loaves and the show bread?

B.   After Scripture has used inclusionary language, it has further used exclusionary language.

C.   What distinguishes these meal offerings is that part of any one of them is tossed onto the altar fires, then excluding the two loaves of bread and the show bread, which yield nothing at all to the altar fires [but which the priests consume entirely on their own].

D.   But then the meal offering that accompanies the drink offerings [specified at Num. 15:1ff.], which is wholly tossed onto the altar fires, also should require bringing near!

E.   Scripture states, "[And it shall be brought to the priest] who shall take it up to the altar."

3.   A.   Why then have you encompassed all varieties of meal offerings but excluded the meal offerings that accompany drink offerings?

B.   After Scripture has used inclusionary language, it has further used exclusionary language.

C.   What distinguishes these meal offerings is that they come in their own account, which then excludes meal offerings that accompany drink offerings, for these do not come in their own account at all.

D.   But is it not the fact that the meal offering of priests and the meal offering of a priest that is anointed come on their own account.

E.   Is it possible that they too require being brought near?

F.   Scripture says, "who shall take it up to the altar."

4.   A.   Why then have you encompassed all meal offerings and at the same time excluded the meal offering of priests and the meal offering of the anointed priest?

B.   After Scripture has used inclusionary language, it has further used exclusionary language.

C.   What distinguishes these meal offerings is that part of them is tossed on the altar fires, and, further, they come on their own account, and they yield a residue for the priests.

D.   That then excludes the two loaves and the show bread, none of which is put on the fire, and it further excludes the meal offering that accompanies drink offerings, which does not come on its own account, and, finally, it excludes the meal offering of priests and the meal offering of the high priest, none of which yields a residue for the priests to eat.

The exquisite exercise reaches a conclusion, having encompassed every possible meal offering and shown the relationships of the one to the next throughout. I cannot imagine a more comprehensive exercise of classification – all in the service of the proposition that classification by itself does not yield valid results. Most impressive is the power of taxonomic logic to draw together all manner of data and to set them into relationship with one another. In that context, the strength of argument of our authorship is manifest: the capacity to demonstrate how diverse things relate through points in common, so long as the commonalities derive from a valid source. And that leads us to the central and fundamental premise of all: Scripture, its picture of the classifications of nature and supernature, its account of the rightful names and order of all things, is the sole source for that encompassing and generalizing principle that permits scientific inquiry into the governing laws to take place.

Does the Mishnah's authorship know the principle of polythetic taxonomy? Indeed it does, as a mere glance at the opening pericopes of Mishnah-tractate *Baba Qama* Chapter 1: 1–4 tells us: "The distinctive feature of the ox is not the same as that of the crop destroying beast, nor is the indicative feature of the crop destroying beast the same as that of the ox; nor is that of either of these, which are animate, the same as that of fire, which is inanimate, nor is the indicative trait of any of these, who ordinarily go out and do damage, the same as that of the pit, which does not go out and do damage. What they have in common is that the may cause injury and you are responsible to take responsibility for them, and if one of them caused injury, whoever is responsible pays restitution by handing over land of the highest quality that he has," so Mishnah-tractate Baba Qamma 1:1. Polythetic taxonomy presents no surprises to the framer of the cited passage. Not only so, but a glance at the exegesis of this passage supplied in the successor writings will reassure us that the framers of the Mishnah surely have made reference, in defining the indicative traits of the taxa under discussion, to Scripture. Where our authorship will take issue with that of the Mishnah is in those cases, and they are exceedingly numerous, in whch the Mishnah's authorship effects its taxonomy, and, consequently, its hierarchical classification, without reference to the dictates of Scripture. In our authorship's view, that is never a reliable procedure. To borrow language that originally served another debate altogether: At stake is the principle, systematically advanced by Sifra, of proof *sola Scriptura.*

IV. The Rehabilitation of Taxonomic Logic Within the Re-presentation of the Torah

In consequence of Scripture's provision of valid taxa, we can, of course, proceed to invoke and utilize precisely that logic of hierarchical classification that the framers of the Mishnah employed. Here is a full statement of the consequence of adopting Scripture's categories. We find the appeal to comparison and contrast time and again, and at no point do we distinguish one category from another so as to make comparison no longer logical. Let us now examine specific illustrations of the right way of pursuing that same taxonomic logic of hierarchical classification that the Mishnah's framers have carried out in the wrong way. Our first example allows us to see an unimpeded flow of classification: this is like that, therefore this falls under the rule of that, pure and simple.

209. Parashat Qedoshim Pereq 11

CCIX:I.1   A.   ["If a man lies with a beast, he shall be put to death, and you shall kill the beast. If a woman approaches any beast and lies with it, you shall kill the woman and the beast; they shall be put to death, their blood is upon them" (Lev. 20:13–16).]

B.   "If a man:"

C.   excluding a minor.

D.   "lies with a beast:"

E.   whether large or small.

2.   A.   "he shall be put to death:"

B.   through stoning.

C.   You say that it is through stoning. But perhaps it is some another of the modes of execution decreed by the Torah.

D.   Scripture says, "and you shall kill the beast."

E.   Here we find reference to "killing," and elsewhere likewise we find the same ["If a woman approaches any beast and lies with it, you shall kill the woman and the beast; they shall be put to death, their blood is upon them"].

F.   Just as elsewhere "killing" involves stoning [as is proven presently], so here too, "killing" involves stoning.

3.   A.   We thereby derive the penalty for one who commits sexual relations upon a beast. Whence do we find the penalty for serving as the passive partner in sexual relations with a beast?

B.   Scripture says, "Whoever lies with a beast will surely die" (Ex. 22:18).

C.   Since [in the context of the present verse] it cannot speak of one who commits sexual relations upon a beast, interpret it to provide an admonition against serving as the passive partner in sexual relations with a beast.

4.   A.   We have derived the penalty for both the active and the passive partner to sexual relations with a beast.

B.   Whence then the admonition?

C.   Scripture says, "And you shall not lie with any beast and defile yourself with it, [neither shall any woman give herself to a beast to lie with it; it is perversion]" (Lev. 18:23).

D.   We thereby derive the admonition for the active partner. Whence the admonition for the passive partner?

E.   "Scripture says, 'No Israelite man may be a cult prostitute' (Dt. 23:18).

K.   "And further: 'And there were also cult prostitutes in the land' (1 Kgs. 14:24)," the words of R. Ishmael.

L.   R. Aqiba says, "It is not necessary to derive proof from those passages. Lo, Scripture says, 'And you shall not lie with any beast [and defile yourself with it],' you shall not lie as passive partner."

5.   A.   "If a woman approaches any beast and lies with it, you shall kill the woman and the beast; they shall be put to death, [their blood is upon them]:"

B.   You maintain that it is through stoning, but perhaps it is through any one of the other forms of inflicting the death penalty that the Torah specifies?

C.   Scripture says, "his blood is upon him,"

D.   and elsewhere we find the same language, "their blood is on their head" (Lev. 20:27).

E.   Just as that usage elsewhere refers to inflicting the death penalty through stoning, so the same language here involves stoning.

6.   A.   We thereby have derived the penalty. Whence the admonition?

B.   Scripture says, "Neither shall any woman give herself to a beast to lie with it; it is perversion" (Lev. 18:23).

The predictable materials, Nos. 1–6, go through the necessary motions. What is important is the givenness of the classifications. This demonstrates beyond doubt that our authorship accepts the principles of *Listenwissenschaft*, with like following the rule of like, unlike following the opposite of that rule. Once categories are defined, no one will call into question the basic logic of comparison and contrast in a system of hierarchization.

The second example in context allows us to see how one classification generates another, or how we may encompass a number of species within a single genus. This is accomplished through the dictate of Scripture.

CCIX:II.1   A.   ["If a man takes his sister, a daughter of his father or a daughter of his mother, and sees her nakedness and she sees his nakedness, it is a shameful thing, and they shall be cut off in the sight of the children of their people; he has uncovered his sister's nakedness, he shall bear his iniquity"] (Lev. 21:17).

B.   "If a man:"

C.   excluding a minor.

2.   A.   "takes his sister, a daughter of his father or a daughter of his mother:"

B.   I know only the cases of the daughter of his father and the daughter of his mother. I know that encompassed under the prohibition are the daughter of his mother but not his father, or the daughter of his father but not his mother. But what about his sister through the same father and mother?

C.   Scripture says, "his sister" – under all circumstances.

3.   A.   But if Scripture had not made the point explicit, I could have proven it through a logical argument:

B.   If one is liable for his sister by his father but not by his mother, or by his mother but not by his father, all the more so that he will be liable for his sister through the same father and mother!

C.   But if you argue in this way, you have imposed a penalty only on the basis of logical argument [which is not to be done].

D.   Therefore Scripture makes the matter "his sister" entirely explicit, to indicate that one should not impose a penalty only on the basis of logical argument. . . .

6.   A.   "and they shall be cut off in the sight of the children of their people:"

B.   We thereby learn the penalty. Whence the admonition?

C.   Scripture says, "You shall not uncover the nakedness of your sister, the daughter of your father or the daughter of your mother" (Lev. 18:9).

D.   I know only the case of the daughter of his father but not the daughter of his mother, or the daughter of his mother but not the daughter of his father. Whence do I learn the admonition against sexual relations with the sister who is daughter of both the same father and the same mother?

E.   Scripture says, ". . . sister," covering all cases.

What is interesting in the following is an explicit limitation on the use of logic untempered by Scripture. Even if I can make a point through the logical means available, there are consequences that I am permitted to draw only if Scripture makes them clear and explicit. Such an intervention, in the following, invokes a principle of limitation on the logic of comparison and contrast of the traits of things independent of Scripture's identification of taxa – even when it works.

7.   A.   But if Scripture had not made the point explicit, I could have proven it through a logical argument:

B.   If Scripture gave an admonition for his sister by his father but not by his mother, or by his mother but not by his father, all the more so that must there be an admonition for his sister through the same father and mother!

C.   But if you argue in this way, you have imposed an admonition only on the basis of logical argument [which is not to be done].

D.   Therefore Scripture makes the matter "his sister" entirely explicit, to indicate that one should not impose an admonition only on the basis of logical argument.

8.   A.   If one is admonished against "your sister," then even a bondwoman, even a gentile [should be subject to admonition]?

B.   Scripture says, "You shall not uncover the nakedness of your father's wife's daughter [begotten by your father, since she is your sister]" (Lev. 18:11).

C.   If covered is the daughter of your father's wife, then would the prohibition extend to her even if she had a different father altogether?

D.   Scripture says, "begotten by your father, [since she is your sister]."

E.   If so, why is it said also, "whether born at home or born abroad" (Lev. 18:9)?

F.   Whether people tell [the father (Hillel)] to confirm the marriage or whether they tell him to divorce her [whether or not the father's daughter derives from a valid or an invalid marriage, the son may not marry the daughter].

We go through the same exercise as before, now dealing with the inclusionary problem, worked out at Nos. 2 and 3. No. 4 makes a point particular to our case. No. 5 goes over matter not required for the exposition of this passage but invited by the use of the word that means both "shameful" and, in context, "merciful." Nos. 6 and 7 cover the ground of Nos. 2 and 3. The conclusion completes an exclusionary, then inclusionary program.

V.   Silence and the Articulated Critique of the Mishnah's Logic: When Sifra's Authorship Does and Does Not Demolish the Logic of Comparison and Contrast

While setting forth its critique of the Mishnah's utilization of the logic of comparison and contrast in hierarchical classification, the authorship of Sifra is careful not to criticize the Mishnah. Its position favors restating the Mishnah within the context of Scripture, not rejecting the conclusions of the Mishnah, let alone its authority. Consequently, when we find a critique of applied reason divorced from Scripture, we rarely uncover an explicit critique of the Mishnah, and when we find a citation of the Mishnah, we rarely uncover linkage to the ubiquitous principle that Scripture forms the source of all classification and hierarchy.[2] In the following passage we see how our authorship treats the Mishnah when it wishes to cite passage of the Mishnah and also to set into the correct relationship categories of things that the Mishnah sets forth.

21. Parashat Vayyiqra Dibura Denedabah Pereq 12

XXI:I.1   A.   "If your offering is a meal offering on a griddle, [it shall be of choice flour with oil mixed in, unleavened. Break it into bits and pour oil on it; it is a meal offering:]"

B.   This teaches that the offering requires the use of a utensil [for its preparation and presentation].

2.   A.   Reference is made twice to the word "your offering" ["If your offering is a meal offering on a griddle, it shall be of choice flour with oil mixed in, unleavened. Break it into bits and pour oil on it; it is a meal offering. If your offering is a meal offering in a pan, it shall be made of choice flour in oil."]. This serves to establish an analogy.

B.   Here "your offering" forms the basis for a classification. Just as "your offering" here involves adding oil and saturating the meal with oil, so "your offering," used later invokes the requirement of adding oil and saturating the meal with oil.

C.   And, further, just as the classification of "your offering" noted below involves putting on oil in a utensil prior to the preparation of the offering, so "your offering" in the present instance also involves putting on oil in a utensil prior to the preparation of the offering.

Here the classification of two species into a single genus does succeed, so No. 2, with both species subject to the same rule. No objection is raised.

XXI:II.1   A.   ". . . choice flour with oil mixed in:"

B.   This teaches that one mixes the oil into the fine flour. [**M. Men. 6:3A–B: All meal offerings prepared in a utensil (baking pan or frying pan) require three applications of oil: pouring oil into the utensil, stirring the meal into the oil, and then again putting oil into the utensil.**]

C.   Rabbi says, "And as to the loaves [baked in an oven, one stirs them with oil (M. Men. 6:3C)] ["In the case of loaves, they stir oil into them . . . as it is said, 'Loaves mixed with oil' " (Lev. 7:12) [T. Men. 8:7B–C]."

D.   They said to him, "But in connection with the cakes that accompany the thank offering, is it not said, 'Flour mixed with oil' (Lev. 23:13)" (T. Tos. 8:7C)?

E. "And it is possible to stir in only with flour. [B. Men. 75a: It was not possible to mingle the cakes with oil but only the flour.]

F. How does one do this? One puts oil into the flour and stirs it in, then oil into a utensil and prepares it, and stirs it, and mixes [the flour] with oil. [Tosefta's version: **"How does one do this? He puts oil into the utensil and fries it. Then he puts oil into the flour and stirs it and breaks it up. And he then pours oil on it as one pours oil on pounded beans"** (T. Men. 8:5C–D)].

G. Rabbi says, "One puts oil into a utensil and prepares it, and stirs it, and then mixes the flour with oil, and then goes and pours oil on it."

All I see here is a reworking of the language we find, also, in the Mishnah and the Tosefta. I see no motif of critique of the Mishnah for its omission of proof texts. Perhaps it is implicit or tacit; but, if so, in it I find no stakes at all. Our authorship knows that the Mishnah contains the Torah, and that is why, I maintain, it has undertaken the work it presents to us here.

XXI:III.1 A. "unleavened:"

B. Might one suppose that this is merely the desirable way of doing the deed [but still, optional]?

C. Scripture says, ". . . it will be . . .,"

D. meaning that it is a firmly established requirement of the rite.

2. A. "Break it into bits:"

B. Might one suppose that that means into two pieces?

C. Scripture says, "bits."

3. A. Might one suppose one should turn it into crumbs?

B. Scripture says, ". . . it . . ."

C. *It* is to be broken into pieces, but the pieces are not to be broken into pieces.

4. A. **As to the meal offering of an Israelite, one folds it one into two, then two into four parts, and divides it at each fold. As to the meal offering of priests, one folds it one into two, then two into four parts, but does not divide it. As to the meal offering of the anointed priest, one did not fold it up. R. Simeon says, "The meal offering of priests and the meal offering of an anointed priest are not subject to the requirement of breaking up, because they are not subject to the taking of a handful, and anything which is not subject to the taking of a handful is not subject to breaking up"** [M. Men. 6:4B–G].

The systematic exegesis leads to a restatement of the Mishnah's rule in the Mishnah's language. However, the point important to the Mishnah, which is the definition of the rule of breaking up in accord with the hierarchization of castes, is utterly outside the frame of reference.

XXI:IV.1   A.   "Break it into bits and pour oil on it; it is a meal offering:"

B.   This serves to extend the rule of breaking up to all meal offerings.

C.   Might one suppose that that same rule extends also to the two loaves and the show bread?

D.   Scripture says, "it . . ."

E.   How come you encompass all meal offerings but exclude the two loaves and the show bread?

F.   After Scripture has used inclusionary language, it has then made an exclusion.

G.   Just as these are distinguished in that part of the offering is placed on the altar fires, so excluded are the two loaves of bread and the show bread, none of which is put on the altar fire [but all of which is given to the priests to eat].

2.   A.   "Break it into bits and pour oil on it; it is a meal offering:"

B.   This serves to extend the rule of pouring oil on the offering to all meal offerings.

C.   Might one suppose that that rule extends also to a meal offering that is baked?

D.   Scripture says, "on it."

E.   I shall then exclude the loaves, but not the wafers?

F.   Scripture says, "it is [a meal offering]," [encompassing wafers under the rule of applying oil].

The clarification introduces other forms of meal offering and speciates them.

XXI:V.1   A.   "If your offering is a meal offering in a pan, it shall be made of choice flour in oil:"

B.   **What is the difference between a baking pan and a frying pan? "The frying pan has a cover, and the baking pan has no cover," the words of R. Yosé the Galilean. R. Hananiah b. Gamaliel says, "A frying pan is deep, and what is cooked in it is spongy, and a baking pan is flat, and what is cooked in it is hard"** [M. Men. 5:8C–E].

2. A. ". . . it shall be made of choice flour in oil:"

    B. This teaches that preparing this meal offering requires putting oil in a utensil prior to preparing the flour.

Once more we review the Mishnah's clarification of Scripture, now representing the Mishnah as merely a secondary amplification of what Scripture says.

The laconic passage at hand contains an important fact. When the Mishnah is cited by our authorship, it will be presented as part of the factual substrate of the Torah. When the logic operative throughout the Mishnah is subjected to criticism, the language of the Mishnah will rarely, if ever, be cited in context. The operative language in dealing with the critique of the applied logic of *Listenwissenschaft* as represented by the framers of the Mishnah ordinarily is, "is it not a matter of logic?" Then the sorts of arguments against taxonomy pursued outside of the framework of Scripture's classifications will follow. By contrast, when the authorship of Sifra wishes to introduce into the context it has already established a verbatim passage of the Mishnah, it will ordinarily, though not always, use, *mikan amru,* which, in context, means, "in this connection [sages] have said." It is a simple fact that when the intent is to demolish improper reasoning, the Mishnah's rules in the Mishnah's language rarely, if ever, occur. When the authorship of Sifra wishes to incorporate paragraphs of the Mishnah into their re-presentation of The Torah, they will do so either without fanfare, as in the passage at hand, or by a neutral joining of language "in this connection [sages] have said."

VI. The Torah as a Proper Noun and the Rehabilitation of Hierarchical Classification

The authorship of Sifra never called into question the self-evident validity of taxonomic logic. Its critique is addressed only to how the Mishnah's framers identify the origins of, and delineate, taxa. But that critique proves fundamental to the case that that authorship proposed to make. For, intending to demonstrate that *The Torah* was a proper noun, and that everything that was valid came to expression in the single, cogent statement of The Torah, the authorship at hand identified the fundamental issue. It is the debate over the way we know things. In insisting, in agreement with the framers of the Mishnah, that there are not only cases but also rules, not only species but also genera, the authorship of Sifra also made its case in behalf of the case for The Torah as a proper noun. This carries us to the theological foundation for Sifra's authorship's sustained critique of applied reason.

Notes

[1] I need hardly add, in light of Chapter Seven, *and Scripture alone!*

[2] What I present here is an impression based on my translation. To understand how Sifra unites the dual Torah, it suffices to underline its utterly affirmative reading of the oral Torah. My first reading of Sifra, represented by my *History of the Mishnaic Law of Purities. VII. Sifra* (Leiden, 1976: E. J. Brill), led me to see the authorship of Sifra as critical of the Mishnah for not citing proof texts and for supposing that we can have law without scriptural proof. But I now realize that I was right in general but wrong as to the explanation of matters. It was only more than a decade later that the issue of the inner logical structure of the whole came to my mind. That is what required me to return to Sifra and translate the entire document, with the results presented here and in the companion study.

CHAPTER NINE

Torah as Proper Noun and the Structure of the Logic of Creation

I. Sifra's Theology of Revelation

The reader may now wonder whether I have entered a circular argument. When I accounted for Sifra's authorship's critique of the Mishnah's utilization of taxonomic logic for the proof of propositions, I claimed that at stake was not merely omission of proof texts but a (to our authorship) flawed use of a valid logic. Yet I further stressed that the correct utilization of that logic can be shown to occur not only in Sifra but, by Sifra's authorship's own standard, in the Mishnah. I further stipulated that Scripture can have been, and probably was, the source of that appearance in the Mishnah of the kind of polythetic classification of which Sifra's authorship will have approved, if not explicitly, then at least implicitly in the Mishnah's introduction of the same polythetic taxonomy.[1] Therefore, does it not all come down to the presence, or absence, of citations of verses of Scripture? And if all that separates Sifra from Tosefta and the two Talmuds is that the latter suffice with the inclusion of proof texts while the former insists upon rewriting the whole of Scripture in line with the Mishnah, then does not the effort invested in Sifra seem a bit excessive. The result, after all, can have been, and was, accomplished in a much simpler way by the authorships of the successor documents to the Mishnah. Why then the reversion to Scripture in Sifra's rewriting of Scripture, that is, its writing with Scripture?

In appealing to the principle, for taxonomy, of *sola Scriptura*, I mean to set forth what I conceive really to be at stake. It is the character of The Torah and what it is, in The Torah, that we wish to discern. The answer to that question requires theological, not merely literary and philosophical, reflection on our part. For I maintain that in their delineation of correct hierarchical logic, our authorship uncovered, within The Torah (hence, by definition, written and oral components of The Torah alike) an

182

adumbration of the working of the mind of God. That is because the premise of all discourse is that The Torah was written by God and dictated by God to Moses at Sinai. In the end, that will explain why our authorship for its part has entered into The Torah long passages of not merely clarification but active intrusion, making itself a component of the interlocutorial process. To what end we know: It was to unite the dual Torah. But on what basis? To answer this question let me start once again from the very beginning: the place of Sifra in its canonical context.

II.   The Singularity of Sifra

The authorship of Sifra stands by itself in the canon of the Judaism of the dual Torah. Its reading and uses of Scripture put together in the way in which Sifra presents its statement of Scripture and the Mishnah within the context of Scripture, enjoy virtually unique standing.[2] True, in formal terms, Sifra falls into the standard classification of verse by verse commentary to a book of the written Torah. In general, in making Midrash compilations, redactors would gather materials of Scripture exegesis and organize them in the order of appearance of verses of Scripture or of the unfolding of a story in Scripture. At the outset, people adhered to the exegetical and redactional pattern already established by the Yerushalmi's verse by verse or sentence by sentence reading set forth for the Mishnah. That is to say, they followed the order of verses of a biblical book, just as the framers of the Yerushalmi followed the order of Mishnah sentences of a given tractate. They undertook to explain words or phrases, imposing upon Scripture that set of values they regarded as self-evident and factual, the values of sages' world view and way of life. The same model of exegesis and organization – that is, the same logoi and topoi – that determined the content of self-evident comment in self-evident order on the Mishnah also dictated what would be done on Scripture. So the original work of collecting and arranging the compilations of exegeses of Scripture followed the patterns set in collecting and arranging exegeses of the Mishnah. Just as the Talmud, which is Mishnah exegesis, treats the Mishnah, so the earliest collections of scriptural exegesis treat Scripture. My thesis may be expressed as a simple formula of relationship:

Talmud	*Exegetical Collection*
Mishnah	Scripture

But while the Genesis Rabbah on Genesis is to be compared to a Talmud tractate devoted to a particular tractate of the Mishnah on that tractate, Sifra on Leviticus bears slight resemblance to a Talmud tractate's treatment of a tractate of the Mishnah.

Although Genesis Rabbah is composed of units of discourse as cogent, in their way, as the ones in the Talmud of the Land of Israel, we should look in vain in the Talmud of the Land of Israel for a tractate that, instead of commenting on a Mishnah-tractate, undertakes essentially to rewrite large tracts of it. For when we pass the, admittedly considerable, passages in which words or phrases are amplified, what do we find in Sifra? It is a series of discursive essays, such as we have now examined at length, in which profound reflection on the nature of probative logic is expressed in examples and cases. Whereas the units of discourse of Genesis Rabbah fall into precisely the same taxonomical categories as those of the Talmud of the Land of Israel, the paramount classification of units of discourse in our document surely do not.

That is not to suggest we find in the two Talmuds no counterpart to the critique of applied reason that we have examined with such admiration. It is to state as mere fact that the two Talmuds, and certainly not the Bavli, in no way undertake the deconstruction and recomposition of a Mishnah-tractate in the way in which our authorship has taken apart and then put back together in a different way the book of Leviticus. The Mishnah in the Bavli always retains its paramount and autonomous position, dictating the program of discourse throughout those passages in which the Mishnah is at issue; Scripture fills the rest. Neither Talmud, and certainly not the Bavli, proposes to rewrite the Mishnah-tractate in the way in which our authorship restates, within the setting of Scripture, the language and propositions of the Mishnah; and none, as I said, pretends to penetrate into the deep structure of probative logic in the way in which our authorship has accomplished its purpose.

To appreciate the singular position attained by our authorship, we do well to reflect on the contrary position defined by the framers of Midrash compilations for Scripture, represented by Genesis Rabbah. Their work, in the main, was dictated for them by the program of Mishnah exegesis worked out in the two Talmuds, particularly in the first of the two. Let me explain. What the masters of biblical exegesis did in Genesis in the compilation, Genesis Rabbah, was what the masters of Mishnaic exegesis did in whatever Mishnah-tractate they chose for study. It follows that the compiling of the first collection of biblical exegesis falls into the same intellectual framework as the Talmud of the Land of Israel, whether this was before, at the same time as, or in the aftermath of the composition of the Yerushalmi. Like the Yerushalmi, Genesis Rabbah emerges in two distinct literary stages: first, people worked out its components; second, people arranged them. These may well have been the same people at much the same time, but the literary work divides into separate and distinct stages. First came writing compositions expressive of complex ideas framed in sophisticated ways. Second came selecting and arranging these units of discourse into the composition now before us. As I have stated, the taxonomical framework suitable for all units of discourse of the Yerushalmi moves, without significant variation or revision, to encompass and categorize the materials of the earliest composition of scriptural exegesis, Genesis Rabbah. This fact I demonstrated in *Midrash in Context* (Philadelphia, 1984; second printing: Atlanta, 1988: Scholars Press for Brown Judaic Studies).

Let me make this more concrete. The framer of an exegetical unit of discourse in the Yerushalmi ordinarily would do one of two things: first, an exegesis of the Mishnah phrase by phrase; second, an amplification of the meaning of a passage of the Mishnah. So a Talmudic sage confronting the Mishnah had the choice of explaining the meaning of a particular passage or expanding upon the meaning, or the overall theme, of a particular passage. The same was so for scriptural verses. True, in dealing with Scripture a sage might systematically interpret one thing in terms of something else, a verse of Scripture in light of an autonomous set of considerations not explicit in Scripture but (in his mind) absolutely critical to its full meaning. But that is still not much more than the exegesis of the passage at hand for a given purpose, established a priori. And that is an exercise fully familiar to the framers of the units of discourse of the Talmud in their confrontation with the Mishnah.

Moving on to the taxonomical categories for a scriptural book, there are four, of which the first two are closely related and the fourth of slight consequence. The first category encompasses close exegesis of Scripture, by which I mean an interpretation of a passage word for word or phrase by phrase. In such an activity, the framer of a discrete composition will wish to read and explain a verse or a few words of a verse of the Scripture at hand, pure and simple. This is a commonplace in Sifra as well. The second category, no less exegetical than the first, is made up of units of discourse in which the components of the verse are treated as part of a larger statement of meaning rather than as a set of individual phrases, stichs requiring attention one by one. Accordingly, in this taxon we deal with wide-ranging discourse about the meaning of a particular passage, hence an effort to amplify what is said in a verse. I cannot find a dozen instances of this kind of discourse in Sifra.

Nor is there a parallel in Sifra to the useful third taxon of the other Midrash compilations, which encompasses units of discourse in which the theme of a particular passage defines a very wide-ranging exercise. In this discussion the cited passage itself is unimportant. It is the theme that is definitive. Accordingly, in this third type we take up a unit of discourse in which the composer of the passage wishes to expand on a particular problem (merely) illustrated in the cited passage. The problem, rather than the cited passage, defines the limits and direction of discourse. The passage at hand falls away, having provided a mere pretext for the real point of concern. The fourth and final taxon, also deriving from the Yerushalmi, takes in units of discourse shaped around a given topic but not intended to constitute cogent and tightly framed discourse on said topic. These units of discourse then constitute topical anthologies rather than carefully composed essays. In place of these last three taxa, as we now recognize well, comes the preoccupation with the Mishnah and the problem of the Mishnah, as our sample in Chapter Three makes abundantly clear.

The taxonomic structure just now described derives from the categories inductively discovered for the Yerushalmi, and it serves for other Midrash compilations, but not for Sifra. The upshot is that types of units of discourse that we find in the Yerushalmi and the ones that comprise Genesis Rabbah fall into precisely the same categories and only into those categories. Taxonomically, all that changes from Genesis Rabbah and the compilations like it to the Yerushalmi (or vice versa) is the document subjected to exegesis (as well, of course, as what is said about it). Because the modes of thought and discourse turn out to exhibit precisely the same definitive traits and only those traits, they sustain a remarkably monothetic taxonomy. That is why I propose the simple equation: The Yerushalmi is to the Mishnah as compilations of exegesis are to Scripture. But none of this is the case for Sifra.

III. The Parsimonious Proper Noun and the Capacious Common Noun

We have concentrated upon Sifra's authorship's brilliant critique of applied reason. Its rehabilitation of the available system of reason was accomplished in such a way as to reopen the entire question of the definition of the Torah. By returning to Scripture as the source for taxa, by appealing to Scripture as the sole criterion for like and unlike, and then by restating the whole of Scripture, for the book of Leviticus, to encompass words not in the original, written Torah but only in the other, oral Torah, that authorship exhibited remarkable imagination. Certainly, by any intellectual criterion, their solution to the problem of the Mishnah exhibited the wit and daring that mere exegesis of Scripture and exegesis of the Mishnah, such as had been done in the Bavli, scarcely adumbrated.

Two solutions to the problem of the Mishnah competed, at least in logic and intellect. A brief review at the end places into context the conclusion of the study as a whole. The one, we recall, transformed the word *torah* into a common noun, denoting many things, above all, status and classification. A teaching, book, or person might enter the status of *torah* or the classification of *torah*. That left ample space for actions, persons, books, and a broad range of categories of entities, so that *torah* might serve as an adjective as much as a common noun (e.g., a Torah teaching, a Torah community, and the like). Therefore, although the Torah remained the scroll that contained the Pentateuch, a variety of other meanings broadened the sense of *torah.* In consequence, from the Mishnah onward, the canon of Judaism called *torah,* or *the Torah,* found ample space for endless candidates for inclusion. The other solution preserved the limited sense of the word *torah,* referring always and only to The Torah, that is to say, the Pentateuch. But then this other approach reread The Torah, the written Torah, and found space for a variety of fresh candidates for inclusion. This was accomplished through a vast restatement of the whole Torah, oral and written, as one, a new and extraordinarily widened statement of what was encompassed within the written Torah.

IV.   Why the Bavli Won

It was for good and substantial reason that the Bavli has formed the definitive statement of Judaism from the time of its closure to the present day. The excellence of its composition, the mastery and authority of those who everywhere studied it and advocated its law, the sharpness of its exegesis and discussion, the harmonious and proportionate presentation of all details, these virtues of taste and intellect may well have secured for the document its paramount position. The Bavli moreover incorporated a far broader selection of antecedent materials than any other document that reaches us out of Judaism in late antiquity, far more, for instance, than the Yerushalmi. This vast selection, moreover, was so organized and put together that systematic accounts of numerous important problems of biblical exegesis, law, and theology alike emerged. Consequently, the Bavli would serve from its closure as both an encyclopedia of knowledge and a summa of the theology and law of Judaism. But what gained for the Bavli the priority it would enjoy was the comprehensive character, in form and in substance, of its statement, based as it was both on the Scripture's and the Mishnah's redactional framework. No one had done that before; no one had to do it again. However, as we now know, that was not the only way to do the work of uniting the two Torahs.

I should claim that the method of the Bavli emerged from the reading of the word *torah* as a common noun, and the intellectual power of Sifra derived from its reading of the word *torah* as a proper noun. The success of the one and the neglect of the other derive from that same fact. Let us dwell on how the Yerushalmi's and Bavli's authorships understood *torah* as a process, rather than as a set of defined propositions, such as we find in Sifra. For the framers of the Bavli (and the Yerushalmi), *torah,* a common noun, bore a variety of meanings. A brief reprise of the meanings associated with the word *torah* will show us how broad a sense serves in the Bavli, and, by contrast, how our authorship implicitly has restricted matters.

1.   When the Torah refers to a particular thing, it is to a scroll containing divinely revealed words.

2.   The Torah may further refer to revelation, not as an object but as a corpus of doctrine.

3.   When one "does Torah," the disciple studies or learns and the master teaches or exemplifies Torah. Hence, whereas the word *Torah* never appears as a verb, it does refer to an act.

4.   The word also bears a quite separate, generic sense, torah as category or classification or corpus of rules, for example, "the torah of driving a car" is a usage entirely acceptable to some documents.

5.   The word *Torah* very commonly refers to a status, distinct from and above another status, as teachings of Torah against teachings of scribes.

6.   Obviously, no account of the meaning of the word *Torah* can ignore the distinction between the two Torahs, written and oral.

7.   Finally, as I have already explained, the word *Torah* refers to a source of salvation, often fully worked out in stories about how the individual and the nation will be saved through Torah.

If I had to summarize all possible usages, as common noun and even as adjective, that the word *torah* sustains in the Bavli, I should state things in a simple way: for the two Talmuds, *torah* refers to a process, not only to a particular document. Those redactors had no compelling reason, therefore, to revert for the formation of their writing to Scripture and its structure. For them, *torah* as status or as process can characterize persons, gestures, many kinds of objects and actions. Consequently, when according all honor and priority to the written Torah, the authorship found it entirely possible to resort not to Scripture but to the Mishnah. They had nothing to prove that rewriting Scripture, or writing through Scripture, would have demanded. All they wished to demonstrate was the correlative and co-equal standing of the two sources of torah, the written Torah and the oral Torah. To this end, they set the two side by side. That mere formality entirely served their purpose.

When the final organizers of the Talmud of Babylonia, who, it is commonly alleged, flourished circa A.D. 500–600, considered the redactional choices made by their predecessors, two appeared the most likely. The organizers might take up and arrange such materials as they had in their hands around the categories – books or verses or themes – of

Scripture, as had their precursers in bringing into being compositions made up of exegeses of Scripture (Midrashim). Or they might follow the order of the Mishnah and compose a systematic commentary and amplification of that document, as had their precursers who created the Talmud of the Land of Israel a century or so before. So they took up materials, in various states and stages of completion, pertinent to the Mishnah or to the principles of laws that the Mishnah had originally brought to articulation. Second, they had in hand received materials, again in various conditions, pertinent to the Scripture, both as the Scripture related to the Mishnah and also as the Scripture laid forth its own narratives. The decision the framers of the Bavli reached was to adopt the two redactional principles inherited from the antecedent century or so. That is why they organized the Bavli around the Mishnah. But, second, they adapted and included vast tracts of antecedent materials organized as scriptural commentary. These they inserted whole and complete, not at all in response to the Mishnah's program, as the encyclopaedists. Their creation turned out to be the encyclopaedia of Judaism, its summa, its point of final reference, its court of last appeal, its definition, its conclusion, and its closure – so they thought, and so said those that followed, to this very day. They held the two Torahs together through the device of redaction, setting side by side, with very little interchange or interpenetration, amplifications of the two Torahs, oral and written.

The Bavli as a whole lays itself out as a commentary to the Mishnah. So the framers wished us to think that whatever they wanted to tell us would take the form of Mishnah commentary. But a second glance indicates that the document is made up of enormous composites, themselves closed prior to inclusion in the Bavli. Some of these composites were selected and arranged along lines dictated by a logic other than that deriving from the requirements of Mishnah commentary. In these the logic of redaction – what (self-evidently) comes first, what (obviously) follows – emerges from a different sort of exegetical task from Mishnah commentary. People focused upon passages of Scripture in making up their compositions of exegesis. Before the time of the Bavli's authors, three principles of composition and redaction – Mishnah exegesis, Scripture exegesis, and biographical collection – flourished more or less in isolation from one another. How do we know? The first is fully exposed in the Talmud of the Land of Israel, the second in earlier compilations of scriptural exegeses. The third accounts for the available biographical composites. To be sure, these never were gathered into tractates or other large and autonomous units of literary expression before the time of the nineteenth- and early-twentieth- century biographers of talmudic rabbis. What is clear, therefore, is that the antecedent redactors, before the age of the Bavli's own compositors, thought that the three things could be done fairly separately.

The framers of the Bavli drew together the results of these three types of work, which people prior to their own labors already had created in abundance. Using the two I specified as definitive redactional structures, the framers made of them all one document, the Bavli, or, in the later tradition of Judaism, the Talmud. Whatever the place and role of the diverse types of compositions circulating before and in the time of the Bavli – compilations of scriptural exegeses, the Yerushalmi, not to mention the exegeses of Pentateuchal laws in Sifra and the Sifres, the Tosefta, Pirqe Abot and Abot de R. Natan, and so forth – the Bavli superseded them all. It look pride of place. It laid the final seal upon the past and defined not only what would succeed for an unknown tomorrow but the very form, topical order, and program of all that would pass into the hands of the future.

That is why the Bavli became the Torah par excellence, the Torah through which Israel would read both Scripture and Mishnah, the Torah all together and all at once, as God at Sinai had revealed it to Moses, our rabbi. It was because the Bavli's writers accomplished the nearly perfect union of Scripture and Mishnah in a single document that the Bavli became Israel's fullest Torah. Yet the same can be said of Sifra, which united the pertinent passages of the Mishnah with the written Torah. Not only so, but the authorship of Sifra did more than merely set things side by side in the same document. They accomplished a true union between the two Torahs by rewriting the one into the pages of the other. But Sifra remained in the wings whereas the Bavli took center stage. What accounts for the difference?

If the educational differences mattered, so that, at stake was studying the Torah, then the success of the Bavli must be attributed to its remarkable clarity, proportion, balance, composition, and accessibility. The rather abstruse discourses, through cases, on the correct system of probative logic, on comparison and contrast and consequent classification, in their initial statement demanded far more intellectual capacity than did the more discursive exposition of the Bavli. The Bavli's authorship, after all, does more than allude to Mishnah passages. It lays out and explains them. By contrast, someone who does not have a reasonable knowledge of the bulk of the pertinent tractates of the Mishnah and Tosefta will find Sifra allusive and elusive. If the institutional difference mattered, then, of course, we have simply to observe that in the *yeshivot,* or sessions, in which the master–disciple circles were sustained, the Bavli served as the principal document of study. Sifra, among many other writings, was there for reference; it was not treated in a sustained way, with the result that, as a document, it could not make its statement whole and complete and in a coherent way. But our authorship meant to speak from beginning to end, not merely episodically and in random order. If the synagogual setting made a difference, finally, then reading the Torah in the synagogue meant reading the written Torah. No one imagined that Sifra would take the place of the book of Leviticus when the lectionary cycle reached the Third Book of Moses. Consequently, the pretense of (re)writing the Torah to encompass the oral within the written parts in a union of the two bore no consequences for the liturgical life of the community.

Educationally, institutionally, and liturgically, therefore, Sifra's author-ship in no way competed with the Bavli's. They made all the wrong choices, as to the manner in which they proposed to unite the two Torahs. They took the route of penetrating into the deep structures of thought; they proposed to rewrite the written Torah by restating within its lines many of the pertinent rules of the oral Torah; they ignored the requirements of the everyday liturgical world; they paid great respect to, but also placed too heavy demands upon, the audience for their book. They failed because they ought to have failed. But as intellectuals, they succeeded beyond imagining.

But the success was merely intellectual – theological, in particular – and not educational, institutional or liturgical. That is why when the people of the Torah, Israel, the Jewish people, for the next fifteen hundred years, wished to approach the Mishnah, it was through the reading of the Bavli. That is why when that same people wished to address Scripture, it was through the reading of the Bavli. All the other components of the canon, while authentic and authoritative too, stood in line, from second place backward, behind the primary reading of the Bavli. It is no accident that authentic avatars of the classical literature of Judaism even today learn Scripture through the Bavli's citations of verses of Scripture just as much as, commonly, they learn the Mishnah and assuredly interpret it exactly as the Bavli presents it.

V. Uniting the Dual Torah: The Torah Adumbrating the Mind of God

If Sifra had taken first place in the curriculum of Judaism, its representa-tion of the written Torah and the oral Torah all together and all at once would have opened a different path. For it is one thing to absorb the Torah, oral and written, and it is quite another to join in the processes of thought, the right way of thinking, that sustain the Torah. The authorship of Sifra proposed to regain access to the modes of thought that guided the formation of the Torah, oral and written alike: comparison and contrast in this way, not in that, identification of categories in one manner, not in another. Since those were the modes of thought that, in our authorship's conception, dictated the structure of intellect upon which the Torah, the united Torah, rested, a simple conclusion is the sole possible one. Now to answer the question of the basis on which our authorship represented itself as participants in, and interlocutors of, The Torah, such that they were prepared to re-present, that is to say, simply rewrite (and, therefore, themselves write) The Torah.

In their analysis of the deepest structures of intellect of the Torah, the authorship of Sifra was supposed to enter into the mind of God, showing how God's mind worked when God formed the Torah, written and oral alike. And there, in the intellect of God, in their judgment humanity gained access to the only means of uniting the Torah, because that is where the Torah originated. But in discerning how God's mind worked, the intellectuals who created Sifra claimed for themselves a place in that very process of thought that had given birth to The Torah. Our authorship could rewrite the Torah because, knowing how The Torah originally was written, they too could write (though not reveal) The Torah.

Notes

[1] I did not trouble to adduce in evidence all examples of polythetic taxonomy presented by the framers of the Scripture, since, in the nature of the argument of this book, a single instance sufficed to raise the question which I wish to confront.

[2] In the companion volume, *Sifra in Context,* I shall work out the detailed comparisons that validate this statement.

The Distinctive Character of Sifra Among Midrash Compilations

The labor of classification through analysis of shared and unique qualities further tells us in what ways a writing replicates traits of aesthetics (e.g., rhetoric), philosophy (e.g., logic), and even theology (e.g., topical program) with other writings of its larger genus. What we will see is the singular character of Sifra when compared with other Midrash compilations of its time and place, and that fact places into perspective the results set forth in the preceding study. Specifically, we will see that the authorship of Sifra stands as a distinct group and sets forth a well-crafted position of its own. It shares with other writings some of its traits of rhetoric, logic, or topic, but with them never all. Therefore, my representation of a document that addresses issues and takes a position is sustained by the comparison of that document with others, both as to the indicative traits of the base document, and also as to the general traits characteristic of them all.

I undertake two distinct exercises of comparison, one for one species of writings in the canon of the dual Torah, one for the other. One species, universally defined by all parties to study, is that of "halakhic Midrashim," by which is meant Midrash compilations of Midrash exegeses of legal passages of the Pentateuch. These are generally held to be Sifra and the two Sifrés, the one to Numbers, the other to Deuteronomy, as well as the Mekhilta attributed to R. Ishmael.[1] There are sufficient points in common among Sifra and the two Sifrés to justify deeming all three documents a single species, allowing us to compare and contrast them. The clear and self-evident points in common are the aesthetic and the philosophical, that is, rhetorical and logical conventions that operate among all three writings. The second species into which our document falls is the one defined by the book of Leviticus, hence commentaries (broadly defined) to that book. There is another important compilation of Midrash exegeses, Leviticus Rabbah, that permits us to compare and contrast the

193

topical and propositional program (if any) of our document to those of another document of the same species: Leviticus commentary. In that context, further, I draw upon two other documents that fall for other reasons into the same species as Leviticus Rabbah, which are Genesis Rabbah and Pesiqta deRab Kahana. All three form one taxon, Sifra a different taxon, when we compare the traits of program and even topic. At the end I ask about the ways in which Sifra is like, and unlike, other documents and suggest why I find it singular among them all.

Forms and Rhetoric: The rhetorical plan of Sifra leads us to recognize that the exegetes wished to show their results through details, masses of details, and, like the rigorous philosophers that they were, they furthermore argued essentially through an inductive procedure, amassing evidence that in its accumulation made the point at hand. The syllogism I have identified about the priority of the revelation of the written Torah in the search for truth is no where expressed in so many words, because the philosopher-exegetes of the rabbinic world preferred to address an implicit syllogism and to pursue or to test the syllogism solely in a sequence of experiments of a small scale. Sifra's authorship, therefore, finds in the Mishnah and Tosefta a sizable laboratory for the testing of propositions. We have, then, to ask, at what points do Sifra and Mishnah and Tosefta share a common agenda of interests, and at what points does one compilation introduce problems, themes, or questions unknown to the other? The answer to these questions is that Sifra and Mishnah and Tosefta form two large concentric circles, sharing a considerable area in common. Sifra, however, exhibits interests peculiar to itself. On the criterion of common themes and interests, Mishnah and Tosefta and Sifra exhibit a remarkable unity. If I had to compare the rhetorical program of Sifra's authorship with that of their counterparts in our document, I should say that the latter group has taken over and vastly expanded the program selected by the former. More to the point, the two documents intersect, but, for Sifré to Deuteronomy, the rhetorical intersection covers only a small segment of the whole plan governing the formulation of the document. In that sense, we have to say that our authorship has made choices and has not simply repeated a restricted program available to all rabbinic authorships and utilized at random by each.

A simple formal program, consisting of three types of forms, served the entire document. An author of a pericope could make use of one or more of three forms but of no other forms at all. Since a sizable repertoire of other forms were utilized by other authorships, we may state with finality that our authorship made choices about the formal plan of its document. These choices corresponded to the authorship's polemical purpose in framing the document. What were these three forms? They were, as we recall, commentary, dialectical–analytical analysis, and citation form. It follows that Sifra's authorship planned to produce a commentary to the book of Leviticus, and that commentary would encompass as two major, though not ubiquitous, concerns: first, the demonstration that if we wish to classify things, we must follow the taxa dictated by Scripture rather than relying solely upon the traits of the things we wish to classify; and, second, the citation of passages of the Mishnah or the Tosefta in the setting of Scripture. As we saw in the shank of this book, the forms of the document admirably expressed the polemical purpose of the authorship at hand. What they wished to prove was that a taxonomy resting on the traits of things without reference to Scripture's classifications cannot serve. They further wished to restate the oral Torah in the setting of the written Torah. And, finally, they wished to accomplish the whole by rewriting the written Torah. The dialectical form accomplished the first purpose, the citation form the second, and the commentary form the third. Let us now compare our document's formal program and plan with those of other documents.

Having shown the presence of a restricted range of choices, I still have not proved that this particular authorship made choices distinctive to itself. I have demonstrated only that, in a given rabbinic writing, a fair amount of formalization or patterning of discourse has characterized the expression at hand. That does not delineate the limits of this particular document and establish a prima facie case, on superficial, rhetorical grounds, that I deal with a systematic statement of an authorship. To the contrary, we may conceive that the formal patterns before us were general to rabbinic writings, not particular to the authorship of a single document (or closely aligned group of documents). Accordingly, a brief set of comparisons is now required, to show that this authorship not only conformed to the requirement that all speech be public and formal, not private and idiosyncratic in form, but also made its own choices as to the particular formalized modes of rhetoric that that authorship would utilize. For that purpose, only a complete survey of the results of the form analysis of all rabbinic writings suffices. Having undertaken form analysis of most of the canonical documents of the Judaism of the dual Torah, I should not find onerous such a systematic and complete survey. Though the results are in hand, readers may concur that a brief overview suffices. And for a preliminary result, a comparison with the results of my studies of other documents' formal characteristics will validate the simple claim at hand, that in Sifra, as in every other rabbinic compilation of Midrash exegeses I have studied, we deal with a consensual authorship, not merely with a random sample of the kinds of formalized writings that occur here, there, and everywhere in the rabbinic canon. To state matters again, what we see is not merely how people happened to say things, but choices people made in how they wished to say things: this, not that.

Let me begin with a catalogue of the forms of Sifré to Numbers. The rhetorical program of Sifré to Numbers is substantially larger than that of the authorship of Sifra, and it is also different from one guiding the authorship of Sifré to Deuteronomy.

1. Extrinsic Exegetical Form:

The form consists of the citation of an opening verse, followed by an issue stated in terms extrinsic to the cited verse. That is to say, no word or phrase of the base verse (that is, the cited verse at the beginning) attracts comment. Rather a general rule of exegesis is invoked. C then introduces a broad range of items not at all subject to attention in the verse at hand. The formal traits consist of: (1) citation of a base verse from Numbers, (2) a generalization ignoring clauses or words in the base verse, and (3) a further observation without clear interest in the verse at hand. But the whole is linked to the theme of the base verse – and to that alone. So an extrinsic exegetical program comes to bear. We will call this the extrinsic exegetical form. I cannot find a counterpart in our document among the rhetorical forms I have identified. But those propositional compositions that merely cite, in a context established by a generalization, a verse of Deuteronomy do run parallel to what, in Sifré to Numbers, I called the syllogistic argument on the meaning of the words or phrases, in which the base verse of Numbers occurs as one among a set of diverse items. I do not find Sifra's commentary form to constitute a counterpart, since the ordinary purpose of commentary form in Sifra is not to develop a generalization. It is rather to identify the sense of a passage by asking what is included or excluded within the rule of the passage.

2. Intrinsic Exegetical Form:

The verse itself is clarified. In the first instance, the exegesis derives from the contrast with another verse that makes the same point. But the formal trait, the focus on the base verse and not on a broader issue, should not be missed. We may call this an intrinsic exegetical form, in that the focus of exegesis is on the verse, which is cited and carefully spelled out. We will know that we have it when the base verse is cited, clause by clause, or in other ways, and then given an ample dose of attention. Here we do have an exact formal counterpart, a rhetorical pattern shared by the authorships of all three documents – Sifra and the two Sifrés. It is the smallest, and also the most common, building block of formal expression I can identify in the diverse compilations of scriptural exegesis. It consists of a verse plus a simple declarative sentence that states the meaning.

Dialectical exegesis pointed toward proving the fallacy of logic uncontrolled by exegesis of Scripture that is common in Sifra and in Sifré to

Numbers. The formal indicator is the presence of the question, in one of several versions: but is it not a matter of logic? That is the unfailing formal indicator. From that clause we invariably move on to a set of arguments of a highly formalized character on taxonomic classification: what is like, or unlike? The exegesis of the verse at hand plays no substantial role, beyond its initial introduction. What is critical is the issue of the reliability of logic. The base verse before us contributes virtually nothing and in no way serves as the foundation for the composition at hand. Formally, items in this pattern can readily have found a comfortable home in the other Sifré, our Sifré, as much as in Sifra. So too the variation, which gives us a citation of the verse plus a law in prior writing (Mishnah, Tosefta) that the verse is supposed to sustain, is common among all three writings. The formal traits require (1) citation of a verse, with or without comment, followed by (2) verbatim citation of a passage of the Mishnah or the Tosefta. Sifré to Deuteronomy presents a far more propositional composition than either Sifra or Sifré to Numbers. Our classification of the patterns of rhetoric in that document, therefore, draws attention to the manner in which propositions are set forth, a classification that, in general, cannot serve in Sifra at all. I may state very simply the results of already published research. Nine recurrent patterns prove dominant in Sifré to Deuteronomy. We distinguish among them by the presence of propositions, explicit, and then implicit, and how these are argued or proved:

1. Propositions Stated Explicitly and Argued Philosophically (By Appeal to Probative Facts)
    1. The Proposition and its Syllogistic Argument
    2. The Proposition Based on the Classification of Probative Facts
    3. The Proposition Based on the Recurrent Opinions of Sages
    4. The Narrative and its Illustrated Proposition: Parable
    5. Narrative and its Illustrated Proposition: Scriptural Story
2. Propositions Stated Implicitly but Argued Philosophically (As Above)
    6. The (Implicit) Proposition Based on Facts Derived from Exegesis
    7. The Priority of Exegesis and the Limitations of Logic
3. Facts That Do Not Yield Propositions Beyond Themselves
    8. Exegetical Form with No Implicit Proposition. This is one form with a clear counterpart in Sifra.
4. Facts That Do Not Yield Propositions Particular to the Case in Hand
    9. Dialectical Exegesis with No Implicit Proposition Pertinent to the Case at Hand but with Bearing on Large-Scale Structural Issues. This form is the same as our dialectical-exegetical one.

Let me now review the catalogue just provided and spell out the formal traits of the patterns I have identified.

I. Propositions Stated Explicitly and Argued Philosophically

1. The Proposition and its Syllogistic Argument:

This form is made up of simple sentences that, in one way or another, set forth propositions and demonstrate them by amassing probative facts (e.g., examples). The patterning of the individual sentences of course varies. But the large scale rhetoric, involving the presentation of a proposition, in general terms, and then the amassing of probative facts (however the sentences are worded), is essentially uniform. What we have are two or more sentences formed into a proposition and an argument, by contrast to those that are essentially single sentences, rather than components of a more sustained discourse. These items ordinarily deal with matters of proper conduct or right action, hence *halakhic* issues. There is a two-layer discourse in them, since, at the superficial level, they yield only a detail of a law, that is, thus and so is the rule here; but at the deep layer of thought, they demonstrate a prevailing and global proposition, that applies – it is implied – throughout, and not only to a single case. Overall, rhetorical analysis draws our attention to modes of stating a middle level proposition, affecting a variety of verses and their cases, in the present list. Then we move onward, to the low level proposition, that pertains only to a single case, and, finally, we turn to a global proposition, that affects a broad variety of cases, left discrete, but homogenizes them. These distinctions are meant to explain the classification system represented here. The absence of a counterpart in Sifra hardly requires proof.

2. The Proposition Based on the Classification of Probative Facts:

The prevailing pattern here is not vastly changed. This is different from the foregoing only in a minor matter. We will propose to prove a proposition (e.g., the meaning of a word) by classifying facts that point toward that proposition. In the foregoing, the work of proof is accomplished through listing proofs not made up of diverse facts. The difference between the one and the other is hardly considerable, but we can successfully differentiate among the formal patterns through the stated criterion. However, one may reasonably argue that this catalogue and the foregoing list essentially the same formal patterns of language or argument. In many of these instances, we have a complex development of a simple exegesis. It is by way of this complexity – the repeated use of a simple pattern – that the propositional form(s) reach full exposure. Sifra's authorship has no use for such a pattern.

3. The Proposition Based on the Recurrent Opinions of Sages:

This is another variation, in that the nature of the evidence shifts, and, it follows, also the patterning of language. Here we will have the attributive constantly present (e.g., X says), which forms an important rhetorical indicator. We may say flatly that this form is not characteristic of our authorship and accomplishes none of their goals. It is a commonplace in the Mishnah, inclusive of tractate Avot, and in the Tosefta; large-scale compositions in the Yerushalmi and the Bavli follow the same pattern; and other large-scale compositions will be drawn together because a sequence of simple declarative sentences on diverse topics, whether or not related in theme, bears the same attributive. The omission of this pattern here, therefore, is noteworthy and constitutes a decision for one pattern and against another. I know of no material equivalent in Sifra.

4–5. The Narrative and its Illustrated Proposition: The Scriptural Story. Also: The Parable as Illustration of an Established Proposition:

The construction in which a proposition is established and then illustrated in a narrative, whether parable, scriptural story, or other kind of narrative, is treated in a single rubric. The formal–structural uniformity justifies doing so. We may find varieties of patterns of sentences (e.g., parables as against stories). But the narrative is always marked by either, "he said to him . . . he said to him . . .," for the story, or counterpart indications of a select pattern of forming and arranging sentences, for the parable.[2] The authorship of Sifré Deuteronomy has resorted to a very limited repertoire of patterns of language, and "narrative," a gross and hardly refined, classification, suffices. For narratives, viewed as an encompassing formal category, do not play a large role in defining (therefore differentiating) the rhetorical-logical program of our authorship. Sifra's authorship scarcely presents stories of this kind.

II. Propositions Stated Implicitly but Argued Philosophically

6–7 Implicit Propositions:

These items involve lists of facts, but lack that clear statement of the proposition that the facts establish. What we have here are complexes of tightly joined declarative sentences, many of them (in the nature of things) in that atom pattern, "commentary form," but all of them joined into a much larger set of (often) highly formalized statements. Hence I characterize this form as an implicit proposition based on facts derived from exegesis. For obvious reasons, there is no counterpart in Sifra.

III. Facts That Do Not Yield Propositions Beyond Themselves

8. Exegetical Form with No Implicit Proposition

This simple exegetical form presents a single fact, a discrete sentence, left without further development and without association or affinity with surrounding statements – once more, "commentary form." The form is as defined: clause + phrase. In Sifra this is the single most common pattern, as we saw. But in Sifré to Deuteronomy that same form in propositional compositions rarely occurs without development. Indeed, if I had to specify the one fundamental difference between nonpropositional exegetical form (such as we find in Sifra and Sifré to Numbers and, in some measure, in Sifré to Deuteronomy) and all other forms, it is the simplicity of the one as against the complexity of the other. Or, to state matters more bluntly, excluding narrative, the sole rhetorical building block of any consequence in Sifra, Sifré to Numbers, and Sifré to Deuteronomy is the simple exegetical one, consisting of *clause + phrase = sentence.*

As a result, the differences from one document to the other have to be specified. What differentiates Sifra and Sifré to Numbers from Sifré to Deuteronomy? In the last-named document, what happens is that all other forms develop the simple atom into a complex molecule, but the "exegetical form with no implicit proposition" remains at the atomic level (if not an even smaller particle than the atom) and never gains the molecular one. These, therefore, constitute entirely comprehensible sense units, that is, on their own, simple sentences, never formed into paragraphs, and define the lowest rhetorical form of our document. The other rhetorical forms build these simple sense units or sentences into something more complex. That fact of rhetoric accounts, also, for our having – willy-nilly – to appeal to consideration of logical cogency in our analysis of rhetoric and form.

IV. Facts That Do Not Yield Propositions Particular to the Case at Hand

9. Dialectical Exegesis with No Implicit Proposition Pertinent to the Case at Hand but with Bearing on Large-Scale Structural Issues

Here we deal with the same pattern that, in Sifra, we have called dialectical–exegetical form. The purpose of the form in Sifra is limited to the two purposes of, first, exclusionary–inclusionary inquiry, and, second, the critique of nonscripturally based taxonomy, whereas in Sifré to Deuteronomy a variety of propositions will be served. This form is made up of a series of closely joined thought units or sentences. Hence they present us with two or more sentences that constitute joined, propositional paragraphs. But their rhetorical traits are so much more particular, and their net effect so much more distinctive, that I treat them as a quite distinct rhetorical phenomenon. Moreover, these are the most patterned, the most formed, of all formal compositions at hand. They require sustained exposition of a proposition plus probative facts. They all make two points, as I have already pointed out, one at the surface, the other through the deep structure. Strictly speaking, as sustained and complex forms, all of these items conform to the fundamental definition of a rhetorical form, language that coheres to a single pattern – and the pattern is one of both rhetoric and logic.

Two such patterns are, first, the systematic analytical exercise of restricting or extending the application of a discrete rule, ordinarily signified through stereotypic language; second, the demonstration that logic without revelation in the form of a scriptural formulation and exegesis produces unreliable results. There are other recurrent patterns of complex linguistic formation matched by sustained thought that conform to other indicative traits yielded by these two distinct ones. The form invariably involves either the exercise of generalization through extension or restriction of the rule to the case given in Scripture, or the demonstration that reason unaided by Scripture is not reliable. The formal traits are fairly uniform, even though the intent – the upshot of the dialectical exegesis – varies from instance to instance. Very often these amplifications leave the base verse far behind, since they follow a program of their own, to which the base verse and its information is at best contributory. One of the ways in which this formalization of language differs from the foregoing is that the exegesis that is simple in form always is closely tied to the base verse, whereas the one that pursues greater structural issues frequently connects only loosely to the base verse. Another persistent inquiry, external to any given verse and yielding, in concrete terms, no general rule at all, asks how to harmonize two verses, the information of which seems to conflict. The result is a general proposition that verses are to be drawn into alignment with one another. Here, however, we are entirely at home. Sifra and Sifré to Deuteronomy have in common the usage of the dialectical–exegetical form for much of the same purposes. On the other hand, Sifra bears affinities of patterning of language with both Sifrés, but also differs in noteworthy ways from each of them. The three have traits in common and also traits particular to themselves. In form–analytical terms they form three species of a single genus, as comparisons with the Rabbah compilations will now show us.

To show that the two Sifrés together with Sifra form three species of one genus of form, we turn to a counterpart set of documents, which have their own shared preferences. We begin with Genesis Rabbah. The atom of formal composition in Genesis Rabbah is what I call the ex-

egetical form. But how it is used in the construction of molecules –
sustained propositional thought – differentiates one document from the
next.

I find three formal patterns in Genesis Rabbah. One juxtaposes a given
verse of the book of Genesis with a verse chosen from some other
biblical writing; the second focuses upon a verse of the book of Genesis,
read by itself; the third makes use of a verse of the book of Genesis in
establishing a proposition of a syllogistic character. There is no counterpart to any of this in Sifra, because Sifra's authorship deals with verses in
Leviticus and rarely invokes verses from other books, except in the
context of demonstrating propositions. To state matters differently, the
citation of a verse from some book other than Leviticus never forms part
of the established formal or structural pattern of a pericope of Sifra. But it
is constant in the Rabbah compilations.

All three formal patterns aim at conveying propositions, and the formal
traits dictate whether the topic at hand is (**I**) the interplay of the base
verse with some other verse, (**II**) the meaning of the base verse, or (**III**)
the proof of a proposition abstracted from the context established by the
base verse (that is, the book of Genesis) in particular. Our formal criterion for differentiating the first two forms is the placement of a verse
(e.g., at the beginning or at the end of a passage). The criterion for
identifying form **III** is no more subjective, since anyone can tell that
verses derive from a variety of books of Scripture and equally serve as
proof for a proposition distinct from them all. Form **I** has absolutely no
counterpart in the formal repertoire of Sifré to Deuteronomy. Form **II**
has corresponding forms, and so does form **III**. Therefore, what differentiates the formal repertoire of Genesis Rabbah from that of Sifré to
Deuteronomy is clear; one authorship has made use of a form the other
authorship has not found useful. Let me briefly describe the forms to
which I have alluded, for a closer look will now show that forms **I** and **II**
have no substantial equivalent in our document, though form **III** does.

Form **I**: When a verse from a biblical book other than Genesis occurs at
the beginning of the passage, a single formal pattern follows: exposition
of that other verse, which I have called the intersecting verse, followed
by juxtaposition of the intersecting verse with a verse of the book of
Genesis.

I. The Intersecting-Verse/Base-Verse Form
    1. Attribution + joining language + intersecting verse.
    2. Exposition of the intersecting verse.
    3. Reciprocal exposition of the base verse and the intersecting
        verse.

Form **II**: When a verse from the book of Genesis occurs at the beginning of the passage, then the focus of discourse will rest upon the exposition of that verse alone. The difference from Sifra is self-evident.

II.   Exegesis of a Verse of Scripture
    A.   Citation of the base verse (which will always be a verse chosen from the larger passage subject to interpretation, not a verse chosen from some other book of the Scripture).
    B.   Comment of a given rabbi. The comment is formulated in diverse ways.
    C.   Secondary, miscellaneous materials will be appended. Sifra exhibits no counterpart.

Form **III**: When a given syllogism comes to expression at the beginning of a passage, followed by a broad range of verses, made up ordinarily as a list exhibiting fixed syntactic preferences, then the focus of discourse will require proof of the syllogism, not exposition of the verses cited in evidence for the facticity of that syllogism.

III.   Syllogistic Composition
    A.   Statement of a syllogism or proposition.
    B.   Verses of Scripture that prove or illustrate that syllogism listed in a catalogue of relevant evidence.
    C.   Secondary expansion: miscellanies (e.g. stories) on the syllogism, providing further illustration.

We have counterparts or parallels to this form, commonly in Sifré to Deuteronomy, only very rarely in Sifra. The formal requirement invariably is the composition of a list, a repertoire of facts ordinarily formulated in a single syntactic pattern. A syllogistic composition makes a point autonomous of the verse at hand. In this type of composition, the point of interest is not in the exposition of a verse but the proposition that is subject to demonstration, the proofs, of course, deriving from various verses of Scripture.

Leviticus Rabbah is made up of thirty-seven *parashiyyot*, and each *parashah* is comprised of from as few as five to as many as fifteen subdivisions. These subdivisions in the main form cogent statements. Some of the *pisqaot* of Sifré to Deuteronomy form cogent demonstrations of a single proposition; most do not. A taxonomy of units of discourse of Leviticus Rabbah proves congruent to that of Genesis Rabbah. The first (form **I**) is familiar: (1) a verse of the book of Leviticus will be followed by (2) a verse from some other book of the Hebrew

Scriptures. The latter (2) will then be subjected to extensive discussion.
But, in the end, the exposition of the intersecting verse will shed some
light, in some way, upon (1) the base verse cited at the outset. The
second form (form **II**) is the exegetical one, in which a verse of Leviticus
is cited and then explained. The sustained analysis and amplification
makes no reference to an intersecting verse but to numerous proof texts,
or to no proof texts at all. The third form (form **III**) is simply the citation
of a verse of the book of Leviticus followed by an exegetical comment,
corresponding to form **II** in Genesis Rabbah. Form **IV** represents a
miscellany, no formal traits at all being discernible.

In the intersecting-verse/base-verse pattern we have an intersecting
verse, then the base verse, then interpretation of the latter in terms of the
form. Therefore, the base verse is read in light of the intersecting verse,
which itself is not unpacked. In form **II**, the verse by verse exegetical
construction, the base verse is cited and then subjected to systematic
amplification in some way or other. The form is characterized by the
preliminary citation of the base verse (not much of a formalization of
syntax or composition, to be sure). It corresponds, overall, to the exegetical form of Sifré to Deuteronomy. I find in Leviticus Rabbah no
sustained formal counterpart to the methodical–analytical syntactic pattern of Sifré to Deuteronomy, and, it follows, none whatsoever to the
formal preferences of the authorship of Sifra.

Another important difference between the rhetorical programs of
Leviticus Rabbah and Sifré to Deuteronomy and Sifra is that the former
follows a rigid pattern in ordering its rhetorical types, always placing at
the head of a sustained unit of thought (corresponding to our *pisqa*) the
intersecting-verse/base-verse form, following with its other forms. There
is in Sifré to Deuteronomy simply no single form that always stands at the
head of a sustained exposition of a verse or set of verses. That is to say,
the framer of a passage intended for use in Leviticus Rabbah ordinarily
began with a base-verse/intersecting-verse construction. In addition, he
very commonly proceeded with an intersecting-verse/base-verse construction (a distinction important in my analysis of Leviticus Rabbah).
These would correspond to both sorts of form **I** in Genesis Rabbah. As a
result, Leviticus Rabbah strictly follows a clear program in laying out
types of forms or units of discourse, nearly always preferring to place
form **I** prior to form **II**, and so on down. Does this careful ordering of
types of forms represent a clear choice? It can be shown that it does,
simply by pointing out a contrary fact.

The organizers of Genesis Rabbah, by contrast, did not so con-
scientiously follow a similar program. What would the authorities who
ordered Leviticus Rabbah choose for the secondary amplification of their
composition? First, as is clear, the framer would take a composition in

form I. Then he would provide such exegeses of pertinent verses of Leviticus as he had in hand. He would conclude either with form III (parallel in Genesis Rabbah: form II) or form IV constructions, somewhat more commonly the latter than the former. When we observe that Genesis Rabbah does not appear so carefully arranged in the order of types of forms of units of discourse, that judgment now appears to rest upon the comparisons of two documents, Leviticus Rabbah and Genesis Rabbah. It no longer rests upon foundations of impressions and rough and ready guesswork. Therefore, Leviticus Rabbah consists of two main forms of units of discourse; first, in position, expositions of how verses of the book of Leviticus relate to verses of other books of the Hebrew bible; second, in position, exposition of verses of the book of Leviticus viewed on their own, and, varying in position but very often concluding a construction of miscellaneous materials. We have already noted the indifference of Sifra's authorship to the order of types of forms.

By focusing upon the gross and blatant traits of formalization, examining a rough and ready mixture of rhetorical and logical traits, I have specified what I believe at the level of large-scale composition and formation of sustained units of thought, beyond the level of discrete sentences, the specific options were. This brings us back to our original question, which we may answer now succinctly. Does a prevailing, miscellaneous rhetorical repertoire circulate more or less promiscuously among the authorships of diverse documents? In that case, the formal plan of our document (as of all the others) is random and not indicative. Or can we show that one authorship has made choices different from those affected by another authorship? In that case, the formal plan of our document also bespeaks deliberation. The answer is that Sifra's authorship appeals to three forms: simple, complex, and Mishnaic. In the simple form, with its many variations, we always have a citation of a passage of the book of Leviticus followed by amplification. In the complex form we have a sustained demonstration concerning the requirements of taxonomy. In citation form we have a joining of a passage from Mishnah or Tosefta to Scripture. And that covers, even in gross definition, the entire formal program of Sifra.

So too various other documents' authorships make choices as to form and even as to the ordering of forms and the cogency of their sustained units of thought. Some documents choose one set of forms and order them quite deliberately, making a single point in a given sustained unit of thought. Others choose other forms and do not make a single point in a sustained unit of thought (e.g., treatment of a single theme or set of verses). Among the authorships that have chosen a limited repertoire of forms and ordered types of forms with great care so as to establish a single, encompassing proposition (not merely so as to discuss from various viewpoints a shared theme) are those of Leviticus Rabbah and Pesiqta deRab Kahana. Other authorships – that of Sifré to Deuteronomy, for instance – chose a set of forms that differed, in part if not entirely, from the choices made by the authorships of Leviticus Rabbah and Pesiqta deRab Kahana, not treated here, and that authorship has also taken no interest in the order of the types of forms that they have chosen. Furthermore, the compositors of Sifré to Deuteronomy had no large-scale propositional program in mind in the composition of sustained units of thought, which, in scale, are substantially smaller than those in Leviticus Rabbah and Pesiqta deRab Kahana. One may both group Sifra and the two Sifrés in accord with indicative traits, differentiating all three from Genesis Rabbah, Leviticus Rabbah, and Pesiqta deRab Kahana, and, moreover, differentiate Sifra and the two Sifrés from one another. But to do so would carry us far afield and is not required for the important, but simple, proposition at hand.

We now may treat as an established fact the proposition that a set of highly restricted repertoires of formal possibilities confronted the writers of materials now collected in the diverse Midrash compilations. Set side by side, as I have laid matters out, each of the Misrash compilations may be distinguished from all the others on purely rhetorical (formal) grounds. The highly formalized character of the rhetoric in any given document shows us a convention of that particular authorship within the canon of the dual Torah, whereas the equally singular definition of the formal program paramount in any given document tells us that each authorship made its own choices. They chose some and neglected others. A long list of formal possibilities not utilized in Sifra but extensively employed in other documents could easily emerge from large-scale comparisons of the forms of diverse writings of the canon of the Judaism of the dual Torah.

Logic

Whether we explore the extrinsic traits of formal expression or the most profound layers of intelligible discourse and coherent thought that hold sentences together and form of them all propositions or presentations that can be understood, we produce a single result. It is that each document's authorship does make choices. Choosing modes of cogent discourse and coherent thought involves a repertoire that is exceedingly limited. Options in rhetoric by contrast prove quite diverse. But the work of comparison and contrast in both sorts of choices proves entirely feasible. With regard to both rhetoric and logic, we are required to compare fixed and external traits. There is no appeal to subjective taste and judgment.

The operative logics in Sifra are mainly propositional and inclusive of propositional, teleological, and methodical–analytical compositions. An authorship intending a commentary will have found paramount use for the logic of fixed association. However, that logic clearly served only a modest purpose in the context of the document as a whole. To review the established results: First, our authorship developed a tripartite program. It wished to demonstrate the limitations of the logic of hierarchical classification, such as predominates in the Mishnah. Second, it proposed to restate the Mishnah within the context of Scripture, that is, to rewrite the written Torah to make a place for the oral Torah. This is worked out in the logic of propositional discourse. Third, it wished in this rewriting to re-present the whole Torah as a cogent and unified document. Through the logic of fixed association it, in fact, did re-present the Torah. The three logics correspond, in their setting within the inner structure of cogent discourse, to the three paramount purposes to which our authorship devoted Sifra.

The four logics catalogued for Sifra originated in my study of Sifré to Deuteronomy.[3] The logic that links one sentence to the next by focusing on a proposition to be proved appeals for connection to the principles of philosophical syllogism. I included in this catalogue the passages that wish to turn a detail of a case into a general rule, in which the generalization is not of a methodical character but important for a particular detail of law. In Sifré to Deuteronomy I count 690 individual units of thought in which two or more sentences are joined together by a connection defined through a proposition. There may be more than that number, but I do not believe any count will yield less.

I find remarkably slight resort to narratives in legal contexts. But that is only a general impression. I count 61 narratives of various kinds, or, more accurately, units of discourse that find cogency in narrative rather than in proposition. My best sense is that it was not through narrative that the bulk of the units of completed thought, resting on making connections between two or more sentences, was composed. Narrative logic of connection is treated as null in some writings, such as The Fathers, while it does predominate in other compositions, such as The Fathers According to Rabbi Nathan.

Fixed-associative discourse in Sifré to Deuteronomy yields 159 entries in this catalogue. Compared to the whole, it is not a sizable proportion. Most documents establish connections between two sentences or among three or more sentences not through appeal to fixed-associative cogency, but through resort to propositional logic of one kind or another (inclusive of methodical analysis).[4] Cogent discourse attained through fixed-analytical method in Sifré to Deuteronomy produces 232 entries. But that understates the proportion, to the whole, of major units of discourse that hold together through methodical analytical logic. The prevailing logic of Sifré to Deuteronomy is not exegetical but propositional. Most units of cogent discourse in Sifré to Deuteronomy appear for cogency to propositions, not to fixed associations, such as characterize commentaries and other compilations of exegeses of verses of Scripture. Let us begin with a rough statistical summary comparing Sifra's to Sifré to Deuteronomy's choices among the four logics at hand.

Sifra:

Type of Logic	Number of entries	Percentage of the whole
Propositional	73	30.4%
Teleological	1	0.4%
Fixed Associative	43	17.9%
Methodical Analytical	123	51 %
	240	99.7%

Sifré to Deuteronomy:

Type of Logic	Number of Units	Percentage of the whole
Fixed-Associative	159	13.9%
Propositional	690	60.4%
Narrative	61	5.3%
Methodical Analytical	232	20.3%
	1142	99.9%

In Sifré to Deuteronomy, of the propositional units of cogent discourse, 60.4% in fact constitute propositional discourse, 5.3% find cogency in narrative, and 20.3% in the methodical–analytical mode. Since that mode presents not one but two propositions, we find ourselves on firm ground in maintaining that the logic of Sifré to Deuteronomy is a logic not of exegesis but of sustained proposition of one kind of another. Our document's authorship links one sentence to another by appeal to connections of proposition, not mere theme, and only occasionally asks the structure of a verse or sequence of verses to sustain the intelligible joining or two or more sentences into a coherent and meaningful statement.

The differences between Sifra and Sifré to Deuteronomy are these:

1. Propositional logic: Sifré to Deuteronomy contains two times the proportion of propositional compositions. We see in Chapter Four that Sifré to Deuteronomy is a highly propositional compilation, whereas Sifra is not.

2. Teleological logic: Sifré to Deuteronomy contains thirteen times the proportion of narrative compositions than does Sifra. Since teleological logic is propositional in its foundation, that disproportion is readily understood.

3. Fixed-associative logic: The two documents make use of approximately the same proportions of this mode of stringing sentences or facts togethers, 17.9% against 13.9%, a differential of 1.2 times the proportion in Sifra over Sifré to Numbers. That does not seem to me a significant difference, given the rough and ready mode of classification employed at this stage in the work.

4. Methodical-analytical logic: Sifra's authorship presents *two and a half* times the proportion of completed units of thought held together by the logic of systematic methodical analysis than does that of Sifré to Deuteronomy. The message of Sifra depends upon repetition of a single highly abstract proposition expressed in concrete terms. Hence the repetition of the same inquiry over a sizable number of diverse entries makes the point Sifra's authorship wishes to make. Sifré to Deuteronomy makes its points as propositions, not as repeated demonstrations of fundamental attributes of thought, such as in the paramount medium of thought and expression of Sifra.

The striking difference, therefore, comes at the end. The authorship of Sifra has a very clear notion of precisely the question it wishes persistently to address and it follows that program through the majority of the pericopes of its document. These questions then form the distinctive trait of mind of Sifra in comparison to Sifré to Deuteronomy. The resort to teleological logic in both documents is negligible in proportion to the whole; the utilization of fixed-associative logic is pretty much in equal proportions. Sifré to Deuteronomy is characterized by an interest in propositional discourse, whereas in Sifra that mode of discourse is subsumed under the logic of fixed analysis. This underlies what is particular, in this context, to our authorship: It knows precisely what it wishes to ask to a majority of passages of the book of Leviticus, and that concerns not proposition but the correct mode of thought and analysis.

Do the rhetoric and logic of the two documents derive from the (supposed) purpose of the authorship of forming a commentary? Not at all. To the contrary, in general, the logic of Sifra and of Sifré to Deuteronomy is sustained, propositional, mostly philosophical, and not that of commentary. What holds things together for our authorships only a fifth of the time relies upon the verses at hand to impose order and cogency upon discourse. Both authorships ordinarily appeal to propositions to hold two or more sentences together. If, by definition, a commentary appeals for cogency to the text that the commentators propose to illuminate, then ours are documents that in no essential way fall into the classification of a commentary. The logic is not that of a commentary, and the formal repertoire shows strong preference for other than commentary form.

Like Sifré to Deuteronomy, Sifra is, in fact, a highly argumentative, profoundly crafted and cogent set of propositions. We may indeed speak of a message, a topical program. A commentary that in form appeals to a clause of a verse and a phrase of a sentence, and in logic holds things together through fixed associations, is not apt to set forth a coherent statement, for commentary makes statements about meanings of verses, but it does not make a set of cogent statements of its own. Nonetheless, in rhetoric and in logic, Sifra like Sifré to Deuteronomy takes shape in such a way as to yield a statement, or a set of cogent statements.

Topic

Does the remarkably cogent and propositional discourse paramount in our document mean to present a detailed program of doctrines, such as is the case in some other Midrash compilations, one that distinguishes this document from others? We ask what subject an authorship has chosen to discuss, and, further, what the propositions concerning that subject an authorship sets forth are. When we describe a document's topic and the problematic of the topic – the thing the authorship wants to know and say about that topic – we correlate the topical program with the rhetorical and logical traits of a piece of writing. Now that we know how our authorship has chosen among a repertoire of modes of expression and thought a distinctive manner of patterning language and a singular means of conducting cogent and intelligible discourse, the next question confronts us. In particular, this question concerns the correspondence between medium of expression and of thought and the message conveyed in one way and not in some other.

The comparison is best set forth through our pertinent example, the two compilations of Midrash exegesis organized around the book of Leviticus: Sifra and Leviticus Rabbah. When in the case of a Midrash compilation addressed to the book of Leviticus, we ask about the components of a topical program, we should like to know whether an authorship has focused upon the topics of that book or upon some other list of topics altogether. Specifically, the book of Leviticus concerns sacrifice and the cult, the sanctity of Israel and, in particular, its priestly caste, the distributive economics of Temple effected through the disposition of crops and land, and the like. Are these the principal foci of discussion? In addressing these topics, an author can introduce a wholly different program (e.g., allegorically reading one thing in terms of something else). Then the exposition of the topics of the book of Leviticus will enjoy only slight attention. A different topical program will attach itself to the book of Leviticus, from the range of subjects that the book covers. In the case of the book of Leviticus, a set of historical questions of a salvific character can take the place of the inquiry into cultic questions concerning sanctification with which the priestly writers originally dealt. That example may not be restated in terms pertinent to a variety of documents. In more general terms an authorship may follow the topical program of the biblical writing on which it chooses to comment, or it may well treat that program as a pretext for discourse on entirely other matters. I define the two broad questions with which we now deal.

1.   Does the document at hand deliver a particular message and viewpoint or does it merely serve as a repository for diverse, received materials?
2.   Does the authorship deliver its message, its choices as to form and meaning, or merely transmit someone else's?

To broaden the question let us consider secondary questions. First, do we have a cogent statement or a mere scrapbook? Comparing one compilation to another yields the correct way of finding the answer. A document may serve solely as a convenient repository of prior sayings and stories, available materials that will have served equally well (or poorly) wherever they take up their final location. A composition may exhibit a viewpoint, a purpose of authorship distinctive to its framers or collectors and arrangers. Such a characteristic literary purpose would be so particular to one authorship that nearly everything at hand can be shown to have been (re)shaped for the ultimate purpose of the authorship at hand. These then are collectors and arrangers who demand the title of authors. Context and circumstance form the prior condition of inquiry, the result, in exegetical terms, the contingent one.

The framers of Leviticus Rabbah treat topics, not particular verses. That formal difference from Sifra underlies a more substantive one. The authorship of Leviticus Rabbah makes generalizations that are free standing and demonstrated through sustained presentation of appropriate evidence and even implicit argument. The writers or compilers express cogent propositions through extended compositions, rather than (at best) emoting episodic ideas. By contrast, in Sifra (as in Genesis Rabbah), things people wished to say were attached to predefined statements based on an existing text, constructed in accord with an organizing logic independent of the systematic expression of a single idea. That is to say, the sequence of verses of Leviticus, for Sifra, Genesis, and Genesis Rabbah, played a massive role in the larger-scale organization of each of the Midrash compilations and expression of its propositions. But in each of its thirty-seven chapters or *parashiyyot,* the authorship of Leviticus Rabbah so collected and arranged its materials as to present an abstract proposition. That proposition is not expressed only or mainly through episodic restatements, assigned, as I said, to an order established by a base text (whether Genesis or Leviticus or a Mishnah-tractate for that matter). Rather it emerges through a logic of its own. What is noteworthy in Leviticus Rabbah is the move from an essentially exegetical mode of logical discourse to a fundamentally philosophical mode. It is the shift from discourse framed around an established text to syllogistic argument organized around a proposed theorem or proposition. What changes, therefore, is the way in which cogent thought takes place, as people moved from discourse contingent on some prior principle of organization to discourse autonomous of a ready-made program inherited from an earlier paradigm.

Reading one thing in terms of something else, the builders of Leviticus Rabbah systematically adopted for themselves and to their own circumstance the reality of the Scripture, its history and doctrines. Specifically, they transformed that history from a sequence of unique events, leading from one place to some other, into the fixtures of enduring tableau of an ever-present mythic world. Persons who lived once now operate forever; events take on that circularity that allows them to happen again and again, every day. No longer was there one Moses, one David, one set of happenings of a distinctive and finished character. Now whatever happens, of which the thinkers propose to take account, must enter and be absorbed into that established and ubiquitous pattern and structure founded in Scripture. History is, therefore, transformed into social structure. It is not that biblical history repeats itself. Rather biblical history no longer constitutes history as a story of things that happened once, long ago, and as a prefiguring of some moment in the future. Biblical history becomes an account of things that happens every day.

That mode of thought explains why, in Leviticus Rabbah, Scripture as a whole does not dictate the order of discourse, let alone its character. In this document they chose in Leviticus itself a verse here, a phrase there. These then presented the pretext for propositional discourse commonly quite out of phase with the cited passage.[5] The verses that are quoted ordinarily shift from the meanings they convey to the implications they contain, speaking about something, anything, other than what they seem to be saying. This "as if" perspective brings renewal to Scripture, a fresh vision. The result of this vision was a reimagining of the social world envisioned by the authorship of the document, that is, the everday world of Israel in its Land in that difficult time. For what the sages now proposed was a reconstruction of existence along the lines of the ancient design of Scripture as they read it. From a sequence of one-time and linear events, everything that happened was turned into a repetition of known and already experienced paradigms. As a result, a mythic being itself was revindicated. The source and core of the myth, of course, derive from Scripture – Scripture reread, renewed, and reconstructed along with the society that revered Scripture.

If we now ask about important and recurring themes or topics in Leviticus Rabbah, there is one so commonplace that we should have to list the majority of paragraphs of discourse in order to provide a complete list of representations of it. It is the list of events in Israel's history, meaning, in this context, Israel's history solely in scriptural times, down through the return to Zion. The events of the generation of the flood, Sodom and Gomorrah, the patriarchs and the sojourn in Egypt, the exodus, the revelation of the Torah at Sinai, the golden calf, the Davidic monarchy and the building of the Temple, Sennacherib, Hezekiah, and the destruction of northern Israel, Nebuchadnezzar and the destruction of the Temple in 586 B.C., the life of Israel in Babylonian captivity, Daniel and his associates, Mordecai and Haman – these events recur again and again. They serve as paradigms of sin and atonement, steadfastness and divine intervention, and equivalent lessons. In fact, we find a fairly standard repertoire of scriptural heroes or villains, on the one side, and conventional lists of Israel's enemies and their actions and downfall, on the other. The boastful, for instance, include the generation of the flood, Sodom and Gomorrah, Pharaoh, Sisera, Sennacherib, Nebuchadnezzar, and the wicked empire (Rome) – contrasted to Israel, "despised and humble in this world." The four kingdoms recur again and again, always ending, of course, with Rome, with the repeated message that after Rome will come Israel. But Israel has to make this happen through its faith and submission to God's will. Lists of enemies ring the changes on Cain, the Sodomites, Pharaoh, Sennacherib, Nebuchadnezzar, and Haman.

Accordingly, the mode of thought brought to bear upon the theme of history remains exactly the same as before: list making, with data exhibiting similar taxonomic traits drawn together into lists based on common monothetic traits or definitions. These lists then, through the power of repetition, make a single point. They prove a social law of history. The catalogues of exemplary heroes and historical events also serve a further purpose. They provide a model of how contemporary events are to be absorbed into the biblical paradigm. Since biblical events exemplify recurrent happenings—sin and redemption, forgiveness and atonement—they lose their historical character. At the same time and in the same way, current events find a place within the ancient, but eternally present, paradigmatic scheme. As a result, no new historical events, other than exemplary episodes in lives of heroes, demand narration. This mode of dealing with biblical history and contemporary events produces two reciprocal effects. First is the mythicization of biblical stories, their removal from the framework of ongoing, unique patterns of history and sequences of events and their transformation into accounts of things that happen all the time. Second is that contemporary events also lose their specificity and enter the paradigmatic framework of established mythic existence. Therefore, the Scripture's myth happens every day, and every day produces reenactment of the Scripture's myth.

Now let us compare the topical program of Leviticus Rabbah with that of Genesis Rabbah. The mode of thought paramount in Leviticus Rabbah proves entirely congruent with the manner of reflection characteristic of Genesis Rabbah, and the propositions concerning history and the social laws of Israel are the same. But there are sufficient differences to show that each document is meant to bear its distinctive message. Where the two authorships differ is in detail; the main points are identical. We see that fact in a simple survey of the propositions of Genesis Rabbah. For example, in it I Genesis Rabbah, the story of the beginnings of creation, humanity, and Israel, we find the message of the meaning and the end of the life of the Jewish people. This appeal not to history but rule-making precedent runs parallel to the equivalent interest in regularities in Leviticus Rabbah. Where the authorship of Genesis Rabbah differs is the choice of the paradigm, which is now the beginnings, but that choice leads to quite distinctive propositions, which, to be sure, prove quite congruent to those important in Leviticus Rabbah. As the rules of Leviticus set forth the social laws of Israel's history in Leviticus Rabbah, so the particular tales of Genesis are turned into paradigms of social laws in Genesis Rabbah.[6] The deeds of the founders supply signals for the children about what is going to come in the future. So the biography of Abraham, Isaac, and Jacob also constitutes the paradigm by which to interpret the history of Israel later on.

We may further compare the topical program of Leviticus Rabbah with that of Pesiqta deRab Kahana. Closely related to Leviticus Rabbah in that its authorship has borrowed five *parashiyyot* from the earlier writing, Pesiqta deRab Kahana move beyond the appeal to scriptural history (as in Genesis Rabbah) or to scriptural case law (as in Leviticus Rabbah). Rather they set forth propositions entirely independent of the received Scripture and so produced the most sustainedly theological compilation, worked out in the modes of argument of philosophy and in the idiom of scriptural exegesis, or Midrash exegeses that derives from late antiquity. In Pesiqta deRab Kahana I see three independently argued propositions.

The first is that God loves Israel, that love is unconditional, and Israel's response to God must be obedience to the religious duties that God has assigned, which will produce merit. Much of the argument for this proposition draws upon the proof of history as laid out in Scripture and appeals to history transformed into paradigm. The second proposition moves us from the ontology to the history that sui generis social entity that is Israel. It is that God is reasonable and when Israel has been punished, it is in accord with God's rules. God forgives penitent Israel and is abundant in mercy. The third proposition is that God will save Israel personally at a time and circumstance of his own choosing. Whereas I take for granted that the hope for future redemption animates the other compilations, we look in vain in some of them, Sifra for a prime example, for an equivalent obsession with messianic questions.

In this regard, I will now depict what I conceive to be the topical and propositional programs of Sifré to Deuteronomy. In that document we do find a highly propositional statement, well within the range of the type of discourse we have noted in other Midrash compilations. The matter of Israel's relationship with God and the responsibilities of a convenanted relationship is primary. It encompasses, first of all, the theme of Israel and God and the implications of the covenant. The basic proposition, spelled out in detail, is that Israel stands in a special relationship with God, and that relationship is defined by the contract, or covenant, that God made with Israel. The covenant comes to particular expression, in Sifré to Deuteronomy, in two matters: first, the land, second, the Torah. Each marks Israel as different from all other nations, on the one side, and as selected by God, on the other. In these propositions, sages situate Israel in the realm of heaven, finding on earth the stigmata of covenanted election and noncommitent requirement of loyalty and obedience to the covenant. These propositions find a place in the foreground of Sifré to Deuteronomy, whereas they do not form the centerpiece of interest and discourse in the Rabbah compilations.

Sifré to Deuteronomy also presents an account of the structure of the intellect. The explicit propositional program of our document is joined by a set of implicit ones. These comprise repeated demonstrations of a point never fully stated. The implicit propositions have to do with the modes of correct analysis and inquiry that pertain to the Torah. Let me give a minor example. One may utilize reason in discovering the meaning and the rules of Scripture. For example, analogy provides adequate ground for extending a rule. There are many instances in which the same mode of reasoning is placed on display. Therefore, although they are not made explicit, the sytematic and orderly character of Scripture is repeatedly demonstrated, with the result that out of numerous instances, we may on our own reach the correct conclusion. Two implicit propositions predominate. The first, familiar from Sifré to Numbers as well as Sifra, is that pure reason does not suffice to produce reliable results. Only through linking our conclusions to verses of Scripture may we come to final and fixed conclusions. The implicit proposition, demonstrated many times, may, therefore, be stated quite simply. The Torah (written) is the sole source of reliable information. Reason undisciplined by the Torah yields unreliable results. These items may occur, also, within the rubrics of the specific propositions that they contain. Some of them moreover overlap with the later catalogue, but, if so, are not listed twice. Our authorship will have found itself entirely at home in this corner of Sifré to Deuteronomy. And in the following, it will have claimed for itself the position of role model for the other authorship, for Sifra's authorship did what seemed important, also to that of Sifré to Deuteronomy.

The second of the two recurrent modes of thought is more important. It is the demonstration that many things conform to a single structure and pattern. We can show this uniformity of the law by addressing the same questions to disparate cases and, in so doing, composing general laws that transcend cases and form a cogent system. What is striking, then, is the power of a single set of questions to reshape and reorganize diverse data into a cogent set of questions and answers, all things fitting together into a single, remarkably well-composed structure. Not only so, but when we review the numerous passages at which we find what, in the logical repertoire I called methodical–analytical logic, we find a single program. It is an effort to ask whether a case of Scripture imposes a rule that limits or imparts a rule that augments the application of the law at hand. A systematic reading of Scripture permits us to restrict or to extend the applicability of the detail of a case into a rule that governs many cases. A standard repertoire of questions may be addressed to a variety of topics, to yield the picture of how a great many things make essentially a single statement. This seems the single most common topical inquiry in Sifré to Deuteronomy. It covers most of the laws of Deuteronomy 12–26. The list of explicit statements of the proposition that the case at hand is subject to either restriction or augmentation, that the law prevailing throughout is limited to the facts at hand or exemplified by those facts, is considerable. The size, the repetitious quality, the obsessive interest in augmentaion and restriction, generalization and limitation – these traits of logic and their concomitant propositional results form the centerpiece of the whole. Nor is this merely subjective judgment, but a result that others can replicate with little difficulty. There can be no doubt that, as to a highly propositional program, Sifré to Deuteronomy falls into the same classification as Leviticus Rabbah, Genesis Rabbah, and Pesiqta deRab Kahana. The authorship proposed to explore not only modes of thought and argumentation but also profound propositions as to Israel's condition, context, and expectations.

When we come to Sifré to Numbers, we enter a document in which we cannot present a similar topical plan. In this aspect, as we will see, Sifra is more like Sifré to Numbers than any other Midrash compilation of late antiquity. Indeed, to establish in Sifré to Numbers some programmatic coherence, we find that we have to resort solely to a reconstruction of the formal traits of the document, then to a translation of those traits into implicit propositions they seem to contain. For as to its sequence of topics, the topical program derives from the book of Numbers and consists in the paraphrase and gloss of what Scripture says, and, as to its distinctive propositions, I see none of that transcendant quality that so impresses us in Leviticus Rabbah, Genesis Rabbah, Pesiqta deRab Kahana, and Sifré to Numbers. In the 116 chapters of Sifré to Numbers that I translated, I could find any number of episodic propositions, but no sustained and coherent program such as I just now set forth on the foundations of the other Sifré. The kind of generalizing paragraphs that I offered in the characterization of not merely the topics but the problematics and propositions of the Rabbah compilations I simply could not compose for this writing. Accordingly, we turn immediately to those things that do recur, formally and forcefully, in this Sifré: the formal patterning of langauge. I see these important traits of form, which lead me to deduce propositions expressed by the form.

1. *The Syllogistic Composition:* Scripture supplies hard facts, which, properly classified, generate syllogisms. By collecting and classifying facts of Scripture, therefore, we may produce firm laws of history, society, and Israel's everyday life. The diverse compositions in which verses from various books of the Scriptures are compiled in a list of evidence for a given proposition – whatever the character or purpose of that proposition – make that one point. And given their power and cogency, they make the point stick. I see no proposition with which the Rabbah authorships will not have unanimously concurred. But when we come to Sifra, we look in vain for this mode of argument. I can point to only a few syllogistic compositions in the document; most of the propositional compositions derive from the Mishnah or the Tosefta. In this respect, in the aggregate Sifra differs.

2. *The Fallability of Reason Unguided by Scriptural Exegesis:* Scripture alone supplies reliable basis for speculation. Laws cannot be generated by reason or logic unguided by Scripture. Efforts at classification and contrastive–analogical exegesis, in which Scripture does not supply the solution to all problems, prove few and far between. Here, of course, we are entirely at home. Sifra's authorship sustainedly and brilliantly carries

forward not only the critique of hierarchical classification and the logical arguments deriving from it, but also, as I will show, the rehabilitation, on proper foundations, of that same mode of thought.

In the context of Sifré to Numbers, this polemic forms the obverse of the point above. So when extrinsic issues intervene in the exegetical process, they coalesce to make a single point. Let me state that point with appropriate emphasis on the recurrent and implicit message of the forms of external exegesis: Scripture stands paramount, logic, reason, analytical processes of classification and differentiation, secondary. Reason not built on scriptural foundations yields uncertain results. The Mishnah itself demands scriptural bases.

However, what about the polemic present in the *intrinsic* exegetical exercises? This clearly does not allow for ready characterization. As we saw, at least three intrinsic exegetical exercises focus on the use of logic, specifically, the logic of classification, comparison, and contrast of species of a genus, in the explanation of the meaning of verses of the book of Numbers. The internal dialectical mode, moving from point to point as logic dictates, underlines the main point already stated: logic produces possibilities, Scripture chooses among them. Again, the question – why is this passage stated? – commonly produces an answer generated by further verses of Scripture (e.g., this matter is stated here to clarify what otherwise would be confusion left in the wake of other verses). So Scripture produces problems of confusion and duplication, and Scripture – and not logic, not differentiation, not classification – solves those problems. To state matters simply: Scripture is complete, harmonious, perfect. Logic not only does not generate truth beyond the limits of Scripture but also plays no important role in the harmonization of difficulties yielded by what appear to be duplications or disharmonies. These forms of internal exegesis then make the same point that the extrinsic ones do.

In so stating, of course, we cover all but the single most profuse category of exegesis, which in both Sifra and in Sifré to Numbers I have treated as simple and undifferentiated: a verse of Scripture or a clause followed by a brief statement of the meaning at hand. This is the single paramount form in Sifré to Numbers, by contrast to Sifra occupying the central position in the repertoire of forms. Here, in the process of paraphrase and amplification of successive phrases of verses, I see no unifying polemic in favor of, or against, a given proposition. The most common form also proves the least pointed: X bears this meaning, Y bears that meaning, or, as we have seen, citation of verse X, followed by, "what this means is". . . Whether simple or elaborate, the upshot is the same. What can be at issue when no polemic expressed in the formal traits of syntax and logic finds its way to the surface? What do I do when I merely clarify a phrase? Or, to frame the question more logically: what premises must validate my *intervention,* that is, my willingness to explain the meaning of a verse of Scripture? These seem to me propositions that must serve to justify the labor of intrinsic exegesis as we have seen its results here:

1. My independent judgment bears weight and produces meaning. I – that is, my mind – may join in the process.
2. God's revelation to Moses at Sinai requires my intervention. I have the role, and the right, to say what that revelation means.
3. What validates my entry into the process of revelation is the correspondence between the logic of my mind and the logic of the document.

Why do I think so? Only if I think in accord with the logic of the revealed Torah can my thought processes join issue in clarifying what is at hand: the unfolding of God's will in the Torah. To state matters more accessibly: If the Torah does not make statements in accord with a syntax and a grammar that I know, I cannot so understand the Torah as to explain its meaning. But if I can join in the discourse of the Torah, it is because I speak the same language of thought: syntax and grammar at the deepest levels of my intellect.

4. Then affirmatively and finally to present what I conceive to be the generative proposition: Because a shared logic of syntax and grammar joins my mind to the mind of God as revealed in the Torah, I can say what a sentence of the Torah means. I too can amplify, clarify, expand, revise, rework: that is to say, create a commentary. Therefore, the intrinsic exegetical forms stand for a single proposition:

Whereas Scripture stands paramount, man's mind through logic, reason, and analytical processes of classification and differentiation, joins God's mind when man receives and sets forth the Torah.

Beyond all concrete propositions, the document as a whole through its fixed and recurrent formal preferences or literary structures makes two complementary points.

1. Reason unaided by Scripture produces uncertain propositions.
2. Reason operating within the limits of Scripture produces truth.

It remains to observe that just as Genesis Rabbah bears formal and substantive affinity to Leviticus Rabbah – the plan and program of both documents present an essential congruity – so too in plan and in program alike Sifra and Sifré to Numbers form a community. The forms and polemic of Sifra and Sifré to Numbers cohere, with the forms so designed as to implicitly state and so to reenforce the substantive argument of both books. In topical traits we may classify Sifra, serving Leviticus, and Sifré to Numbers as inner directed, that is, toward issues of the interior life of the community vis-a-vis revelation and the sanctification of the life of the nation, and, intellectually, as centered on issues urgent to sages themselves. For to whom are the debates about the relationship between Torah and logic, reason and revelation, going to make a difference, if not to the intellectuals of the textual community at hand? Within the same classification scheme, Genesis Rabbah and Leviticus Rabbah and Sifré to Deuteronomy appear outer directed, addressing issues of history and salvation, taking up critical concerns of the public life of the nation vis-a-vis history and the world beyond. Sifra and Sifré to Numbers address sanctification, Sifré to Deuteronomy, Genesis Rabbah, and Leviticus Rabbah, salvation.

As to Sifra, we have found three basic and definitive traits: first, total adherence to the topical program of the written Torah for order and plan; second, common reliance upon the phrases or verses of the written Torah for the joining into coherent discourse of discrete thoughts (e.g., comments on, or amplifications of, words or phrases) and, third, dependence upon the oral Torah for its program of thought: the problematic that defines the issues the authorship wishes to explore and resolve. Sifra seen whole and complete, as we now recognize, nonetheless does set forth an urgent and compelling set of propositions.

Beyond doubt each document of Midrash compilations follows its distinctive topical and propositional program, as much as a particular rhetorical and logical one. And the correspondence between the topical–propositional program and the rhetorical and logical choices is established, at least, for some of the compilations, clearly including this one. If we now ask ourselves a simple question – is the message of Sifra or Sifré to Numbers the same as that of Leviticus Rabbah or Genesis Rabbah? – the answer is obvious. No, these are four different books. The former two make distinct points of their own, respectively. The latter produce a coherent statement, but each with its own emphases. So, in all, the several documents make different points in answering different questions. In plan and in program they yield more contrasts than comparisons. Since these *are* different books, which *do* use different forms to deliver different messages, it must follow that there is nothing routine or given or to be predicted about the point that an authorship wishes to make. Why not? Because it is not a point that is simply "there to be made." It is a striking and original point. How, again, do we know it? The reason is that, when the sages who produced Genesis Rabbah read Genesis, they made a different point from the one that the book of

Leviticus precipitated for the authorships of Sifra and, as a matter of fact, also Leviticus Rabbah. So contrasting the one composition with the other shows us that each composition bears its own distinctive traits of mind, traits of plan, and traits of program.[7]

Sifra and the other documents we have reviewed do not merely assemble this and that, forming a hodgepodge of things people happen to have said. In the case of each document we can answer the question of topic as much as of rhetoric and logic: Why this, not that? That is to say, why discuss this topic in this pattern of language and resort to this logic of cogent discourse, rather than treating some other topic in a different set of language patterns and relying on other modes of making connections and drawing conclusions? These are questions that we have now answered for Sifra, and, in the contrasts already drawn, for the other writings as well.

The writings before us, seen individually and also as a group, stand not wholly autonomously but also not everywhere forming a continuity of discourse, whether in rhetoric, or in logic, or in topic and problematic. They are connected. They intersect at a few places but not over the greater part of their territory. For they are not compilations but free standing compositions. They are not essentially the same, but are articulately differentiated. They are not lacking all viewpoint, serving as a single undifferentiated task of collecting and arranging whatever was at hand. Quite to the contrary, these documents emerge sharply differentiated from one another and clearly defined, each through its distinctive viewpoint and particular polemic, on the one side, and formal and aesthetic qualities, on the other.

What, in the context of Midrash compilations, can we then conclude concerning the singularity and particularity of Sifra? Sifra is like, but also unlike, every other writing with which we make comparisons. Sifra is somewhat like Sifré to Numbers and Sifré to Deuteronomy in rhetoric and logic, but different from them in its topic and program of propositions. In many important ways, as to rhetoric and logic, moreover, Sifra differs from the other two even in its rhetorical and logical classification. For although the same repertoire of forms occur in the two Sifrés and Sifra, they appear in different proportions, and we are able to explain the formal preferences of Sifra. Furthermore, we can account for the logics that particularly well serve Sifra's authorship: why this, not that. Sifra's principal messages prove congruent, but not wholly similar, to those of Sifré to Numbers, but still quite distinctive to its authorship. If what seems to me important in Sifré to Numbers stands up under examination when the document is read whole, then the two documents are by no means wholly symmetrical. Sifra's topical program and propositional repertoire is simply out of phase with those of Sifré to Deuteronomy.

As to the Rabbah compilations, Sifra is like Leviticus Rabbah in its topic, the book of Leviticus, but utterly out of phase with Leviticus Rabbah in its treatment of its topic. What concerns our authorship is a range of issues that is utterly outside of the perspective of Leviticus Rabbah. Whereas, one may surmise, our authorship will have concurred in the propositions that are set forth by Leviticus Rabbah, Genesis Rabbah, and Pesiqta deRab Kahana, in point of fact not a single paramount proposition in those documents plays a sustained role in ours. Therefore, seen in context, Sifra is a remarkably singular document, in which rhetoric and logic are so framed as to serve the expression of a statement highly particular to this piece of writing. Like some compilations in rhetoric, but unlike those same compilations in topic and proposition, congruent with others in logic, but not in rhetoric and certainly unlike in proposition, Sifra presently appears to be singular in its classification, distinct among all pertinent Midrash compilations. Sifra bears some traits in common with a variety of documents, but proves identical to none of them.

Notes

[1]   But that writing is quite different from the two Sifrés and Sifra and we will not deal with it here. My translation and study of Mekhilta Attributed to R. Ishmael may be consulted.

[2]   Further differentiation, to identify the diverse forms of narrative, is not required here. I have carried out that work of differentiation in my *Judaism and Story*. (Chicago, 1990: The University of Chicago Press).

[3]   As stated earlier, since I have not systematically analyzed the logics of any prior document, I cannot conduct any comparisons here except for the one between Sifra and Sifré to Deuteronomy. The result, however, demonstrates that there are significant differences between the two texts and shows that analysis and comparison of the logics operative in other documents should prove interesting. My sense is that the logics that are utilized serve the larger proposition and polemic of a document, just as do the types of rhetoric that are found paramount. Hence, there is a correspondence between the programmatic intent of an authorship and its rhetorical and logical media for expressing its message.

[4]   That matter of methodical analysis covers both Talmuds' reading of the Mishnah, which is so remarkably disciplined as to serve as the finest example of the matter that we have. Any notion that Mishnah exegesis in the Talmuds is free association is based on impressions formed merely in episodic reading of this and that, skipping from here to there in search of thematically pertinent items, such as characterizes *yeshiva* study in this country, or (merely) the guesswork of the romantic and wildly uninformed literary critics of the day. Anyone who has studied either Yerushalmi or Bavli Mishnah exegesis knows how a fixed and rigorous program imposes its agenda everywhere.

[5]   A principal exercise of exegetes, therefore, has been to explain why a given base verse yields the lesson that is attached to it. The subtlety of the explanations

underlines the simple fact that in this context the verse does not generate the proposition and is not meant to.

6   The parallel mode of thought in Sifré to Deuteronomy and in Sifra is the exercise of inclusion and exclusion, which turns a case or an example into a law with clear-cut application or exclusion. That mode of generalizing law forms the counterpart to the interest in generalizing laws from incidents or anecdotes characteristic of Genesis Rabbah. In both cases we observe the move from an essentially ad hoc and episodic mode of thinking to a philosophical and scientific one. The profound interest in generalization, rather than merely precedent or ad hoc observation, characteristic of the authorships of Sifra and Sifré to Deuteronomy, for law, and of Leviticus Rabbah and Genesis Rabbah, for history, seems one of the deepest and most indicative traits of mind of the Judaism of the dual Torah in its intellectual origin and marks that Judaism as deeply philosophical. No student of the writings of the Church fathers can find that fact surprising, even though the idiom of the formative intellects of the Judaism of the dual Torah is less accessible, within the philosophical mode, than that of the formative intellects of Christianity, particularly Catholic (not Gnostic) Christianity.

7   My comparison of Genesis Rabbah and Leviticus Rabbah, in *Comparative Midrash: The Plan and Program of Genesis Rabbah and Leviticus Rabbah* (Atlanta, 1986: Scholars Press for Brown Judaic Studies) underscores this result.

Bibliography

Prior studies of Sifra have provided us with a variety of texts and commentaries, but none has addressed the issues I raise in this book. It suffices, therefore, to refer to some of the basic works on the document, then to place this study into the context of my own previous writings.

This Work in the Context of Prior Studies of Midrash Compilations

With this work, I near the final part of a sustained project of Midrash studies. After I systematically translated and analyzed nearly all of the successor documents to the Mishnah of the Judaism of the dual Torah produced in the formative age, that is, Tosefta (presented for the first time as a systematic commentary to the Mishnah and repository of relevant supplementary materials), and the two Talmuds (twenty-five tractates of the Yerushalmi, seven of the Bavli, with more planned later on), I turned to the Midrash compilations. In each case I translated, or retranslated, a document and then subjected it to a systematic study in the comparative method. In that way I have worked through the following midrash compilations:

Judaism and Scripture: The Evidence of Leviticus Rabbah. Chicago: The University of Chicago Press, 1986.

Genesis Rabbah. The Judaic Commentary on Genesis. A New American Translation. I. *Genesis Rabbah. The Judaic Commentary on Genesis. A New American Translation. Parashiyyot One through Thirty-Three. Genesis 1:1–8:14.* Atlanta: Scholars Press for Brown Judaic Studies, 1985.

The Judaic Commentary on Genesis. A New American Translation. II.
224

Genesis Rabbah. The Judaic Commentary on Genesis. A New American Translation. Parashiyyot Thirty-Four through Sixty-Seven. Genesis 8:15–28:9. Atlanta: Scholars Press for Brown Judaic Studies, 1985.

The Judaic Commentary on Genesis. A New American Translation. III. *Genesis Rabbah. The Judaic Commentary on Genesis. A New American Translation. Parashiyyot Sixty-Eight through One Hundred. Genesis 28:10–50:26.* Atlanta: Scholars Press for Brown Judaic Studies, 1985.

Sifré to Numbers. An American Translation. I. *1–58.* Atlanta: Scholars Press for Brown Judaic Studies, 1986.

An American Translation. II. *59–115.* [III. *116–161:* William Scott Green]. Atlanta: Scholars Press for Brown Judaic Studies, 1986.

The Fathers According to Rabbi Nathan. An Analytical Translation and Explanation. Atlanta: Scholars Press for Brown Judaic Studies, 1986.

Pesiqta deRab Kahana. An Analytical Translation and Explanation. I. *1–14.* Atlanta: Scholars Press for Brown Judaic Studies, 1987.

An Analytical Translation and Explanation. II. *15–28. With an Introduction to Pesiqta deRab Kahana.* Atlanta: Scholars Press for Brown Judaic Studies, 1987.

Sifré to Deuteronomy. An Analytical Translation. I. *Pisqaot One through One Hundred Forty-Three. Debarim, Waethanan, Eqeb, Re'eh.* Atlanta: Scholars Press for Brown Judaic Studies, 1987.

An Analytical Translation. II. *Pisqaot One Hundred Forty-Four through Three Hundred Fifty-Seven. Shofetim, Ki Tese, Ki Tabo, Nesabim, Ha'azinu, Zot Habberakhah.* Atlanta: Scholars Press for Brown Judaic Studies, 1987.

An Introduction to the Rhetorical, Logical, and Topical Program. Atlanta: Scholars Press for Brown Judaic Studies, 1987.

In addition to the analytical translations are the following monographic studies:

The Integrity of Leviticus Rabbah. The Problem of the Autonomy of a Rabbinic Document. Chico: Scholars Press for Brown Judaic Studies, 1985.

Comparative Midrash: The Plan and Program of Genesis Rabbah and Leviticus Rabbah. Atlanta: Scholars Press for Brown Judaic Studies, 1986.

From Tradition to Imitation. The Plan and Program of Pesiqta deRab Kahana and Pesiqta Rabbati. [With a fresh translation of Pesiqta

Rabbati *Pisqaot* 1–5, 15.] Atlanta: Scholars Press for Brown Judaic Studies, 1987.

Canon and Connection: Intertextuality in Judaism. Studies in Judaism series. Lanham: University Press of America, 1986.

Midrash as Literature: The Primacy of Documentary Discourse. Studies in Judaism series. Lanham: University Press of America, 1987.

Invitation to Midrash: The Working of Rabbinic Bible Interpretation. A Teaching Book. San Francisco: Harper & Row, 1988.

What Is Midrash? Philadelphia: Fortress Press, 1987.

Judaism and Scripture: The Evidence of Leviticus Rabbah. [Systematic analysis of problems of composition and redaction.] Chicago: The University of Chicago Press, 1986.

Judaism and Story: The Evidence of The Fathers According to Rabbi Nathan. Chicago: University of Chicago Press, 1989.

Other studies of Midrash compilations, produced alongside the translations and analytical works listed above, are as follows:

The Foundations of Judaism. Method, Teleology, Doctrine. Philadelphia, 1983–5: Fortress Press. I–III. I. *Midrash in Context. Exegesis in Formative Judaism.* Second printing: Atlanta: Scholars Press for Brown Judaic Studies, 1988.

The Oral Torah. The Sacred Books of Judaism. An Introduction. San Francisco: Harper & Row, 1985.

Editor: *Scriptures of the Oral Torah. Sanctification and Salvation in the Sacred Books of Judaism.* San Francisco: Harper & Row, 1987.

Mekhilta Attributed to R. Ishmael. An Analytical Translation. I. *Pisha, Beshallah, Shirata, and Vayassa.* Atlanta: Scholars Press for Brown Judaic Studies, 1988.

An Analytical Translation. II. *Amalek, Bahodesh, Neziqin, Kaspa and Shabbata.* Atlanta: Scholars Press for Brown Judaic Studies, 1988.

An Introduction to Judaism's First Scriptural Encyclopaedia. Atlanta: Scholars Press for Brown Judaic Studies, 1988.

Writing with Scripture: The Authority and Uses of the Hebrew Bible in the Torah of Formative Judaism. Philadelphia: Fortress Press, 1989.

I plan to return to work on the Mishnah in its political, philosophical, and jurisprudential context, with monographs completed or projected as follows:

The Economics of Judaism: The Initial Statement. Chicago: University of Chicago Press, 1989.

The Politics of Judaism: The Initial System in its Greco-Roman Philosophical Context (in press)

The Philosophy of Judaism (in press)

General Index

229

Index to Biblical and Talmudic References